POST-CONTEMPORARY INTERVENTIONS

Series Editors: Stanley Fish and Fredric Jameson

AESTHETICS AND MARXISM   Chinese Aesthetic

Marxists and Their Western Contemporaries

Liu Kang   *Duke University Press   Durham and London 2000*

© 2000 Duke University Press

All rights reserved

Printed in the United States of America on acid-free
paper ∞

Typeset in Trump Mediaeval by Wilsted & Taylor
Publishing Services

Library of Congress Cataloging-in-Publication Data appear
on the last printed page of this book.

Parts of chapters 3 and 4 appeared in *New Literary History*
27, no. 4 (1996). Another part of chapter 4 appeared in a
slightly different form in *positions: east asia cultures
critique* 3, no. 1 (1993). Part of chapter 5 appeared in
Social Text 10, nos. 2–3 (1992).

For Yazeng

CONTENTS

This book analyzes the relationship between aesthetics and modern Marxism by focusing on the Chinese case. At the same time, it highlights connections, parallels, and differences between the Chinese aesthetic Marxists and their Western counterparts. The heroes are a diverse cast, ranging from writers and philosophers to political leaders, playing in the various acts of the historical drama lasting nearly a century. Common among them, obviously, is a strong emphasis on "culture" and "aesthetics" in theory and practice. This historical study of the formation of aesthetic discourse in modern China, especially in Chinese Marxist traditions, is combined with theoretical reflection on wider political and cultural issues pertaining to the problems of modernity, alternative modernity, and postmodernity. The key questions raised in this book not only traverse a broad spectrum of fields of inquiry, but also involve a host of historical and intellectual traditions, Marxist ones in particular. Although these issues cannot be comprehensively covered in one volume, the chapters that follow alert readers to some important, yet often unnoticed and neglected links among the distinct theories and practices within modern Marxist traditions on issues of culture and aesthetics.

In light of the centrality of "culture" in contemporary society and social thought, we need to examine these connections to deepen our understanding of discrete and heterogeneous modern aesthetic traditions, as well as to seek new alternatives in both theoretical and practical senses. It is possible that some alternative model of cultural criticism could be extrapolated out of Chinese aesthetic Marxism, as indeed its major thinkers have aspired to do. I would be gratified if readers found this study useful as an introduction to that Marxism and its principal theorists. The Chinese Marxist "model" does not claim universal validity in the manner of some current Western theories, paradoxically by way of fetishizing difference and otherness. Nevertheless, it contains implications beyond regional and geopolitical boundaries.

Rather than a "detached" observation, this book is an "intervention," in a small way, into the subjects under discussion. I try to apply dialectical method in both the historical description and explanation of Chinese theories and my own critical position. This dialectical thought is intrinsically self-reflexive, as is evidenced by the use of Chinese aesthetic Marxist practices in rethinking modern traditions and the legacies of revolution and modernity. Analogies to this thought are noted in the ways that modern Western Marxists reflect on capitalist modernity and postmodernity. Rethinking the "rethinking" of culture, politics, and aesthetics, I examine historical events and the less tangible historicity of the concepts and categories by which events are mapped out. Insofar as the dialectic of "practice" (or history proper) and "theory" constitutes the very problematic of Marxism (which as the "principal contradiction," lies at the heart of Chinese Marxist traditions), the reinscription of "self-reflexivity" as a proper Marxian dialectic represents a renewed effort at cultural critique.

The central thesis of this book is that culture and cultural revolution are inextricably related to the Marxist projects of critiquing capitalist modernity and constructing an alternative modernity. Aesthetics and culture have been of primary concern in Chinese Marxist circles. In this respect, the diverse practices and designs of Chinese Marxism are similar to those of Western Marxism, or an equally distinct variety of Euro-American Marxist intellectual enterprises. But save for a partial grasp of Maoism, Western Marxists had little awareness of what their Chinese colleagues were doing in a different context. Thus, although it is generally understood that Maoism transformed the ways that Europeans thought about Marxism, by comparing Chinese aesthetic Marxism and Western Marxism we can gain insight into the historical development of modern Marxism.

Chinese aesthetic and Western Marxism both create a theoretical space for critical interventions by empowering cultural politics. European and North American cultural politics have fostered an oppositional vision centered largely on the problems of domination and resistance, manipulation and self-government, and consent and coercion in modern capitalist society. In contrast, aesthetic Marxism in China has served the twofold mission of critiquing the intrinsic contradictions of revolutionary hegemony and offering a constructive vision of culture in a postrevolutionary society. Herein lies the value of Chinese aesthetic Marxism, with implications that reach beyond China proper in the world of global cultural critique. Moreover, being non-Western, Chinese aesthetic Marxism has self-consciously questioned the inherent Eurocentrism in Marxism itself. If this Eurocentrism is to be challenged and problematized, questions posed by Chinese aesthetic Marxists cannot be neglected. Its originality, as well as its historical and structural limitations, has allowed Chinese aesthetic Marxism to make a crucial difference in the struggles of the real world. Hence, it is a significant development within Marxist tradition, deserving critical attention.

Searches for an alternative modernity by Chinese Marxism (including, of course, its "first stage," represented by Mao Zedong) have critiqued not only capitalist modernity, but also its determinism and teleology. Yet the Chinese critique, like that of modern Western Marxism, privileges "culture" as both a means and an end in itself in constituting an alternative modernity. In Mao's version, the role of cultural revolution is second only to that of peasant guerrilla warfare, and key to the establishment and development of a revolutionary hegemony, the predominant feature of his socialist alternative. Such a privileging of "culture," however, has resulted in the neglect of other critically important areas of social life, the economic in particular. In the postrevolutionary period, cultural revolution and revolutionary hegemony gradually lapsed into massive politicization and instrumentalization of aesthetic and cultural life. This severely undermined social and economic reconstruction, or the constitution of a socialist mode of production, as another central goal of an alternative modernity. Mao's privileging of culture, as a way in its inception to counter the economic determinism of classical Marxism, was eventually turned into a "culturalist" determinism and essentialism. His plan for a socialist China as an alternative to both Soviet-style socialism and Western capitalism became a liability, and even long after Mao's era ended, the Maoist legacy has left a huge amount of vastly complex problems in ideological and cultural terrains.

Yet contrary to the widely accepted view that Chinese Marxism—primarily represented as Maoism—is monolithic, there have always been different Marxist positions in China. This book analyzes these discrete practices of Chinese Marxist intellectuals, emphasizing the construction of autonomous cultural space in a postrevolutionary society. The tragic consequences of Mao's Cultural Revolution and revolutionary hegemony compelled Chinese aesthetic Marxists to reflect on Mao's privileging of culture, first, as a betrayal of the Marxist principle of the primacy of the economic, and second, as an impediment to constructive and systematic social transformation. Chinese aesthetic Marxism, especially Li Zehou's "philosophy of practical subjectivity," reaffirms historical materialist concepts as well as the categories of material "practice" and "mode of production" vis-à-vis the language of contemporary cultural criticism.

This is not to suggest that Chinese aesthetic Marxists followed the agenda of Western Marxism; the Chinese have self-consciously critiqued

Western Marxism and its Maoist connections. Significantly, the Chinese Marxist experience in a postrevolutionary society and the vision that has emerged from it have drawn a different cognitive map, an alternative "cultural topology" for contemporary cultural studies. They offer us an epistemic alternative for understanding the genealogy of the critical notions and conceptual schemes by which modern Chinese cultural history has been interpreted. *Aesthetics and Marxism* investigates these "topological cultural spaces" from the critical perspective informed by Chinese theories themselves, while also juxtaposing these theories with Western Marxist ones, so that their assumptions can be mutually challenged in illuminating ways. Granted, it is only a preliminary experiment, and as such, subject to the most relentless scrutiny of history.

In this book, I craft a narrative of the genealogy of the aesthetic discourse in modern China within the context of its conceptual migrations, modifications, and divergences, from classical German thought to modern Western Marxism and cultural criticism. Most of the Chinese theorists discussed—with the exception of Mao—are generally unknown to intellectuals in the West. While Lu Xun is perhaps familiar to a larger audience, the names Qu Qiubai, Hu Feng, Zhu Guangqian, and Li Zehou, have little or no resonance to English readers. Their Western "counterparts," however—including Georg Lukács, Theodor Adorno, Antonio Gramsci, and Louis Althusser, to name a few—are now household names in Western academic circles. While the positivist model of "influence studies" may have lost some of its credibility of late, it would be dangerous to absolutize and fetishize difference and otherness, and thus externalize the internal tensions and contradictions within modernity. The disciplinary division of "area studies" in European and North American academies, although not a result of the contemporary fetishization and institutionalization of difference, has nonetheless externalized and fragmented "modern China" as an object of knowledge from mainstream cultural and literary studies. The dominant binary oppositions within "China studies"—such as modernity/tradition, West/East, First World/Third World—further dichotomize and externalize the intrinsic conflicts of modernity, which has primarily designated the modernity of the capitalist West as a totalizing model by which all alternatives are understood as other. This account of the genealogy of the aesthetic in China's alternative modernity tries to dismantle the totalizing myth by recuperating it as a diverse body of paradoxical and heterogeneous experiences and conditions of possibility. The concept of the aesthetic, with its unique versatility and ambiguity, incarnates the contradictory nature of modernity. Therefore, it serves as a prism through which to examine the internal contradictions and structural relations mediated and negotiated by the aesthetic itself, without either totalizing or externalizing its overdetermined internal contradictions.

The first chapter, in remarking generally on these theoretical and historical questions, serves both to clarify key issues and problematics, and to make a genealogical query to the epistemic as well as institutional machinery in current historical and cultural studies that identify and categorize "China," "modernity," and "culture." This entails discussing the relationship between aesthetics and modernity—from its origins in eighteenth-entury Europe (Germany in particular) to the nineteenth and early twentieth centuries, when the prospect of an alternative modernity arose. That is, when Western capitalist modernity expanded from a local historical experience into a global movement, it spawned at once fragmentation and universalization, and opened up alternate possibilities. China's passage into modernity unquestionably constituted one alternative, with culture and aesthetics playing significant roles. When Marxism entered the arena of China's struggles, it transformed aesthetics from a preeminently bourgeois discourse of autonomy and separation into a powerful weapon for revolution. The relationship between aesthetics and politics, then, became a most compelling issue. The implications of this historical transformation of aesthetic discourse need to be evaluated within the context of modern Marxist traditions, in which politics (in terms of "cultural politics" and realpolitik), ideology, hegemony (in prerevolutionary and postrevolutionary societies), and subjectivity (or the "death of subject") have constituted the "core" problematics. Because these issues are crucial to contemporary cultural criticism as well, it is necessary to show the connection between earlier experiences and the 1990s. The pre-Marxist Chinese appropriations of aesthetic discourse from the late nineteenth to the early twentieth century were primarily motivated by the cultural politics of encountering a Western modernity. A brief investigation of Liang Qichao, Wang Guowei, and Cai Yuanpei's endeavors to bring aesthetic discourse to bear on China's modernity and searches for an alternative modernity will demonstrate the importance of aesthetics and culture in modern Chinese history.

The remaining chapters, which focus on the development of Marxist aesthetics in China, are organized primarily by historical periods—from the May Fourth enlightenment and cultural critique in the 1910s to the Cultural Reflection of the 1980s—and concentrate on the question of interpretation. A critical feature of the Chinese Revolution was the contradiction between the two principal forces: urban Marxist intellectuals and peasants. The formation of Marxist aesthetic and cultural theories reflected this fundamental incongruity, especially in the shifting of revolutionary cultural work from Shanghai, arguably the most cosmopolitan and modern city in early-twentieth-century Asia, to the backward rural areas, first to Jiangxi, then to Yan'an, as the revolutionary base areas, and finally, after the victory of the revolution, back to the cities again. This phenomenon has been explained either by the modernity/tradition or urban/rural models, which externalize the contradictions within the Chinese Marxist movement. Here, this contradiction is examined by probing Lu Xun's aesthetics of negativity and allegory along with Qu Qiubai's critique of Europeanization and promotion of national popular culture as manifestations of the politics/culture and urban/rural conflicts within the global experiences of modernity. Urban Marxist intellectual Lu Xun's writings are compared with the works of his Western counterparts, Walter Benjamin and Adorno, and Qu Qiubai's with Gramsci's projects, since both represent revolutionary strategies devised independently by two Communist leaders facing similar historical conditions.

As for the role of aesthetics and culture in Mao's thought, Gramsci's notions of hegemony and counterhegemony are useful in an alternative reevaluation, largely because they were derived from comparable strategic considerations and historical conditions. Yet, there are serious inadequacies and ambiguities in Gramsci's theoretical reflections. In Mao's theory and practice, the aesthetic question of "form" or "national form" was the focal point. Mao's projects of revolutionary hegemony and cultural revolution by promulgating "national form" entailed, among other things, the "thought-reform" that aimed to transform urban Marxist intellectuals into "true" revolutionaries, modeled after the revolutionary army of peasants. This involved a massive politicization and instrumentalization of culture and aesthetics in postrevolutionary China. But such things cannot be sufficiently understood from a Gramscian perspective, for Gramsci, though close in many ways in his thought on cultural revolution, was never able to envision a postrevolution cultural space. Moreover, in exploring the key issue of constructing a revolutionary culture in a postrevolutionary society, which constituted Chinese aesthetic Marxism's main problematic, many serious misappropriations by contemporary Western cultural studies of Gramsci's strategies of communist revolution come to light. The displacement of commodification and economic inequality with erratic, fragmented "war of positions," "identity politics," and so on reveals the ahistorical and idealist tendencies of certain Western Left academicians or anarcho-liberalist "post-Marxists." It is interesting to note that many radical claims made by postcolonialist critics against Western "epistemic violence" or "subalternity" had already been put forth by Qu Qiubai and Mao in the early 1930s and 1940s. Postcolonialism, which derives much of its theoretical presuppositions from Gramsci as part of the above-mentioned strategic displacement, not only says hardly anything new about modern China; when used in China studies, the postcolonialist paradoxical debunking of a radical revolutionary legacy from which s/he finds a mirror image of her/himself, only obfuscates the real question of coming to grips with the complex legacy of Chinese revolution and revolutionary hegemony.

The notion of "civil society" in Gramsci's formulation, for instance, emerged from his strategic thinking on the establishment of a socialist society, drawing on the experience of civil society/state formations in the bourgeois society of the West. These considerations can be illuminated by Hu Feng's insistence on constructing a semiautonomous, independent cultural space in postrevolutionary society, where subjectivity or "subjective fighting spirit" can resist both coercion and the consensus of bourgeois-feudalist hegemony, as well as the political instrumentalization of the revolutionary hegemony itself. The discussion of "civil society" in general and in China in particular, therefore, needs to rigorously challenge the epistemic assumptions underlying concepts based merely on the experience of capitalist modernity.

The emergence of an "aesthetic Marxism" in postrevolutionary China since the 1950s, first marked by the eight-year debates about aesthetics during the 1950s and 1960s, presents yet another interesting cluster of issues concerning the role of culture and aesthetics, discussed in chapter 4. Represented primarily by academic Marxists, especially Zhu Guangqian and Li Zehou, the aesthetic Marxists broached a wide range of problems similar to those raised by contemporary critical theorists: specifically, the matters of subjectivity in aesthetic experience; praxis/practice in the cultural terrain; and the relationship between humanity and nature, and between aesthetics and ideology. The differences between Chinese aesthetic and Western Marxists, however, have far-reaching implications. The Chinese insist on the historical materialist notions of "practice" in terms of material production, while Western Marxists—whether the existentialist humanist Jean-Paul Sartre, antihumanist structuralist Louis Althusser, or cultural materialist Raymond Williams—invariably stress "praxis" in cultural and aesthetic realms as opposed to the "economism" and "productivism" of classical Marxism. Subjectivity as a "bourgeois humanist" concept has been under relentless assault in the West, while Chinese aesthetic Marxists have invested not only the utopian aspiration of a true humanity in the notions of sovereign subjects and human agents, but also in the political and ideological legitimation and rationality of subjectivity as a new political identity. While "alienation" has long been a master trope for the Western Marxist deconstructive and negative critique of capitalist modernity, "humanized nature" in the young Marx's *1844 Manuscripts* became the rallying cry for Chinese aesthetic Marxists's vision of an alternative modernity.

A last difference is noted in the widely interrelated "postmodern" debates in the West and "Cultural Reflection" in China in the 1980s, the ideological underpinnings of which are traceable to the upheavals of the 1960s, epitomized by the Chinese Cultural Revolution and the May 1968 Parisian student movement. The political and hermeneutic questions that these debates have posed, now in hindsight, involve a paradoxical dialectic of historicizing impulses that simultaneously project some ahistorical, transcendental "cultural" and "aesthetic" categories by which actual historical events and the historicity of concepts are displaced. "Sign," "language," and "discourse"—and lately, Gramscian "subalternity," "micropolitics," and the like—have displaced and suspended indefinitely the compelling issues of social injustice and economic inequality, invoking the seemingly perpetual moment of "interregnum." The Chinese, on the other hand, vacillated between a politically engaged, interventionist position and an eminently "aestheticist" and even metaphysical stance clamoring for transcendence over worldly issues and politics. Nevertheless, significant and powerful theoretical formations have emerged from the 1980s' cultural ferments across the globe, providing us with the ways, conceptual schemes, and problematics to think through historical conjunctures and look for alternatives.

I find the vision of Chinese aesthetic Marxism original, not only because of the conceptual framework that it offers, but also because its own discerning positions and agenda constitute a crucially different voice that may demystify the current preoccupation of difference and otherness in cultural studies. It is ironic, therefore, that this distinct voice, arising from and self-consciously critical of the radical legacy that has helped nurture the contemporary "politics of otherness," has remained ignored by the practitioners of that radical cultural politics.

This is not to suggest that Chinese aesthetic Marxism affords a grand, systematic theory for cultural studies, one that may replace the current "models." I have only begun in this book to raise some questions, and we are only beginning to search for answers that affect our thinking about culture and the world.

ACKNOWLEDGMENTS

In the course of writing this book I learned a great deal from numerous friends and colleagues. I am deeply indebted to Fredric Jameson, without whom this book could not have been written. I want to thank those friends and colleagues whose insights, helpful comments, and supports in many ways made the writing of this book a rewarding experience. They include Masao Miyoshi, Arif Dirlik, Rey Chow, Tonglin Lu, Stanley Abe, Jonathan Arac, Ralph Cohen, Paul Bové, Xudong Zhang, and Qiguang Zhao in the United States; Wang Fengzhen, Li Zehou, Liu Zaifu, Yue Daiyun, Zhang Fa, Zhang Yiwu, Wang Ning, Zhao Shilin, and Xu Dai in the People's Republic of China. I am especially grateful for the unflinching support of my colleagues at Penn State University, including Caroline Eckhardt, Stanley Weintraub, and Thomas Beebee. I owed greatly to Jianping Wu, who, as a friend and a student of mine for many years, helped me crystallize many ideas in this book and made the otherwise lonely labor of thinking and writing this book delightful through numerous conversations. I received fellowships and research grants from the American Philosophical Society (1992), and from the Institute for Arts and Humanistic Studies (1992) and the College of Liberal Arts (1993) at Penn State University, for which I remain thankful. I am extremely grateful to Reynolds Smith, Senior Editor at Duke University Press, for his patience and understanding during the rather prolonged process of completing the book. My wife Yazeng Zhang has given me invaluable encouragement since we fell in love some thirty years ago when we were "playmates under the plum trees, riding bamboo horses," as the Chinese proverb goes. No words can express my deepest love and gratitude for her.

CHAPTER 1

Aesthetics, Modernity, and Alternative Modernity:

The Case of China

The fascination with the aesthetic is inexorably tied to modernity—understood now as a historical condition of existence and experience, cutting across temporal and geographical boundaries. As such, the question of the aesthetic pertains to modern European thought beginning with the Enlightenment, when philosophers assigned high priority to it in their reflections on modernity. The aesthetic question, however, hardly dominates discourses of modernity, which center instead on objective science and scientific reason. As Max Horkheimer and Theodor Adorno put it, the "rationality of the Enlightenment" promised "the disenchantment of the world, the dissolution of myths and the substitution of knowledge for fancy."[1] But as the course of history since the Enlightenment has shown, scientific rationality has failed to live up to the expectation that it would not only subsume, but also transcend natural and human existence. Instead, it increasingly betrayed its limitations in coping with the complex problems of humankind. Diverse cultures and histories have not, and cannot, be contained by a particular way of reasoning, be it scientific or otherwise. Serious challenges to scientific reason's applicability to and capacity to resolve all human dilemmas were only raised after the unbridled faith in ideas of science, progress, and freedom began to turn against itself, and transform Enlightenment rationality into an "instrumental rationality" that served the twentieth-century powers of domination and oppression. Then, cultural and anthropological dimensions, and indeed the aesthetic dimension so dear to many thinkers of the Enlightenment, were recovered once again, as in the Renaissance when the values of humanity dimmed that of God, in the critique of modernity and searches for an alternative modernity.

If science, technology, and scientific reason are the dominant themes of modernity, then "culture" becomes a key category for contemporary Western social thought in the analysis and understanding of the world, centering on the issues embedded in postmodernity. Hence, aesthetics has acquired or regained prominence among modern Western thinkers, ranging from Friedrich Nietzsche and Sigmund Freud to Martin Heidegger, and from Sartre and Adorno to Michel Foucault and Jacques Derrida. It now serves as an immanent critique of modernity, and a way to measure the social, political, and economic movements of postmodernity. In modern Western Marxist thought, the ascendancy of the aesthetic from Lukács to Adorno is even more glaring, and aesthetic thinking has come to identify, to a great degree, the diverse projects of contemporary Western Marxism as a critique of modernity.

Yet the negative, critical function of the aesthetic in modern Marxist traditions is only part of the story. Aside from the largely repressive role it played in so-called "really existing socialism"—that is, the former Soviet Union and Eastern European countries—aesthetic discourse has been constructive in the People's Republic of China, where Marxism was, and still is, a fundamental feature of modern tradition and social life. This positive function, however, has taken the dialectic form of critique and reconstruction. In other words, it has had both hegemonic and counterhegemonic formations, emerging from China's searches for an alternative modernity.

In the West, the aesthetic has been primarily a bourgeois discourse of modernity, a feature that it retains in the hands of Western Marxist intellectuals despite its challenge to the dominant ideological forms of capitalism. This contradiction also characterizes the diverse undertakings of modern Western Marxist cultural politics. When Marxists in the West critique capitalist modernity, they must assume a bourgeois civil society as a social space from which to mount their attack. In Chinese Marxism, in contrast, the aesthetic underwent a fundamental transformation, from a bourgeois discourse into a revolutionary tool in struggles for state power. After the seizure of state power, the aesthetic strengthened the revolutionary hegemony created by the Chinese Communist Party. This structural shift in aesthetic discourse involved serious contradictions, particularly in a postrevolutionary society.

The genealogy of the aesthetic in modern China, then, may reveal a possible alternative to the Marxist cultural formations of the West. It may also expose internal tensions and contradictions within modernity, understood as a global experience. An examination of the historical role of aesthetics raises the following questions: How have the relationships between culture, aesthetics, modernity (or an alternative modernity), and Marxism been generally perceived and described? What is the relationship between aesthetics and modernity in the West? What is the role of aesthetics in Chinese modernity, or an alternative modernity? What are the main functions of the aesthetic and culture in modern Marxist traditions, from Western to Chinese? And how shall we come to grips with these complex relationships, ones that lie at the heart of contemporary intellectual debates?

Indeed, these issues are pertinent to interrogating the historicity of the concepts and categories with which we engage the subjects of this study. Specifically, "critical theory" is explored as a rubric of contemporary intellectual discourse, and "China studies" as an institution of knowledge production and distribution. Since self-reflexive critiques are often central to today's critical theory, an investigation of the historical conditions of relevant intellectual discourses or institutions is a necessary point of departure.

The Preeminence of Aesthetics in Modern Chinese Thinking

This genealogical inquiry starts from the historical resources of modern aesthetic thought and their social conditions in the West. The aesthetic is a discourse of modernity par excellence, for it articulates the intrinsic contradictions of modernity in the most concrete and "sensuous" of terms. (The term *aesthetic* in its original meaning refers precisely to "sensuousness," or human senses.) Its inception in eighteenth-century Germany is indicative of the contrary character of Western capitalist modernity. From Alexander Baumgarten to Immanuel Kant, Georg Wilhelm Friedrich Hegel, and Friedrich Schiller, aesthetic cognition served as mediation, reconciliation, and negotiation on two fronts: Politically, it moved between the generalities of reason and the particularities of sense; socially, it tried to negotiate between an aspiring modern European bourgeoisie yearning for freedom and autonomy, and the German feudalist absolutism. It should be noted, though, that aesthetic mediation and negotiation are immanently imaginary and utopian. The aesthetic's projection of a free, equal, autonomous, and universal subjectivity speaks at once for all humanity, and for the bourgeoisie in particular. Terry Eagleton's study aptly uncovers the correlation between the contradictory, mediatory, and utopian nature of aesthetic discourse, and the concrete political conjuncture of eighteenth-century Germany. It is in the sense of rigorous historicizing scrutiny that the versatility and ambiguity of the concept of the aesthetic should be understood, both in the Western and Chinese contexts. The aesthetic, as Eagleton argues, has "a certain indeterminacy of definition which allows it to figure in a varied span of preoccupation: freedom and legality, spontaneity and necessity, self-determination, autonomy, particularity and universality, along with several others."[2] This indeterminacy of definition, however, is actually historically determinate:

The category of the aesthetic assumes the importance it does in modern Europe because in speaking of art it speaks of these other matters too, which are at the heart of the middle class's struggle for political hegemony. The construction of the modern notion of the aesthetic artifact is thus inseparable from the construction of the dominant ideological forms of modern class society, and indeed from a whole new form of human subjectivity appropriate to that social order. . . . But my argument is also that the aesthetic, understood in a certain sense, provides an unusually powerful challenge and alternative to these dominant ideological forms, and in this sense an eminently contradictory phenomenon.[3]

It is crucial that Eagleton insists on the specific class character of universal humanist concepts of the aesthetic and subjectivity. Many current cultural and social theories either refuse to recognize, or attempt to obfuscate, the still-dominant class character of contemporary societies. But it must be added that "class" as a social formation is susceptible to structural overdeterminations from a multitude of factors. It is now widely acknowledged that class formation is subject to the influences of race, gender, and ethnicity. Impacts of cultural values and geopolitical differences on social classes must be considered, too. In the Chinese context, for instance, the mediatory and reconciliatory functions of the aesthetic have to be grasped not only with respect to different class formations, but also different cultural and geopolitical formations, which have decisively affected class and discursive formations.

The aesthetic discourse mediates and negotiates the contradictions within Western modernity on several levels: first, the abstract philosophical realm; second and perhaps the least abstract, the realm of social life; and finally, the ambiguous domain of psychology, which itself also mediates between abstract ideas and concrete social practices. On the first level, the aesthetic discourse mediates the fundamental dichotomies of Western metaphysics, between rationality and sensuousness, and between epistemology and ethics. In a political as well as sociological sense, it promises to reconcile the mounting tensions between free, autonomous individuals in a civil society and public sphere, and the regulatory, coercive, and authoritative powers of the state. On the third level, the aesthetic is probably at its most effective: its imaginary, sensuous, and utopian projection of subjectivity promises to unify logic-reason with sense-experience, ontology and ethics with epistemology, and particular individuality with general sociality. During the process of its migration from eighteenth-century Germany to twentieth-century China, however, radical structural changes took place. On the metaphysical or philosophical level, the tension between scientific rationality and ethical, ontological reflection is now compounded by the presence of an alien system of values—an Oriental culture as old as those in the West. Philosophical differences are ultimately connected to practical social issues. From the standpoint of an imperialist power in the West, the Nietzschean "will to power," seen in the Western context as a disruptive and subversive force to scientific reason, served to disseminate and reinforce the Eurocentric rationality of modernity to the rest of the "alien and barbaric" world. Such a reinforcement was largely carried out in reality by the barbarous, brutal means of violence and force. To this aggressive assertion of power, the Chinese responded by intensifying the intrinsic tensions of Western modernity, asserting the *ti-yong* dualism or "Chinese essence or substance versus Western practical use." In other words, the internal contradictions of Western modernity were externalized or fragmented by the various Chinese/Western dichotomies. Formulated after the 1895 Sino-Japanese War, in which China was defeated by its rapidly modernized and aggressive neighbor, the ti-yong dualism was a culturally reassuring position that affirmed basic ethical and cosmological values that gave continuity and meaning to Chinese civilization, and that would enable adaptation and absorption of Western modernity.[4]

The Chinese solution to the external social and political tensions of modernity, embodied by the ti-yong dichotomy, was grounded on the assumption that only internal cultural and psychological (or spiritual) values—perceived as inherently superior to the materialist, instrumentalist, and scientific reason of the West—could empower a materialistically and technologically backward China in its own search for modernity. As the intrinsic tensions of Western modernity were transfigured into the preeminently cultural and geopolitical dichotomy of the "materialist" West against the "spiritual" East, structural transformations in both the cultural and psychological domains took on complex dimensions. Culture must now bear the burden of not only solving the paradoxes of Western modernity, but also reaffirming and empowering China's own national identity. Hence, a crisscrossing and collapsing of the "interior" and "exterior" boundaries become inevitable. "Interior," or psychological and spiritual transformation would provide vital subsistence to "exterior," or social and political transformation.

The aesthetic, then, became a favorable topic for those Chinese intellectuals who wanted to mediate and reconcile the intricate tensions and contradictions arising from China's passage into modernity. In the course of its structural transformation, the inherent contradictions contained within the aesthetic concept became exacerbated. To begin with, the aesthetic discourse that tried to bridge the traditional Chinese value of harmony with Western dualism was unavoidably at odds with modernist ideas of autonomy, independence, and subjectivity. Second, when Marxism was introduced into China, a transference of the class character of subjectivity occurred: it was no longer the bourgeois subject, but a newly emergent, revolutionary subjectivity, that the aesthetic discourse should identify. Such a transference entailed a demystification of the universalism that the aesthetic discourse embodied. Third, the utopian aspect of the aesthetic discourse, in the process of conceptual transgression and transference, became increasingly politicized. The politicization of aesthetics and aestheticization of politics thus became salient features of modern Chinese history.

In other words, aesthetic discourse in modern China is loaded with a mélange of ideological presuppositions: as a historical concept derived from Western bourgeois thought since the Enlightenment, it carries an ideological baggage advocating at once for the political hegemony of the bourgeoisie and a utopian notion of true humanity in opposition to bourgeois utility. Aesthetics is primarily a concept of modernity, in the sense that it bespeaks the autonomy and separation of social spheres, and presupposes a self-determining and self-sufficient subjectivity.[5] Contradictions inherent in aesthetics become most apparent when transplanted into China.

The aesthetic is first hailed by modern Chinese intellectuals around the turn of the century as an indispensable constituent of modernity. Liang Qichao, eminent reformist scholar and ardent advocate of cultural enlightenment, extolled "beauty" or aesthetics as "the most important element of human life." He insisted that "*meishu* [literally, the art of beauty, or fine art] generates science."[6] Wang Guowei, another prominent intellectual regarded as a founder of modern scholarship in China because of his efforts to integrate German philosophy and aesthetics into traditional Chinese thought, devoted his whole life to the promotion of the aesthetic ideal as the paramount model of modern life. Founding President of Peking University and renowned social reformist Cai Yuanpei proposed to replace religion with "aesthetic education."[7] Chinese Marxists, too—from early intellectual leaders such as Li Dazhao and Chen Duxiu, to revolutionary commanders such as Qu Qiubai and Mao Zedong—invariably stress the importance of aesthetics and culture. Lu Xun, modern China's "cultural giant," can be credited with creating an "aesthetics of negativity," responding to the formidable tensions between political revolution and cultural enlightenment. As we shall see, Lu Xun's aesthetic thought, together with Qu Qiubai's idea of fostering a proletarian class consciousness through cultural revolution and popularization, represent Chinese Marxist aesthetics in incipient, yet significant forms. But Lu Xun's urban, cosmopolitan vision of cultural revolution differs greatly from Qu Qiubai's rural-centered, nativist view. The incommensurability between Lu Xun and Qu Qiubai signals the bifurcation of Chinese Marxist cultural and aesthetic theories in the decades that followed, thereby intensifying the tensions within Chinese modernity.

The May Fourth intellectual movement of 1919 was the culmination of China's encounter with modernity in all its antagonistic and contradictory aspects. Of these contradictions, the most salient was the Western intrusion that threatened to destroy China's sovereignty and colonize it entirely. Going hand in hand with this imperialist attempt, though, was the promise of a progressive modernity. It is crucial to bear in mind the complex circumstances under which China entered the modern era in order to understand the breaks, ruptures, discontinuities, revolutions, and violence that dominated modern China's history. In fact, this is also the manner in which modernity itself as a universal, global phenomenon ought to be understood: it is a moment fraught with conflicts and incongruities, breaks and ruptures. Likewise, May Fourth intellectual inquiries and social formations, governed by the historical conditions of modernity, are necessarily fragmented, fractured, and contradictory, even though their ostensible goals and claims invariably call for unity, totality, and universality. The radical iconoclasm and antitraditionalism that characterized the May Fourth movement thus cannot be construed as "totalistic," or as producing totalizing resolutions to China's problems.

The universalist and totalizing claims of the May Fourth intellectuals, however, reflect their awareness of China's social change as an integral part of a global modernity. To be sure, there were inherent connections between the forms of May Fourth cultural radicalism and iconoclasm, and the deep-seated "Chinese cultural predisposition" or "monistic and intellectualistic mode of thinking."[8] But it is equally undeniable, and far more significant, that this radicalism fundamentally transformed traditional values, to which radical intellectuals themselves were thoroughly indebted. Marxism, as Arif Dirlik argues convincingly, represents the single most powerful intellectual, ideological, and political force in modern China, not only contributing to the radicalization and diffusion of China's social formations, but also to the spatial and temporal fragmentation of Marxism itself as both a product and critique of Western capitalist modernity.[9] It is wrong, therefore, to insist that the tenacity of its unique tradition has obstructed China's entry into modernity, for China in modern times has experienced probably the most intense social, political, and economic ruptures and changes of its entire history. Oddly, until today, the immutability of China's culture has been held as a truism in the West. It is not the "immutability of Chinese tradition" but the persistence of such a view that is problematical, based as it is on an assumption of Western modernity that could only see changes in other parts of the world as derivative, reluctant, if not reactionary. It has been hard to see changes in the non-West as positive attempts to create alternatives to Western modernity. These alternatives, then, have often been discounted as either a "historical anomaly" or, in the Chinese case, "the immutability of tradition."

The two most celebrated themes of the May Fourth movement, coined by Chen Duxiu, a major Marxist intellectual and the first leader of the Chinese Communist Party (CCP), were democracy and science. While these two concepts did in general grasp the main features of Enlightenment rationality, they went through a structural transformation during and after the May Fourth period that radically altered their "original" meaning. Already heavily contested and polysemic in their Western context, these notions were further complicated in their new setting. In Chen Duxiu's inaugural formulation, they were offered as "cures" for China's political, moral, and intellectual ills.[10] On the other hand, these concepts were considered mainly as modern alternatives to the Confucian tradition in both a cultural and intellectual sense by Hu Shi, another leading intellectual figure in the May Fourth movement who later crusaded for Anglo-American liberalism.[11]

At first, "science" was enthusiastically embraced by people of diverse political and ideological persuasions; it was seen as an encompassing method or paradigm to comprehend and interpret all phenomena in the world. Not until the 1980s' debate about culture was the predominant "scientific paradigm" challenged, although science or scientific discourse was equally touted by an overwhelming majority of Chinese intellectuals during this period. A prominent critical voice in the debate was, in fact, the scientistic revision of Marxist dialectical materialism and historicism, represented by Jin Guantao.[12]

"Democracy," in contrast, underwent a tortuous journey in modern China. In the minds of May Fourth intellectuals, democracy may be characterized as an "attitude" or "ethos" in the Foucauldian sense, as a mode of relating to the world, or a way of thinking, rather than a concept of political institution or system of jurisprudence and governance.[13] Democracy in China has been entwined with various rival political forces, and its discursive formation and transformation attest to the conflictual and antagonistic nature of China's modernity. The articulation of "democracy" in China has been decidedly "extradiscursive": it was caught first between Guomindang's (Nationalist Party) procapitalist, protofascist ideology and the CCP's revolutionary one. Then, pro-Western liberalists and staunch nationalists all vied for the ownership of the word. The government, masses, and intellectuals often seized on issues of democracy in their conflicts and coalitions alike after the People's Republic of China (PRC) was established in 1949. The most recent episode in which "democracy" was invoked, used and abused, and manipulated and deployed by all sorts of political forces, both domestic and international, was the 1989 Tian'anmen event, labeled by its proponents and supporters as a "democracy movement," but condemned by official opponents as "political unrest." For crusaders of a Western-style democracy, Chinese "socialist democracy" is seen as "anti-democratic," diametrically opposed to democratic principles of an American brand. By such principles, though, both "seeds" and "failures" of the pro-Western, pro-American democratic movements in China are measured in the West.[14]

This brief excursion indicates the extent to which crucial concepts such as democracy and science have been mutilated, rarefied, or extended by different and contentious political forces. Under these circumstances, these terms could hardly have any cohesive and systematic meanings. "Democracy," because of its discursive "hybridity," has often proven, in the Chinese context, to be at once too mighty as a political and ideological catchword, and too vacuous and feeble as an intellectual and critical concept. Although "science" has always been valorized as an infallible and incontestable paradigm of China's modernity and modernization, its much ontologized status risks being manipulated by political powers, too. Scientism, or the valorization of scientific reason, has a troublesome legacy in China, the follies and fallacies of which have yet to be fully exposed.

Aesthetics, contrary to the grandiose and "masculine" status of both science and democracy, is frequently perceived as humble, submissive, and "feminine." Surprisingly, however, it generally holds out a resilient and persistent site in modern China. Aesthetics, or the aesthetic discourse, opened up a significant space in both theory and practice, and performed a decisive role in modern Chinese cultural politics. Nonetheless, for the most part, it has evaded the selective eyes of actors as well as spectators. Captivated by the spectacle of China's political struggle, China observers are unable to cast a glimpse at the structure of the amphitheater, as it were, in which historical dramas are played out, let alone savor the theatrical and aesthetic effects surrounding the scene. These aesthetic effects are neither side effects nor marginal influences; they are often the very loci of dramatic acts, as ideological and political campaigns almost always began in artistic and literary circles.

Li Zehou, China's major proponent of "aesthetic Marxism," formulated his highly influential thesis of China's struggle for modernity largely in political and sociological terms, calling it "a dual variation of enlightenment and national salvation." The thesis was expressed in a musical metaphor ("dual variation"), yet ironically, Li and countless interpreters paid scant attention to the metaphor and its aesthetic effect, that may bear, either inimically or positively, on the concept itself. What Terry Eagleton suggests about the status of the aesthetic as inherently "feminine" makes good sense: "As a kind of concrete thought or sensuous analogue of the concept, the aesthetic partakes at once of the rational and the real, suspended between the two somewhat in the manner of the Lévi-Straussian myth. It is born as a woman, subordinate to man but with her own humble, necessary tasks to perform."[15] But this "feminine" discourse has performed political interventionist functions no less effectively than other discourses. While the existence of a revolutionary "feminism" in China— prompted by Mao's defiant proclamation that "Women can hold up half the sky," and actively pursued by millions of Chinese women during his reign—is perhaps more radical than feminism in the West, at least in an ideological sense, notions of femininity and masculinity carry a different connotation from that of Western feminist theories.

In the West, intense debates about the role of culture have largely focused on the issues of modernity and postmodernity. Contemporary Western social thought now perceives culture as playing a key role in modernity. This is said to be critically related to a "late" capitalist society, where culture, according to Fredric Jameson, has undergone "a prodigious expansion . . . to the point at which everything in our social life—from economic value and state power to practices and the very structure of the psyche itself—can be said to have become 'cultural' in some original and yet untheorized sense."[16] The centrality of culture in contemporary debates about modernity and postmodernity seems to be based on an assumed temporal-spatial correlation: the elevation of culture is presumed possible only today, when realms of culture and material become indistinguishable. In other words, postmodern culture has become thoroughly commodified, while the commodity itself is transformed into cultural or "symbolic capital." The spatial or geopolitical locus of postmodernity is situated unmistakably in the West. The corollary is that in the age of modernity that preceded postmodernity, dominance or pervasiveness of culture would be considered a historical anachronism or anomaly. This is because what distinguished modernity from the Middle Ages was the autonomy and separation of culture from other spheres of social life, and culture's limited role—vis-à-vis the domination of the economy, science, and technology—identified the secular, materialistic, and pragmatic orientation of modernity.

Such an understanding of the relationship between culture and modernity has only limited validity. What is at stake, however, is not so much the historical limits of conceptions, as the universalism underlying such a historical periodization. Modernity, as many critics contend, by virtue of its contradictoriness and nonsynchronicity, revolves around a dialectic that animates every sphere of society, without ever successfully installing a universal telos. Thus, the "culturalist resolution" for constructing modernity in non-Western countries is no more "exceptional" or "abnormal" than the preeminence of "culture" in the postmodern West. The role of culture in historical responses to and critiques of modernity has a genealogy that is far from monolithic and unilinear. It is not merely a "recovery" of Enlightenment aesthetic thought by postmodernist theorists. In China, for instance, the critique of modernity and searches for an alternative modernity have long assumed "culturalist" forms.

But before engaging the issue of why culture has been so central to China's modernity, one must question the ways in which modern Chinese history is perceived and conceptualized both in the West and China. It is now a truism in scholarly circles that the predominance of culture, or a "culturalist tendency," in Chinese responses and solutions to modernity is a main characteristic of modern Chinese history, from the late Qing reforms (circa 1890–1910), to the May Fourth intellectual enlightenment movement (1919), to the Great Cultural Revolution (1966–1976). How to interpret this phenomenon? The critical paradigms in modern China studies have been shaped by the same conceptual frameworks and discourses of Western modernity. Because culture had only a limited role in the construction of Western modernity, the dominance of a certain "culturalism" in China must be seen as a historical anomaly. Many Chinese scholars also tend to subscribe to this view. They see the emphasis on culture and cultural revolution as an impediment, rather than a unique historical solution and alternative, to modernity. Such conventional wisdom has recently been challenged. China's questions and solutions are now placed in the more global context of modernity than in the past. Yet due to the institutional division of labor in Western academia, the examination of China's role in global modernity is still confined within the perimeters of China studies or Sinology. (Japan, by contrast, has recently received more attention from a wide range of disciplines in the social sciences and humanities beyond the field of Japanology and area studies specialists. Japan's success with modernization, and its increasingly self-conscious assertion of its distinctive experience of modernity, have compelled Western students to look at that country's case within the global historical movements of the modern era.)[17]

At the height of the 1960s' worldwide upheavals of cultural revolutions and into the 1970s, French and German thinkers such as Sartre, Althusser, and Herbert Marcuse enthusiastically embraced Maoism and Mao's Cultural Revolution as distinct criticisms of and alternatives to (capitalist) modernity. Interestingly, the Chinese Cultural Revolution had only limited impact on Western Sinology or China studies. In fact, China studies, as an institution deeply entrenched in the cold war politics of the time, had remained hostile to it throughout. Poststructuralists and postmodernists in the West, in comparison, have by and large remained silent or ambivalent about the encounter between Maoism and French radical theories. The Western Left has evidently been puzzled by events in post-Mao China, where Mao's revolutionary legacy has been almost totally denounced. Ironically, while the political interventionist stance is being increasingly asserted in contemporary cultural criticism in the West (mainly in English-speaking countries), ideologies of (capitalist) modernity and modernization, ranging from Daniel Bell's "end of ideology" brand of liberalism to the so-called "neo-Confucian revival," have recently gained considerable currency in China.

Given this, it is little wonder that aesthetic discourse, especially Marxist aesthetics in China, has attracted little attention abroad. Chinese aesthetic Marxists are primarily inspired by classical German philosophy, along with the writings of Marx and Lenin, and their theoretical discourse is suffused with metaphysical and essentialist terms such as the "essence of beauty," "humanized nature as the ultimate fulfillment of man's essence," and so forth, far removed from China's social reality. For a China specialist in the West, who is probably interested in issues directly related to realpolitik Chinese aesthetic discourse appear to be nothing more than an officially sanctioned rehearsal of Marxist-Leninist doctrines, hardly useful for analyses of the political reality in China.[18] To a postcolonialist critic, on the other hand, Chinese Marxist aesthetics, together with other forms of modern thought, seem deeply enmeshed in the Western hegemonic discourse of modernity, particularly in the discursive formation of subjectivity that lies at the heart of modern aesthetics.

But neither "mainstream" China studies in the West nor postcolonialist perspectives, nor some of the newer views emerging in the China field, understand the importance of Chinese Marxist aesthetics in China's modernity or alternative modernity. "Mainstream" China studies, especially in the United States, still remains ensnared by a residual cold war ideology, and hence, largely adopts an anti-Marxist stance; postcolonialist perspectives tend to gloss over the most critical issues of China's revolutionary legacy and ideological hegemony. Such a powerful hegemony renders China's cultural scene fundamentally different from those of other "postcolonial" or "Third World" countries, particularly India and the Arab world, from which most of the assumptions of the postcolonialist and "Third World" cultural criticism are derived.[19]

Just as postmodernism in the West tries to dissolve autonomy and the boundaries between culture and other social spheres, and to place culture at the core of social life, so the Chinese searches for an alternative modernity puts culture at the heart of its project. This may be explained in terms of nonsynchronicity or uneven development, but the concepts themselves must be significantly modified. The conceptual migration and overlap among modernity, an alternative modernity, and postmodernity should be understood as a result of historical multilinearity, and spatial and temporal asymmetry. In other words, one should rigorously challenge assumptions of a historical teleology by which diverse courses and routes are measured as uneven developments, which implies a unilinear temporal progression of premodern, modern, and postmodern. Such a conceptual framework is derived from a recent European strain, the Enlightenment, and has been since misrecognized as the universal model. Now that such models of history are subject to scrutiny, examinations of culture's historical role in China or the "postmodern" West should also be sensitive to the universalist assumptions at work.

The critique of modernity actually began during modernity's inception, and has always assumed different patterns and perspectives. Significant critiques of modernity took the form of social and political revolutions, which swept across the world in the first half of the twentieth century. In China, such a critique and search for an alternative modernity also involved cultural revolution, and thus, cultural and aesthetic realms were key. The primacy of cultural critique in modern China cannot be dismissed as a historical anachronism, an epiphenomenon to uneven, nonsynchronous development, or an anomaly of modernity, nor can it be simply attributed to the uniqueness of Chinese tradition with its "culturalist predisposition." Rather, the preoccupation with cultural and aesthetic issues represents a Chinese attempt to address the problems of modernity, one that bears structural resemblance to the contemporary Western criticism of capitalist modernity.

The successes and failures of this Chinese alternative need to be assessed. It should not, however, be merely measured by Western modernity as a universal model. The Chinese attempt should be seen as an ipso facto alternative to Western capitalist modernity before it is labeled a failure or success. To judge it one must judge modernity as a whole, as a global experience or condition of existence that must include alternatives and challenges across the world. The concept of modernity itself has to be problematized and redefined in the first place. Marshall Berman astutely describes modernity as experiences that "cut across all boundaries of geography and ethnicity, of class and nationality, of religion and ideology." He then argues that modernity as such "can be said to unite all mankind. But it is a paradoxical unity, a unity of disunity: it pours us all into a maelstrom of perpetual disintegration and renewal, of struggle and contradiction, of ambiguity and anguish. To be modern is to be part of a universe in which, as Marx said, 'All that is solid melts into air.'"[20] Modernity must now be grasped as the experience of a general, historical, and universal condition of existence, a structural totality determined and overdetermined by a multitude of particular, local, and irreducible contradictions. The most important feature of modernity is its contradictoriness. Internal, eminent contradictions define modernity as such, in spite of endless efforts to externalize and transport contradictions across geopolitical boundaries. A prominent example of such an externalization or transportation is colonialism, by which European capitalism turned all the social and economic contradictions of capitalist modernization into worldwide ones. Of course, externalization took place at ideological and, indeed, epistemological levels, too. Dichotomies like modernity and tradition, or the modernized West versus the premodern non-West, have been instrumental in the establishment of modern knowledge, or technologies or institutions of knowledge.

Modernity being understood as a global condition of existence, China's entry into it is historically inevitable. But it does not follow that China's passage into modernity is unavoidably predetermined by a European model. Modernity may have begun in the West, but the West does not have a monopoly on it. Even in the beginning, modernity involved most parts of the world (through colonialism, slavery, the opening of world markets, and so on), and contradictions thus spread globally. The monolithic and unilinear model of modernity turned out to be merely a retroactively constructed abstraction, whether by Hegelian self-fulfillment of the "absolute spirit" or by Weberian rationalization of the "ideal-type," which precluded a multitude of contradictory factors in the real historical processes. As Masao Miyoshi points out, the so-called modern period of the "First World" may or may not be modern in other areas of the world, and concepts such as modern, modernity, and so forth "should be regarded as regional terms peculiar to the West."[21] In short, modernity is a necessarily contradictory, fragmentary, and heterogeneous entity, or a paradoxical "unity of disunity." It makes more sense to speak of a multiplicity of modernities or alternative modernities than to define modernity as exclusively a European experience.

The relationship of the aesthetic discourse to Chinese modernity or an alternative modernity, then, tells us as much about China as the intrinsic tensions and conflicts of modernity itself. By the same token, the Chinese aesthetic discourse, especially Marxist aesthetics, unravels both the limits and promises of an aesthetic critique of modernity.

Liang Qichao's Aesthetic of "New Citizenry" and Tensions of Modernity

The first systematic introduction of the concept of aesthetics in China was made in 1915.[22] At the turn of the century, however, late Qing reformist intellectuals such as Liang Qichao had already advocated the notion of beauty as key to China's rejuvenation and passage into modernity. Liang Qichao's notion of beauty is important not only because of his status within modern Chinese thought, but also because, as a transitional figure, Liang's aesthetic ideas embody both radical, revolutionary utopianism and cultural, political conservatism. Moreover, Liang's aesthetic thought contains a valuable critique of capitalist modernity, analogous to that of the Western modernist critics.

Studies of Liang in the West have paid little attention to his aesthetic ideas, a serious oversight since they lie at the heart of his thinking. Joseph Levenson, for instance, traces the inherent contradiction in Liang's cultur-alist attitude toward modernity, in contrast to Marxists who saw moder-nity as both a cultural and economic problem.[23] He also examines Liang's shifting positions: from a strong advocate of Western ideas, to a cosmopol-itan modernizationist, and finally, to a nationalist and cultural conserva-tive, reaffirming Chinese cultural values. Yet Levenson attributes this complex change of mind to a simple duality of reason and emotion, reduc-ing the inner tensions of Liang's thought to an intellectual commitment to Western values and emotional attachment to Chinese tradition.[24] Such a simplistic formulation perhaps tells us not so much about Liang, as about the dualistic mode of thinking to which Levenson unselfconsciously sub-scribed. The dichotomies of reason/emotion and knowledge/experience are but a part of the dualistic conceptualization of Western modernity. At the same time, it is also inadequate to simply ascribe Liang's intellectual vacillation and eclecticism to a "liberalist orientation."[25]

Hao Chang's analysis offers a more sophisticated perspective, focusing on the social formation of a "New Citizenry" as the central project of China's modernity. Chang carefully differentiates Liang's notion of the "New Citizenry" from both Confucianism and modern Western ethical systems. He maintains that Liang drew a distinction between private and public morality, and the necessity to cultivate public morality, or civic virtue, as a collective, social, and state system of ethics. In Liang's judg-ment, Confucian morality emphasized family ethics and lacked a true public morality.[26] The concept of a "New Citizenry" comes close to the ideal of the European bourgeoisie: an autonomous, independent, self-determining, and self-regulating subjectivity, which exists in a civil soci-ety or public sphere. It is significant, as Chang notes, that despite Liang's eminently modern concept of a "New Citizenry," his differentiation of polity and morality "were inseparably fused in the tradition of Confucian practical statesmanship."[27] Confronted with the social reality of China, Liang's evolutionist, reformist, and utopian "New Citizenry" program was politically untenable. Liang ultimately looked toward political and ideological conservatism against socialist revolution. Nevertheless, as

Chang observes, Liang's "popular image of citizenship . . . became a major and abiding part of the ideological ferment of twentieth century China."[28] This "popular image of citizenship," in turn, comes from Liang's aesthetic ideas.

Liang's seminal role in promoting literary reform was exemplified by his 1902 essay, "On the Relationship between Fiction and the Government of the People," in which he articulated the necessity of writing fiction or stories—*xiaoshuo*: "If you want to revitalize a country's populace, you must first revitalize that country's fiction."[29] This extravagant assignment to story writers was in keeping with his belief that "beauty" or aesthetics was "the most important element of human life."[30] It can be said that Liang's notion of modernity itself rests on a historical understanding of Western culture, in which aesthetics or fine arts are privileged over science:

> One who only has some rudimentary knowledge of the history of the West would know modern Western culture evolved from the Renaissance. I do not need to repeat the common knowledge that the foundation of modern culture is science. However, the primary vocation and the greatest contribution of the Renaissance lay in the fine arts. Looking superficially, the fine arts are products of feeling, while science is a product of reason, and the two are incommensurable. But how can such a warm-hearted Mr. Art breed a cold-minded son of Science? It would be extremely interesting to explore the causal relationship between the two. The reason why the fine arts can engender science is solely derived from the notion of "unity of truth and beauty." They [the Renaissance thinkers] considered truth the same as beauty, and what was truthful was also beautiful. So their pursuit of beauty started from the pursuit of truth.[31]

Although Liang accorded high priority to "truth," his notion of it was by no means confined to the epistemological and cognitive categories of scientific knowledge and reason. His perspective was derived from a neo-Confucian and Buddhist idealism that considers "true" as the "state created by mind."[32] Such a definition, when invoked in describing the Renaissance's pursuit of truth and beauty, betrays not only Liang's cultural prejudices, but also his deep-seated utopianism, implied by his interpretation of modern Western culture. Given the predominant rationalist view, Liang's attempt to see Western modernity from an aesthetic angle is radical. It bears heavily on both his idea of a "New Citizenry," which amounts to no less than a concept of subjectivity, and his project of a "moral revolution," which turns out to be a reconciliation and selective synthesis of traditional Chinese and Western cultural values.[33] Liang's view problematized the dichotomy of a "material West/spiritual East" embedded in the dualism of ti-yong (spiritual essence and practical use), and radically rewrote the historical formation of modernity, disclosing its intrinsic contradictions between feeling and reason, the fine arts and sciences.

His notion of aesthetics, however, is also self-contradictory and incomplete. Liang's view of the political function of the aesthetic, conveyed by his exuberant assignment of writing fiction to the messianic mission of changing China, is utopian. His claims had no substantive historical evidence to back them up, nor did he envision any concrete, practical steps to implement change through writing stories and novels—an objective hardly tenable and achievable, given China's immense social, political, and economic crises at the time. On the other hand, the grand social and political mission accorded by Liang to fiction revealed a utilitarian strain of thought as well. His stance on the political role of fiction reaffirmed the presumptions within the ti-yong dualism. By shifting the burden of China's social change exclusively to aesthetic and cultural domains, Liang in effect essentialized China's spiritual and cultural superiority.

The contradictory nature of Liang's aesthetic idea can be further illustrated by his explicit critique of Western modernity. He attributed escalating social conflicts in modern Europe to Western culture's inability to reconcile the tensions between individuality and collectivity in the ceaseless pursuit of progress. Such a pursuit, according to Liang, resulted in excessive expansion and the domination of scientific reason, along with the "massification" of all spheres of social life.[34] Still, Liang did not simply condemn the phenomena of modern capitalist social regulation, centralization, and bureaucratization from a moral standpoint. Nor, of course, did he understand the political economy of the Fordist mode of production, which was characterized by Liang as "massification." Such huge, highly centralized industrial production began to emerge precisely at the time Liang went to Europe. There are, nonetheless, at least two possible directions that Liang's critique may lead. First, by insisting on compromising and negotiating the relationship between private and public life, increasingly dissociated and collapsed by the capitalist mode of production in the phase of Fordism or highly centralized industrial production, Liang carved out an idealist domain for free, civilized individuals in modern China. Second, he offered to solve the problems plaguing humankind by intermingling "the best of all cultures." Liang considered this task a "supreme mission" for China, "to expand our civilization with the Western civilization and to supplement the Western civilization with ours," thereby forming a new syncretic cultural system benefiting all humanity.[35] Undoubtedly, both directions have a strong aesthetic, utopian inclination. Liang hoped to reconcile and unite antagonistic forces by way of "spiritual life" and Lebenswelt. But his solutions are at odds with each other, precisely be-cause the modernist notion of free, civilized, spiritual individuals presup-poses a cultural elitism (and ultimately, a cultural ethnocentrism) that runs counter to the populist and universalist claims underlying his cul-tural syncretism.

Liang saw a possible reconciliation of the public and private in modern European idealist philosophy, especially in Henri Bergson's notion of the "intuition," "duration" (durée), and "vital impulse" (élan vital) of the "free consciousness." While for Bergson, the free flow of consciousness or intu-ition defines human experience as an "aesthetic experience,"[36] in Liang's mind it generates the "spiritual life" or Lebenswelt in which humanity progresses every day. Liang applauded modern European intuitive and ide-alist philosophies, which in his view provided possible "reconciliation be-tween idealism and materialism," "science and religion."[37] His emphasis on "spiritual life" as the principal civic virtue is analogous to that of some European modernists, such as the late-nineteenth-century British intel-lectuals who advocated "intellectual aristocracy" and antimodern elit-ism. As Raymond Williams observes in his analysis of "the Bloomsbury fraction," and Frank Raymond Leavis and his Scrutiny group, these British intellectuals articulated a position of a "free" and "civilized" norm in modern societies: "In the very power of their demonstration of a private sensibility that must be protected and extended by forms of public con-cern, they fashioned the effective forms of the contemporary ideological dissociation between 'public' and 'private' life."[38]

Such an ideological effect can be said to have occurred in Liang's at-tempts to compromise a similar dissociation in China, too. Liang wavered between conflicts between polity and morality, civility and nationhood, in his struggles to create a modern subjectivity or "New Citizenry" as an aesthetic and moral being. But his protomodernist orientation of the au-tonomy and separation of the arts, when pushed to an extreme by a thinker like Wang Guowei, turned out to be self-destructive. It simply pulverized the category of subjectivity, which Liang intended to cultivate as a "New Citizenry."

Autonomy or Self-Destruction: The Modernist Aesthetics of Wang Guowei

Wang Guowei was no social reformist like Liang Qichao. He was primarily a literary scholar, who dedicated himself to the aesthetic ideal of free indi-viduality, autonomy, and separation. He was deeply immersed in Scho-penhauerian, Nietzschean, and Chan (or Zen) Buddhist aesthetics. Wang's aesthetic ideas can be seen as radically modernist and traditionalist at once. As a person, he remains a controversial figure. A scholar of formidable erudition in philosophy, aesthetics, history, and literary criticism, Wang was perhaps the first to incorporate modern Western concepts into studies of Chinese literature in sophisticated ways. Fiercely hostile to social reform and revolution, Wang in his later years occupied himself entirely with Confucian classics. Politically speaking, Wang was a staunch conservative. Many years after the Qing Dynasty was overthrown by the 1911 Republican Revolution, he remained till his death a loyalist to the dethroned emperor. In 1927, at the age of fifty-one, Wang drowned himself in the Lake of Summer Palace in Beijing. His suicide in the prime of life was largely a symbolic gesture, leaving a major enigma in modern Chinese intellectual history. Wang has been denigrated ever since, by liberal reformists and radical revolutionaries alike, as a recalcitrant cultural and political reactionary. Not until the late 1980s was he viewed more favorably in China.[39]

In the 1990s, Wang's posthumous fame suddenly reached an unprecedented height: his interpretations of the classic Chinese novel *Dream of Red Chamber*, from a Schopenhauerian-Nietzschean perspective, is hailed as the inauguration of modern Chinese scholarship. He is credited with establishing a scholarly paradigm that integrates modern Western thinking with the classical tradition of China. As such, he is considered a modern sage. Wang's most significant contribution, in brief, is said to be his unyielding efforts to overcome the political and ideological obstacles to a truly independent, autonomous scholarship.[40] Accordingly, his suicide is now interpreted as a gesture of "cultural will-passing," signaling a profoundly pessimistic vision of prospects of culture and tradition, to which he reacted not with passive acceptance or cynicism, but with unremitting will of resistance, ultimately by giving up his own life.[41]

To be sure, Wang's latest ascendancy has much to do with the political and ideological milieu of the 1990s, in which a so-called "national learning"—*guo xue*—has been "rediscovered" or "revived." National learning has been promoted by a group of Beijing scholars, who intended to recuperate a nonpolitical and nationalist cultural alternative to the disintegrating revolutionary hegemony. As a move to essentialize scholarship in the humanities—primarily in the realms of literature, history, and philosophy—it entails radical debunking of an intellectual tradition in modern China inextricably intertwined with realpolitik, that is, political power struggle as the material condition of social life. National learning posits itself as a neohermeneutics (or posthermeneutics?) reinterpreting modern Chinese intellectual history from a conceptual framework that pits the binarism of the "political-secular/scholarly-transcendental" against that of "tradition/modernity" as a major hermeneutic paradigm in the 1980s' debate.[42] A truly modern national learning, according to its advocates, is concerned not so much with immediate political, secular, and pragmatic issues, as with the nonutilitarian, nonpolitical, and transcendental issue of "truth."[43]

Both the modernist and conservative traits in Wang's thought are highlighted by recent attempts to lionize him as the crowning hero of national learning. To understand Wang's ideas, a quick look at some of the major features of modernism is helpful. Modernist sentiment is well captured by Charles Baudelaire, who saw the artist as the embodiment of the deepest dilemma of modernity. "Modernity," Baudelaire wrote, "is the transient, the fleeting, the contingent; it is the one half of art, the other being the eternal and the immutable."[44] It is this perpetual vacillation and vertigo that characterizes aesthetic modernism in the West, philosophically represented by Wang's two primary sources of inspiration, Arthur Schopenhauer and Nietzsche, among others. But in China, Wang's modernism (and conservatism) has a decidedly political twist. Or, to put it differently, compared to Western aesthetic modernism, politics—that is, power relations of the state and society at large—is far more important in Wang's mind, despite his professed apolitical aestheticism to the contrary.

Wang's radical aesthetic modernism can be seen in two aspects of his thought. First, Wang shared with Nietzsche and Schopenhauer a strong sense of modernity as nothing more than a vital energy or desire, the will to life (and death) and power, in a universe of anarchy, alienation, disorder, and despair. Nietzsche discerned vital yet wild and primitive energies, incarnated by the mythical spirit of Dionysus, "to be at one and the same time 'destructively creative' (i.e., to form the temporal world of individualization and becoming, a process destructive of unity) and 'creatively destructive' (i.e., to devour the illusory universe of individualization, a process involving the reaction of unity."[45] Since Dionysian spirit in Nietzsche's view is the aesthetic spirit par excellence, aesthetics is endowed with a power above that of science, rationality, and politics, "beyond good and evil." Wang's confidence in the power of aesthetics was no less passionate than Nietzsche's, but it was tinged with a Schopenhauerian self-destructive or suicidal pessimism. Schopenhauer argued that the destructiveness of humankind, which in a Baudelairean sense means the fleeting and contingent aspects of modernity, stems from desire itself. Desire in Schopenhauer's opinion is a paradoxical, self-annihilating entity, a burlesque travesty or shoddy mirror image of the Kantian aesthetic. It is the other side of modernity, the eternal and immutable, but only in the sense of an absolute Buddhist quiescence that demolishes subjectivity at one stroke. The destructive force of desire thus denies its own existence, being seen as a perpetual, inferno-like Buddhist Brahman, the resource from which everything originates and must ultimately return. Such a self-abnegating aesthetic state of desire, or attitude of life, seemed to fit Wang perfectly. His intellectual upbringing was deeply ingrained with the submissive and nihilistic strains of Taoism and Chan (Zen) Buddhism. It is little wonder that Wang was enamored with Schopenhauer's thought. Like Schopenhauer, Wang had a strong aversion to Kantian aesthetics, particularly to its Enlightenment optimism.[46]

"What is the essence of life?" Wang asked rhetorically, and then answered with absolute assurance:

> It is nothing but *yu* [desire]. Desire by its nature is insatiable, which originated in the state of lack. To lack is to be in the state of suffering. . . . Our life is like a pendulum, swinging perpetually between suffering and boredom. Of course boredom can also be viewed as a kind of suffering. We call happiness the state in which the two [suffering and boredom] are relinquished. However, we must strive strenuously for happiness, in addition to the suffering we already experience. Striving is a kind of suffering, too. . . . Suffering increases rather than decreases as the world culture expands, for the more progressive culture becomes, and broader it expands [human] knowledge, the more [human] desires. Therefore [a person] suffers more intensely and feels more agony. . . . Desire, life, and suffering, then constitute a triad. . . .
>
> There is only one thing that can allow us to transcend our practical interests and calculations, and to forget the relationship between matter and self. . . . What is this thing that can achieve all these [transcendence and forgetting], if not meishu [fine art]? . . . The task of fine art is to describe the suffering of life, and to point a way out of suffering. It will then allow us, the philistine crowd, to part with struggles of desire in life, within the world as a prison house, so that we may achieve a temporary equanimity. Such is the goal of all fine arts.[47]

This argument was presented in Wang's celebrated study of *Dream of Red Chamber*. What distinguishes this as not only his magnum opus, but also a first in paradigmatic modern literary criticism in China, is Wang's modernist interpretation. Wang's study elucidates the affinities between Western postromantic, modernist sentiments and classical Chinese aesthetics that had fascinated modernist thinkers and poets, such as Karl Jaspers and Ezra Pound. In this classic Chinese novel, Wang saw a mutual illumination of the Schopenhauerian denial of desire and a tragic vision of life. Such a vision looks like an appearance of Heideggerian authentic being, through the wholesale immolation and abnegation of worldly desires, achievable by an unobtrusive Taoist-Buddhist poesis incarnated by the novel itself.

The second characteristic of Wang's modernism was his adamant insistence on the autonomy and separation of art and scholarship. This was posed against Western-inspired reformist or revolutionary ideologies that favored scientific reason. In addition, it was opposed to Chinese utilitarian tradition, which privileged politics and morality over "pure truth," or metaphysics, and aesthetics. Unlike most modern Chinese intellectuals who were preoccupied with China's compelling social problems, and looked invariably to Western scientific reason and social ideologies as cures, Wang remained inordinately critical of such enthusiasm for Western ideas. In particular, he singled out scientific rationality as a pernicious influence. Wang castigated the efforts of scholar Yan Fu to reform China with modern Western notions as "mere interests in British doctrines of utilitarianism and evolution," "sub-branches of philosophy, economics, sociology, and so on." He claimed that "the animus of Mr. Yan's studies is not philosophical but scientific."[48]

Wang critiqued Confucian utilitarianism from the same angle. He contended that most Chinese philosophers were only concerned with moral and political philosophies as means to societal change, without emphasizing a metaphysical basis, which should be an end in itself. Moreover, in Chinese tradition, fine art has never had an independent value of its own. Hence, in order to have truly independent intellectual inquiry, scholarship and fine art must be pursued as ends in themselves, rather than means to other political and social objectives. Invoking the Kantian dictum of "purposiveness without a purpose," Wang expounded the relativity of both useful and useless aspects of scholarship. Scholarship cannot be judged "useful" or "useless" purely in terms of its relationship to specific social issues or historical events; it should be measured by the extent to which it pertains to the "universal truth of life."[49] Autonomy, or independence of scholarship, especially in metaphysics and aesthetics, is in Wang's opinion firmly grounded in the pursuit of truth. Truth in Wang's vocabulary obviously has little to do with scientific knowledge. Instead, it refers to a kind of intuitive revelation about the essence of life, embodied by Schopenhauerian and Taoist-Buddhist aesthetics. In this respect, Wang's notion is akin to that of Liang Qichao, taking truth to be the pure creation of mind, rather than to that of Kant, who tried to reconcile a priori, transcendental rationality with empirical knowledge. What Wang wrote about truth is revealing, telling us as much as about his modernist aesthetics as his conservative politics:

> The aim of philosophy and art is truth. Truth is universal, eternal, and immutable, and he who elucidates truth (the philosopher) or expresses it (the artist) makes a universal and eternal contribution. It is not short-lived. Precisely because it is universal and eternal, truth cannot be in complete harmony with the interests of any particular nation at a particular time. And sometimes truth is incompatible with such interests. But this is where the sacredness of truth lies.[50]

Wang's concern with the pursuit of truth, irrespective of its usefulness or historical specificity, not only contradicts his modernist sensibility and awareness of the ephemeral, transient nature of things (which would include truth itself), but also retreats to an intractable classicism that takes truth as immobile and eternal. Politically, it signals a turn to an antireform, counterrevolutionary standpoint. His ideological allegiance resembled a certain right-wing modernism in the West. As an aside, the so-called Chinese modernism, a marginal movement in the 1930s by a handful of Western-educated writers, showed unequivocal right-wing political and ideological affiliations, whereas the majority of modern Chinese writers, who mostly had left-wing allegiances, tended to espouse nineteenth-century European romanticism and realism as their literary modes.[51]

Western aesthetic modernism can be said to have had two distinct preoccupations. One was with language, or the mode of representation; the other, myth. An obsession with language and representation had to do with the modernist uncertainty of the linguistic medium, and suspicions about language's ability to represent eternal and immutable truths. It was directed against assumptions about the transparency of language, which can represent truth and reality with no distortion, and those of Western metaphysics invested in mimesis itself, as embodied by the aesthetic modes of classicism, realism, and naturalism. The purported "crisis of mimesis" was, in hindsight, a cultural constituent of the experience of modernity. Modernist art, therefore, was conceived first of all as a countermimetic act, or as the manifestation of attitudes of "countermodernity." But the role of art was largely misunderstood by modernists, who transmuted art into an organic, self-referential construct. It was valorized as an ontological being, as a pure innovation of the imagination of the individual artist, divorced from social and historical contexts. By so doing, the modernist artifact—or the "well-wrought urn," to borrow John Keats's celebrated metaphor—became locked up in an aporia, turning itself into a reified and alienated object in the very moment of its own creation. Art was first conceived as a subversion of alienation and the reification of life, but in the end it divorced itself from life entirely, thus becoming alienated from the populace. It also came to be reified as a newfangled commodity when the market began to accept modernist arts as valuable objects. In the hands of certain revolutionary avant-garde writers and artists, experiments with language and multiple perspectives were at once expressive and subversive of alienation, and critical of bourgeois consumerism and lifestyles. But with other modernists, invention or reinvention of myth often performed dubious and ambivalent functions, which can either be absorbed by "mainstream" ideologies or hegemony, or appropriated as a consumer product that can neutralize political struggles. Myth is an ambiguous term for Western modernists, playing multifarious roles in the works of James

Joyce, Thomas Eliot, William Faulkner, and Pablo Picasso, to name just a few. Modern mythology can be construed as a post-Enlightenment countermyth to that of modernity itself, or a proliferation of multiple, pagan myths against medieval Christian mythology.

Yet Wang's generation of Chinese intellectuals believed their cultural traditions and symbolic systems were quite different from Western ones. As modern intellectuals, the Chinese felt no less a deep sense of restlessness and anguish than their Western counterparts. In China, there has never been a strong sentiment against the alleged "tyranny of mimesis," which is predicated on an ontological split between essence and phenomenon, between the world to be represented and the representing medium of language. Unlike the intense apprehension of the unreliable and untrustworthy status of language—which is as old as Western civilization itself since the time of Plato—Chinese poetics, except a certain Taoist agnosticism, are not based on the dichotomous presuppositions or binary oppositions between essence and appearance, reality and representation. Confucian notions of language are largely synthetic, blending a protonaturalist idea of the "organic and natural origins" of the linguistic sign with that of functionalism, taking language as an indispensable means of communication between human beings and the cosmic order, and among human beings themselves. Hence, to insist on the resemblance between Tao and Logos, and thereby draw equations between the "Chinese view" of language (which is actually merely a specific kind of Taoist skepticism) and modern-day deconstruction, neglects the dominant Confucian notion that presupposes a natural bond and reciprocal interaction between signs and things.

Myth, on the other hand, has hardly enjoyed a privileged status in a Confucian cultural ambiance, which concentrated on the secular world and communal intercourse, presided over not by mythological deities, but the spirits of family ancestors. Moreover, in a culture that prizes memory, preservation, and reproduction of traditional values, the Western modernist valorization of innovation and creation would find itself unable to solicit enthusiasm. The only exception in China would be an artistic innovation that directly benefits the moral good or social well-being. Since Western modernism made neither of these claims, it did not easily take root in China, especially since Chinese writers and artists alike were preoccupied, as most Chinese intellectuals were, with the compelling social problems that threatened to tear the nation apart. Western romanticism and realism, by contrast, had all the social and moral appeals that the Chinese needed, and thus, were eagerly embraced.

But cultural differences were by no means the decisive reason for Wang's halfhearted espousal of modernism or his ultimate conversion to Confucian classicism and political conservatism. Granted, cultural differences are significant determinants, especially with respect to the personal dispositions of individuals. But they must be understood as contradictions within a given historical context or condition of existence, which in Wang's time, was precisely the moment of modernity. Cultural differences and predispositions form a habitus, defined by Pierre Bourdieu as "a system of durable, transposable dispositions which functions as the generative basis of structured, objectively unified practices."[52] It should be emphasized that a habitus, as a set of subjective and unconscious dispositions, changes with historical material conditions. Individuals make their choice to be either a radical, avant-garde modernist or an uncompromising conservative, but this depends on concrete social practices overdetermined by a multitude of factors. In Wang's case, his choice to be a traditionalist and conservative was derived primarily from his reaction to China's societal transformation—he was undoubtedly opposed to any reform or evolution, let alone revolution. Such a choice was inevitably filled with internal incoherence and contradictions, as evidenced by his later repugnance of his early advocacy of vernacular literature (*Dream of Red Chamber*) as well as German nihilistic philosophy, incommensurable with his eventual conviction to Confucian morality.

Wang's aesthetics, incorporating the ideas of Western modernist precursors with classical Oriental philosophies (Taoist-Buddhist in particular), is not unrelated to his ideological position, rooted in the agrarian life of traditional China. Of course, there is no simple homology between Wang's aesthetics and the political economy of China. Nor can we pinpoint in his work explicit manifestations of such ideological and political positions. This can only be inferred from Wang's oeuvre, which symptomatically lacked a construction of subjectivity as a self-conscious, autonomous being. By contrast, one can identify a preponderance of self-destructive, self-abnegating quiescence in his thought, pursued with great zeal. His suicide paradoxically signaled not passive acquiescence, but moral resolve. The absence of any interest in constructing subjectivity marks a serious difference between Wang's notions and Liang Qichao's "New Citizenry."

Still, perhaps inadvertently, Wang pointed to a cultural realm that can only be defined as imaginary, existing in a poetic world that intermingled human emotions and natural surroundings. This was fully spelled out in the imaginary world of his tour de force on Chinese aesthetics and poetics, *Renjian cihua* (Remarks on lyrics in the world of men). This "poetic world" or *jingjie*—merging and dissolving at once the boundaries between emotion and scene, mind and matter, self and thing, subject and object[53]—became an ideal state of artistic creation, echoed and studied over and over again by Chinese artists and critics alike. The organic, pastoral, and agrarian "way of life" that Wang's aesthetics/poetics has intimated invites comparison with the British postromantic poets, critics, and intellectuals that Raymond Williams studied.

The mode of life embodied by Wang's aesthetics of a "poetic world" is double-edged: on one side, it could be deployed, with a certain abstraction, to reinscribe an ideology of bourgeois liberalism into Chinese national culture in an Arnoldian fashion, as is the case with the national learning school's latest rediscovery of Wang's significance. On the other, since it reflected the real material condition of China, Wang's poetic world should be grasped as a specific reference to China's agrarian mode of production that revolution aimed to transform. As such, Chinese revolution could not divorce itself from agrarian life, attempting to come to terms with it in cultural and aesthetic realms.

With respect to the liberalist direction in Wang's poetic world, Williams's comment on the ideological function of Matthew Arnold's notion of "culture and anarchy" is illuminating: "Excellence and humane values on the one hand; discipline and where necessary repression on the other. This, then as now, is a dangerous position: a culmination of the wrong kind of liberalism . . . was a culmination of the most honest kind."[54] This would apply to Wang's recent advocates, too. Insofar as Wang's aesthetics is pitted against the legacy and hegemony of the revolution that irrevocably transformed China from the old, agrarian mode of production into a new "socialist" one, any valorization of the poetic world would smack of a nostalgia for pastoral harmony and dignity, however horrendous social injustices may have actually been rendered and legitimated under precisely such social circumstances. It is, nevertheless, interesting that just as concerns with the "way of life" and natural intimacy of culture and social relationships and structures have strongly impacted the British legacy of cultural criticism—from Leavis and Eliot, to Edward T. Thompson, to Williams and Stuart Hall—so too, the Chinese emphasis on communal and natural bonds permeating cultural and social formations has influenced modern aesthetic and cultural criticism—from Liang Qichao and Wang Guowei, to Lu Xun, Qu Qiubai, and Mao Zedong.

When the agrarian mode of life was actually confronted by revolution, from the May Fourth movement to the Communist revolution, a host of new contradictions emerged. Not the least of these was the one between modern, urban, cosmopolitan culture and agrarian, nativist, nationalist cultural formations. It would be a serious mistake to reduce this contradiction to the simple tradition/modernity opposition, for it has been internalized within China's modernization process, and therefore, is intrinsic to China's modernity or alternative modernity. This is especially true in the hegemony of Chinese Marxist revolutionary culture, which has constituted the most powerful historical force in China's modernity.

Enlightenment and Aesthetic Education:
Cai Yuanpei's Incomplete Project

Cai Yuanpei promoted a synthetic notion of a universal cultural system by way of aesthetic education. Unlike Wang, who fought to carve out an autonomous terrain for culture and aesthetics during a time of formidable social conflict, Cai's concern was decidedly with the public domain, continuing Liang's project of an aesthetic and ethical education to foster a modern subjectivity and universal cultural syncretism. Cai's enlightenment aesthetic project, though not a Marxist formation, highlights the intrinsic contradiction between an urban, cosmopolitan vision of modernity and a rural, agrarian, nativist orientation.

Cai's aesthetic concept is twofold. First, the aesthetic was conceived as a preeminent discourse of enlightenment and cultural revolution, against China's stagnant tradition; second, it provided a humanistic and utopian dimension to Chinese modernity, influenced primarily by Western scientific reason. As a utopian discourse, it promised new formations of universalism and cultural syncretism. Underlying his assumptions of the aesthetic is a distinctly urban and cosmopolitan vision. Although his aesthetic idea was extremely influential, Cai was primarily an educator rather than a literary theorist or an aesthetician. His aesthetics, then, is best grasped as a key constituent of his overall project of enlightenment and education.

An eminent leader within the May Fourth intellectual enlightenment movement and cultural revolution, Cai's personal history and outlook were radically different from Wang's.[55] His entire career was dedicated to educational and institutional reforms in cities like Beijing and Shanghai. Until his death, he held a number of important government posts: Minister of Education, president of Peking University (a state-run institution), and chair of the Academia Sinica, along with several other high official positions under the Guomindang administration. His writings often reflected his political views. Cai was primarily a liberal democrat, among the predominantly right-wing associates of Chiang Kai-shek's dictatorial regime. Unlike his friends in the May Fourth movement—such as Chen Duxiu, Lu Xun, and Qu Qiubai, who turned to Marxism and communism—Cai remained committed to changes in education and other societal sectors in urban areas. His politics differed as well from another prominent May Fourth intellectual, Hu Shi, who succeeded Cai in almost all official posts. As a liberalist, Hu was greatly favored over Cai by the Guomindang regime because he remained a conformist to Chiang Kai-shek's policies; and unlike Cai, who never openly condemned the Communists, Hu was often a mouthpiece for Chiang Kai-shek's anti-Communist campaigns. Hu's Anglo-American-style liberalism frequently put him in an awkward position, torn between being a reluctant instrument of Chiang Kai-shek's oppressive state, and a liberal intellectual whose conscience and values were basically at odds with the regime. In the end, until his death in Taiwan, Hu was a willing collaborator with Chiang Kai-shek's regime. It is not surprising that he became a major target of political campaigns on the mainland against "Western bourgeois liberalism."[56]

By contrast, Cai's project of institutional reforms and cosmopolitan cultural revolution retained an enduring legacy in China, even after the establishment of the People's Republic. The appeal lies in the incipient modern civil society or public sphere that Cai's educational reform embodies. Urban, cosmopolitan Marxist intellectuals such as Lu Xun and his disciple Hu Feng, among others, had seen the critical need to construct and maintain a semiautonomous space or public sphere under a revolutionary hegemony. On the other hand, Qu Qiubai, himself an urban and cosmopolitan intellectual, initiated a populist and peasant cultural revolution in order to foster a revolutionary class consciousness. Mao also grounded his project of revolution on primarily rural, agrarian cultural forms and structures. Indeed, the internal conflicts between urban, cosmopolitan Marxists and rural, nativist revolutionaries became one of the key issues underlying aesthetic and cultural debates and movements within the Chinese Marxist tradition. It was not until the 1980s' rethinking of China's revolutionary hegemony and modernity that Cai's incomplete project of enlightenment and urban, cosmopolitan cultural revolution began to receive a positive reevaluation.

Cai's idea of enlightenment was mainly derived from the West, particularly eighteenth-century German thought. Like Liang, Cai was quick to seize on the liberating and revolutionary force of the European Enlightenment, fascinated by its cultural dimensions of philosophical, scientific, and artistic enlightenment. To be sure, Cai was drawn to scientific reason, regarding it as an indispensable means to achieve material progress. But Cai's suspicion of relying on the power of science was aroused when he formulated his idea of enlightenment during his years in Europe (mainly in Germany) in the 1910s. Cai's concept of science was historical and philosophical rather than pragmatic. He insisted on the inseparability of science and philosophy, and the mythological, anthropological, and metaphysical foundations of modern science, cutting across diverse scientific systems, including Greek, Indian, and Chinese. This view allowed him to see an interconnectedness and reciprocity between science and metaphysics, without privileging either as the paramount model for modernity. He observed that ever since Kant distinguished science from philosophy, the relation between the two had been one of dialectic tensions: Hegel, for instance, subsumed science under philosophy, while some modern scientists or scientific philosophers rebuked philosophy as sheer sophistry, based on mysticism and superstition. Yet Cai claimed that modern philosophy and methaphysics already synthesized modern scientific discoveries and rationality with philosophical reflections. Hence, he concluded, modern science and philosophy should not be incompatible and mutually exclusive, but instead mutually complementary.[57]

The disenchantment of the world and dissolution of myths, according to Cai's view, cannot be fulfilled by scientific reason alone, which was itself derived from myth and religion. Cai agreed that demystification was the most urgent task of enlightenment, but rather than science or scientific reason, he proposed aesthetics or aesthetic education as the most effective way of demystification and enlightenment. In a seminal 1917 speech, Cai formulated the thesis of "replacing religion by aesthetic education." He first defined religion as a historical phenomenon, satisfying humankind's basic needs of knowledge, will, and emotion at early, primitive stages. As scientific reason evolved, he contended, it gradually replaced religion as a new explanatory system, disenchanting and demystifying the world by its analytical, rational power, which has significantly enriched humanity's material well-being. Ethics and morality, in contrast, are susceptible to concrete historical changes, and vary from culture to culture. All the eternal solutions that religion promises can no longer resolve conflicts between different cultural, moral, and ethical systems and values in modern times. Religion can retain its effectivity only in the realm of emotion. But its inability to unite all diverse cultures and values also weakens its emotive and affective efficacy. Aesthetic experience, Cai maintained, works precisely in the realm of emotion. Therefore, the role of religion in modern times should be replaced by that of aesthetics.

Cai's concept of the aesthetic was eminently Kantian: it is that which bridges the noumenal and phenomenal worlds, and reconciles reason with experience, rationality with sensibility, freedom with law, through a universal emotional experience. But the thrust of Cai's thesis was that "religion in the West has become a thing of the past, the problem of which has already been solved by modern scientific research. . . . People in Europe still go to churches now because of a habit, inherited from the past."[58] He thought it would be evidently wrong to either promote the Western religion of Christianity in China as a new, modern thing, or to convert Confucianism into a religion, after the model of Christianity.[59] The aesthetic, in short, by replacing "religion," by which Cai actually referred to the whole of old tradition, served a preeminent role in the antitraditionalist modern enlightenment. The primacy of both aesthetic experience and education in Cai's program also indicated that enlightenment was mainly conceived as a project of cultural revolution. This was precisely the sense in which

Cai envisaged and actively promoted the "New Cultural Movement" of 1915, together with Chen Duxiu, Lu Xun, Hu Shi, and other precursors of the 1919 May Fourth movement.

As a humanist movement of self-liberation, enlightenment for Cai was a continuation of Renaissance idealism. As a project of modernity, he also believed it was aimed at reconciling and negotiating tensions between the material world and human consciousness. In Cai's mind, education was of vital importance in the project of enlightenment. The core of his education program is aesthetic. Two aspects of the aesthetic, largely based on Kantian notions, were emphasized by Cai: universality and transcendence.[60] Kant argued in the *Critique of Judgment* that aesthetic judgments are at once subjective and universal. By appealing to human emotion and appreciation of beauty, detached from concrete and practical interests, subjective aesthetic experience becomes universal, or "impersonally personal." Both Cai and Liang were attracted to Kant's utopian view of the aesthetic since they were primarily concerned with the need to construct a new relationship between individual, private life and public, social spheres. At the same time, they hoped to reconcile China's traditional values with those of the West, establishing a universal system in which humankind could coexist in harmony. Cai, like Liang and others, saw pitfalls in both the unrestrained individualism of the West, and the undifferentiated state of private and public spheres within the Confucian tradition. Aesthetic education, thus, would accomplish the goal of fostering a modern subjectivity ("New Citizenry" in Liang's project; "education of men" in Cai's), overcoming the gap between egotism and altruism. The aesthetic ideal was also congenial to Cai's (and Liang's) utopian project of cultural syncretism. Cai, again like Liang, was a passionate advocate of a new universal cultural system. In a 1923 speech delivered in Belgium, "On China's Renaissance," Cai identified the key characteristics of Chinese culture that he considered congruent with and amenable to the ideal of humanity: populism, universalism, pacifism, egalitarianism, and tolerance of different religions. These fundamental Chinese values, Cai argued, when integrated with the best of world cultures, would help bring about China's renaissance—in turn, benefiting all of humankind.[61]

The "transcendental" aspect, on the other hand, was perceived by Cai as that which pertains to the central problem of modernity. The ultimate goal of humanity, Cai maintained, was to transcend the phenomenal world, to attain harmony with the universal will of the noumenal world. Such a goal would be attainable only by way of aesthetic experience:

> Aesthetic experience, combining both beauty and sublime, bridges the phenomenal world and the noumenal world. Kant recognized this

for the first time, and none of the subsequent philosophers have rejected this idea. In the phenomenal world, man always has feelings of love and hate, fear and misery, joy and anger, sadness and happiness. These feelings change as a result of changing circumstances, such as separation and reunion, life and death, fortune and misfortune. Art, however, treats all these phenomena as its own material [of contemplation], turning it into an object to which man responds with only aesthetic appreciation, without concerns of other issues.... Detached from practical concerns of the phenomenal world, man's feelings crystallize into a pure aesthetic experience, whereby he befriends the creative power, and comes close to the noumenal world.[62]

The phenomenal world refers in Cai's vocabulary to the real world, in which injustice, class conflict, and other evils go hand in hand with humankind's pursuit of happiness. The noumenal world, by contrast, turned out to be an ethical and moral entity, subject to historical mutations. It differs from the metaphysical Kantian *ding an sich* (here, Cai's interpretation displays a stronger Confucian leaning). But Cai's transcendental concepts did not transcend reality. His understanding of the Kantian dichotomy of phenomenal and noumenal worlds had an unequivocal historical referent: conflict-ridden modernity. Both universal and transcendental aspects of the aesthetic have a primal heuristic value, central to Cai's project of aesthetic education. Cai's objective was to cultivate a "healthy personality" and "self-realization." It would be a new subjectivity with moral integrity and courage, with determination and will of self-sacrifice, in the face of the ordeals of life.[63]

The goal of Cai's aesthetic education is, in one sense, similar to Schiller's. Like Schiller, Cai wanted to wage a cultural revolution in the psychic realms in order to create an ideal aesthetic state. Such a state resembled a utopian public sphere of freedom and democracy, in which all social hierarchies would be suspended and abolished, and a new human relationship, in the image of disinterested fraternity, would be constituted. But Cai's aesthetic and ethical subjectivity is no replica of a Kantian-Schillerian one, based on the idealism of the European bourgeoisie. Cai's subjectivity has a more socialist, as opposed to aristocratic or bourgeois, bent, for he always stressed the aspects of self-realization and self-sacrifice. Moreover, his notion has a distinct Confucian touch in its ethical and political dimensions. In Confucianism, polity and morality are but two sides of the same coin. Since Cai considered aesthetic education to be the best morally, he never denied that it also served a political purpose. He encouraged Confucian ethical-moral practice in aesthetic education, instead of condoning a moral and political detachment.

Cai's faith in aesthetic education and self-realization is anchored on an urban, cosmopolitan vision of modernity and a bourgeois, humanist concept of subjectivity. Cai considered the social dimensions of beauty to be more important than natural beauty, and the highest kind of beauty in society could only be found in the public domain of a modern city.[64] He laid out a detailed blueprint for aesthetic education, in which the aesthetic concerns of urban planning and construction, as well as urban institutions of aesthetic education such as museums, art galleries, concert halls, and theaters, were carefully deliberated and meticulously charted.[65] Under the historical circumstances, however, plagued as China was by intense social conflict, Cai's ambitious project of institutional reform, indispensable to the building of a modern civil society, was hardly realizable and remained largely utopian. In fact, the absence of any consideration of China's political or economic situation in Cai's project much weakened its effectiveness and viability.

Although Cai's project of enlightenment and aesthetic education revealed serious predicaments in China's modernity, it also signaled certain possible directions for an alternative modernity. The liberalist one, pursued mainly by non-Marxist, procapitalist intellectuals represented by Hu Shi, faced insurmountable difficulties and internal contradictions. Of these, the most important yet somewhat misrecognized contradiction was the dichotomy of Westernization/Sinification. Hu was deeply entrenched in this dichotomy, and consequently, was misjudged as a staunch Westernizer. But Hu's position is more complex. An eminent intellectual leader of China's New Cultural movement (sometimes also named the Literary Revolution), Hu was the first to see that a linguistic revolution was the prerequisite of a cultural revolution. In addition, Hu was an unrelenting iconoclast during the May Fourth era, known for his fierce attacks on Confucian tradition, and impassioned advocacy of literary and cultural revolution and enlightenment. Moreover, Hu was the first proponent of an "alternative modernization" or alternative modernity for China.[66] Hu's notion of an alternative modernity and his radicalism, however, were marred by a lack of cohesive political vision. He was often indecisive when confronted with political issues, wavering between a liberal democratic position that favored individual freedom and a conservative standpoint that leaned toward Chiang Kai-shek's repressive regime. This was partly due to Hu's superficial understanding of Anglo-American liberalism, as well as an uncritical acceptance of Deweyan pragmatism. In the essay where he formulated the concept of an alternative modernity, he dismissed it as conservative. Ironically, Hu thought the idea was smuggled in by self-styled "friends of China" from the West. The only solution for China, he declared, was the "acceptance of modernization," or "wholehearted modernization." Wholeheartedness was alluded to again by Hu himself in his famous (or infamous) assertion of "wholesale Westernization," for which he was stigmatized. Hu bitterly resented this for nearly the rest of his life because, as a dedicated nationalist and patriot, he had not imagined himself being portrayed as a wholehearted pro-Westerner, let alone a traitor, a label he received from the massive anti-Hu campaign in the PRC in the 1950s.[67]

Indeed, the pro-Western liberals were not without their serious problems. A major flaw was their disregard of the intense class conflict in China's process of modernity, significantly enfeebling the liberalist cultural politics, and often exasperating the political stand of liberalists like Hu. Aligning with the right-wing Chiang Kai-shek regime after the 1927 split between the Guomindang and CCP, liberalists were caught in a moral dilemma: they had to endorse the oppressive and protofascist cultural policies of the Guomindang regime, against their own conscience. They felt alienated, too. Pro–Chiang Kai-shek liberalists encountered enormous hostility from the multitude of intellectuals who, at the time, were largely sympathetic to left-wing ideologies. The 1930s' cultural arena was dominated by fierce ideological warfare between intellectuals themselves, only to be aggravated by the interference and manipulation of political factions on both the Right and Left. A serious casualty, in hindsight, was Cai's enlightenment project. The Left-Right battle was exacerbated by the struggle between the Guomindang and CCP, and the Sino-Japanese War that happened intermittently. Given the severe national crisis during those years, it was perhaps impossible to establish an unobtrusive, relatively autonomous civil society. No matter how beneficial it might have proved itself to China's modernity, Cai's project had unfortunately little material condition in China then.

Marxism had a quite different fate. It opened up an alternative way to conceive of and construct modernity in a China facing the modernized West, which brandished the double-edged sword of capitalism and imperialism. First embraced by Chinese revolutionaries as an ideology of change, Marxism guided the social movements that have brought China to its own history of modernity. In the very process of China's modernity, a Chinese Marxism came into being. Significantly, from the outset, this Chinese Marxism had emphasized cultural and aesthetic dimensions in its revolutionary project. From Chen Duxiu and Li Dazhao to Qu Qiubai and Mao Zedong, prominent figures in the May Fourth movement, most Marxist leaders devoted a great deal of attention to aesthetic, artistic issues. Chinese Marxism accepted most classical Marxist assumptions, inherited from European Enlightenment thought, especially universalism and utopianism. Class struggle, of course, was taken to be the core of Marxism by

Chinese Marxists. The dual emphasis on class struggle and cultural revolution resulted in the stress on class struggle in cultural and aesthetic domains. This general orientation inevitably caused formidable internal contradictions, which will be discussed later. Suffice it to say here, these contradictions were inextricably related to the May Fourth cultural enlightenment projects. One of these contradictions was the urban/rural division. An urban, cosmopolitan vision of enlightenment, inherent in Cai's aesthetic theory, was accepted by Marxists, who then highlighted the class character of and class consciousness in the enlightenment. But Mao's communist revolution was largely a rural-centered, nationalist revolution of peasants. Mao's rural orientation had a decisive bearing on his aesthetic and cultural views, which were frequently at odds with urban-centered, cosmopolitan Marxism. Clashes between these orientations occurred often during the course of the struggle for a revolutionary cultural hegemony. After the revolutionary hegemony was established, the conflicts continued, escalating as the Chinese Revolution moved into the phase of social reconstruction and modernization. The culmination of the struggle within Chinese Marxism was the Cultural Revolution. Contrary to the accepted view that the Cultural Revolution was Mao's political move to crash his enemies, the Cultural Revolution was an event that encapsulated the intense contradictions of China's modernity or an alternative modernity. The rural/urban conflict within Chinese Marxist cultural policies was part and parcel of the internal contradiction in Chinese Marxism itself, and was embedded in the struggles of the Cultural Revolution in aesthetic and cultural domains.

The tension-filled genealogy of the aesthetic in modern China, from the beginning, was entangled with politics—either in the sense of realpolitik, power struggles and class conflicts, or in the sense of cultural politics, struggles of hegemony and counterhegemony in aesthetic and cultural domains. As the quintessential discourse of modernity, the aesthetic embodies the contradictory, fragmentary, and transitory nature of modernity. It also promises a dialectic strategy of fragmenting and unifying, resisting and reconfiguring cultural and social formations at the extremely complicated political conjuncture of China's modernity. Aesthetics has been considered unimportant. It appears much less grandiose than do concepts of science or democracy. The aesthetic, however, became a focal point in the history of Chinese revolution and modernity. In the minds of Liang, Wang, and Cai, the aesthetic discourse was primarily deployed in the encounter with Western modernity. Liang considered the aesthetic the central category of his "New Citizenry" project, or modern subjectivity and the construction of a new, universal cultural syncretism. Wang opted for a position analogous to aesthetic modernism in the West, insisting on the autonomy and independence of aesthetic and cultural domains, while paradoxically pursuing a self-destructive resistance to modernization. Contrary to Wang's antimodern attitude, Cai's notion of aesthetic education was crucial to cultural enlightenment and revolution. These thinkers made remarkable efforts to bring the aesthetic discourse to bear on China's modernity and searches for an alternative modernity. Perhaps the most enduring value of their attempts is that their critique of Western capitalist modernity opened up aesthetic and cultural alternatives. But their critiques and alternatives were fraught with inner tensions and contradictions, only to be intensified, transgressed, and internalized by Chinese Marxists. The aesthetic again played a major role in both the establishment of a powerful revolutionary hegemony and the Cultural Revolution, which undoubtedly has profound ramifications for the world.

CHAPTER 2

The Formation of Marxist Aesthetics:

From Shanghai to Yan'an

The Chinese Revolution greatly enriched the meaning and function of the aesthetic. It shifted the location of cultural struggles from the city to the countryside, creating a rural dimension. It also endowed culture with a double mission: as a principal weapon in the political struggle for state power; and as key (that is, hegemonic) to constituting a revolutionary class consciousness or subjectivity in the making of revolution. The aesthetic discourse was thus at the forefront of China's political arena. It was embedded in both realpolitik and cultural politics. In political power struggles, the aesthetic discourse was subject to instrumentalization; in cultural politics, it was often at the center of controversies and functioned as a catalyst in political movements, such as the Cultural Revolution. In short, revolution set into motion the dialectical process of the politicization of aesthetics and aestheticization of politics. It would not be an exaggeration to suggest that the dialectic of aesthetics and politics was a major characteristic of the Chinese Revolution.

In order to appreciate the extent to which the aesthetic has been entangled with the dual problematics of China's modernity or an alternative modernity, namely revolution and reconstruction, it is necessary to situate the genealogy of the aesthetic during both revolutionary and postrevolutionary periods within a global context of modernity, and to juxtapose it with Marxist theories and practices in other parts of the world, Western Marxism in particular. The aesthetic discourse developed not by a one-dimensional progression, but traversed and circulated through a trajectory that was both curvilinear and three-dimensional, at the sociopolitical conjuncture across cultural and national borders. As a universal and utopian discourse, the aesthetic lies at the heart of the Chinese Revolution, with its universal (or international) orientation. The Chinese Revolution always set the emancipation of humanity as its highest strategic goal, by which its local, nationalist objectives and tactics were subsumed. The universal, global, or international dimension was crucial to Chinese Marxism. It not only distinguished Chinese communist revolution from the Guomindang's nationalism, but also rendered the revolution a self-conscious search for an alternative modernity. In other words, Chinese Marxists genuinely believed that the Chinese Revolution was an integral part of worldwide revolution, and that the success of the Chinese Revolution would significantly affect the whole world in addition to altering China's fate.

Of course, the Chinese Revolution actually had only limited impact, mainly confined to its own national boundaries. Indeed, the Chinese Revolution has usually been seen as merely a local, nationalist response to global modernity with the West as its core. In actual and real terms, it was a local event, a peripheral maneuver vis-à-vis the West. Nonetheless, it was also a strenuous and self-conscious effort to challenge and "decenter" the West, as it were, as the center of global modernity. At least in its aspiration, vision, and overall strategies, the Chinese Revolution had a decidedly global and universal orientation, which should not be overlooked. For without recognizing this global dimension, it is hard to understand why Chinese Marxists emphasized aesthetic discourse. And vice versa, the emphasis on the aesthetic is indicative of Chinese Marxists's universal and global view of revolution.

From Enlightenment to Revolution: The Inception of Marxist Aesthetics

Revolution and modernity are inseparable twins.[1] On the one hand, revolution contains all the principal features of modernity: radical and ceaseless discontinuities, ruptures and mutations, and a cutting across of temporal and spatial boundaries. On the other hand, modernity is a lived experience of revolution: it feels simultaneously emancipating and exhilarating, frightening and agonizing. But perhaps the most important link between the two is that revolution, as a fundamental change of power, is constitutive of modernity. It is, in other words, revolution that brought the historical moment of modernity into being. Modernity can be said to have emerged from the bourgeois revolutions in England, France, the United States, and the rest of Western Europe, starting in the seventeenth century. The establishment of a capitalist world market, and the rapid expansion of modern science and technology in industrial production, can be seen as both the cause and effect of political and social revolution. In short, modernity is a complex historical phenomenon, determined and overdetermined by a multitude of forces. Revolution is the catalyst for modernity in Western Europe and North America.

In the rest of the world, revolution not only brought about modernity, but also produced situations in which capitalist modernity was resisted, opposed, and emulated all at once. Socialist revolutions, the Russian Revolution in particular, were the first attempt to create an alternative modernity in the twentieth century. Nationalist, anticolonialist revolutions in the non-West were affiliated with socialism to varying degrees. It is fair to say that socialist revolutions marked most of the worldwide revolutionary movements of the time, although ironically, by the end of the twentieth century, many of the "really existing socialisms" collapsed one after another.

If the Russian Revolution was a socialist revolution largely within the Western hemisphere or capitalist system, then the Chinese Revolution, and revolutions in the rest of the "Third World," were much more complicated. The Chinese Revolution, for instance, not only had the objective of bringing about socialism, but also the task of national liberation from Western imperialism. In many countries, such as India and the Arab world, national liberation and decolonization did not necessarily involve a socialist revolution led by Marxists and communists. But the Chinese Revolution was definitely a socialist, nationalist, and anti-imperialist struggle. Moreover, the Chinese Revolution was conceived of as a way to bring about modernity, with the manifest goal of establishing a socialist alternative modernity instead of a capitalist one. Set in a "Third World" country, the Chinese Revolution was inevitably anti-imperialist and nationalist; socialism became the choice for constructing modernity or an alternative modernity in China. This historical fact distinguished China's experience from the capitalist West, Soviet Russia, and the colonialist or postcolonialist "Third World." Under the current trend of revisionism, it is fashionable to dismiss the Chinese Revolution as a "historical error," or an obstacle to, rather than an engine for, China's modernity. But one cannot confuse a present-day reassessment with what happened in the past. To pronounce the "demise of socialism" and condemn the Chinese Revolution is but an ideological statement that helps little in advancing historical knowledge. Instead, a rigorous historicizing effort is needed, one which can bring to the fore the dialectics of ideologies, strategies, and actual events and consequences, intertwined with subjective vision and intention, and objective, material conditions and contingencies.

Since contemporary debates about modernity and postmodernity have, for the most part, concentrated on the Western model of modernity, and non-Western responses and reactions to it, the characteristics of the Chinese Revolution have become obliterated by the assumptions underlying the discussion. Modern Chinese history is now resituated within the context of global capitalist modernity, centered in the West. Reassessments of it come from various ideological positions, be they bourgeois liberalist, modernizationist, or postcolonialist, all summoned under the rubric of modernity. Despite the fact that some of these positions may appear quite radical, such as postcolonialism, they often reinforce Eurocentrism in their value judgment by insisting on a pervasive "Western hegemonic discourse of modernity" in diverse experiences of modernity or alternative modernities in non-Western countries.

Under such circumstances, it is difficult to rethink the Chinese Revolution in ways other than current ideological indictments. It seems that one is forced to choose between two options. First, to adhere to the older, but still predominant "hegemonic discourse." In the China field, this entails little more than repeating the cold war anticommunism that either condemns China as the only remaining nemesis of (Western capitalist) democracy and human rights, or obversely, applauds China's recoil from its communist dead end, back onto the right track of capitalism. The other, newer option is to embrace postcolonialist positions, chastising the Chinese Revolution as but an episode of blind Westernization, copying the *grand récit* of totalizing modernity and liberation. But even the dominant discourses of China studies have watered down their stringent ideological rhetoric in order to adapt to the changed atmosphere in the era of post–cold war globalization. Insofar as today's transnational capitalism puts economic interests over and above ideological contentions, it is politically unwise to keep brandishing anticommunism to bash China, a country that global capitalism needs badly as a crucial labor and consumer market.

Postcolonialism, however, encounters great difficulty in confronting China's revolutionary legacy on its own terms. Indeed, it can be argued that by inverting the roles of the postcolonial critic as interrogating subject and China as the object of interrogation, we may see both postcolonialism and the Chinese Revolution in a new light. It may be helpful, then, to examine the underlying presuppositions of postcolonial criticism through the prism of the Chinese Revolution. By virtue of the fact that it constituted an alternative to capitalist modernity, the Chinese Revolution preemptively unmasks the intrinsic contradictions and discrepancies of postcolonialism. A major theoretical source of postcolonialism is Marxism. From Antonio Gramsci's notion of hegemony to Edward Said's critique of Orientalism, postcolonial critics have invariably acknowledged their indebtedness to Marxism, especially Marxist cultural theories. A curious dismissal, or severance, of the link between Marxist *theory* and actual revolutionary *practice* is often evident in postcolonialist criticism. Given this, it is difficult to see that the Chinese Revolution has in actual practice already put much of Marxist theory to the test, and that the Chinese experience could debunk many a claim made by postcolonialists concerning aesthetic, ideological, and psychological formations in the non-

West or "Third World." To rethink the Chinese Revolution in a new historical context not only serves to better understand China's modernity, but helps to dismantle the contradictions and paradoxes inherent in contemporary cultural theories as well.

While aesthetic discourse played a crucial role in modern China, the Chinese Revolution also redefined it. In the Western context, the aesthetic—from the Enlightenment to today's postmodern debates—has largely functioned as an arbiter, mediating and compromising the conflicts of the practical world in the imaginary and emotive realms, particularly in bourgeois civil society and the public sphere. It was primarily a bourgeois discourse prior to the emergence of Marxism. Even in classical Marxism and modern Western Marxism, the role of the aesthetic is confined mostly to cultural spheres within bourgeois civil society.

Chinese reformers of the late Qing period and intellectuals of the May Fourth movement espoused aesthetic discourse in cultural spheres, too, hoping to carve out the contours of China's modernity by way of cultural enlightenment, and by fostering a new subjectivity and syncretic cultural system. In spite of geopolitical and cultural differences, Chinese intellectuals invoked aesthetic discourse in a modern public sphere analogous to the bourgeois civil society of Europe.

Around the turn of the century, Shanghai evolved into a major modern metropolis in Asia. Here, an incipient civil society emerged, particularly in the Western concessions or virtual colonies within the city, where intense capital and commercial exchanges between European headquarters and local branches concomitantly brought in cultural exchanges, with their fundamental infrastructures and institutions, such as the modern press, media, and schools. Meanwhile, in Beijing, these cultural institutions, especially the modern universities, grew rapidly. Undoubtedly, these developments owed much to Western powers, specifically American missionaries, whose objective was clearly to transform Chinese social consciousness with Western ideas. This colonialist cultural strategy, as in many colonial or semicolonial countries, in effect laid the foundation for a modern civil society in China. Of course, it was definitely not a civil society comprised primarily of independent bourgeoisie, as in Western Europe. Rather, it was a segment of civil society in a country dominated by both local imperial or military rulers and Western colonialists who controlled either all or some parts of the country.

This Chinese civil society, to be sure, was only a semblance of what a "real" civil society—say, in nineteenth-century London or New York— would look like. But it contained the basic infrastructural components of a bourgeois civil society, and therefore, deserved to be seen as such, even if somewhat "imperfect." Much of contemporary talk about why China did not develop a modern civil society neglect this historical fact. An obvious reason is that historians adhere too stubbornly to the Weberian "ideal-type" within the Western European model to allow any "anomaly." A less obvious reason is that a foregone conclusion of China's lack of capitalism (and therefore, an urgent need to build one) dictates such an outright denial of its existence. It would be more fruitful to view the emergent, fragmented civil society in China's major cities in the context of global modernity. The existence of such a phenomenon is then a particular instance in the nonsynchronous, uneven development of modernity. In other words, Western colonial powers and capitalists, in effect, brought all the intrinsic contradictions of capitalism itself into the "Third World," along with the social formations in which the contradictions were generated. The tremendous growth of modern cultural institutions in Shanghai and Beijing is thus attributable to the global development of capitalist modernity, however uneven and fragmented it appeared.[2]

It is equally important that in most parts of China, especially the vast rural areas, civil society was either primitive or nonexistent. This was largely a result of China's traditional social structure, which did not encourage the growth of a modern bourgeoisie and capitalism. It is true that China's lack of capitalist development was responsible for an underdeveloped civil society. But it does not follow that China needed capitalism in order to allow a modern civil society to flourish. In fact, to either deny or focus merely on the emergence of modern bourgeois civil society in China misjudges history. China's passage into modernity involved intensely uneven economic and sociopolitical developments, irreducible to the simple dichotomy between capitalism and noncapitalism (or lack thereof). The corollary dichotomy between the state and civil society also has limited use. China's modernity was characterized precisely by the disjuncture between the fledgling modern cities and civil society and the oppressive, coercive state, disintegrated and enfeebled by regional warlordism as well as political and economic fragmentations.[3] Simply put, in modern China, both the state and society had been devastated by incessant crises, with little chance to stabilize their basic formations.

The Chinese Revolution precipitated the fragmentation and disintegration of the state by centering on rural transformation as the key issue of China's modernity. Evidently, its very success hinged on fundamental structural changes in China's vast rural areas and population. The revolutionary hegemony that the Chinese Revolution intended to build, then, shifted its focus from modern civil society in a metropolis decidedly to rural areas, where formations of social groups and structures of domination differed essentially from those in the cities. Hence, the Gramscian concept of hegemony needs to be reassessed and modified in light of the Chinese

Revolution. Indeed, not only in relation to China, but in general, Gramsci's cultural theory can be seen from a different perspective when the Chinese Revolution is taken into account. The revolution, in effect, put into practice the theories of cultural revolution and leadership formulated by Chinese Marxists, Qu Qiubai and Mao Zedong in particular. There is a remarkable resemblance between the observations and conclusions of Qu, Mao, and Gramsci—arrived at, of course, without any real contact. As political leaders of communist revolutions at roughly the same historical period, facing comparable social and political conditions, the Chinese and Italian Marxists shared common views on culture, hegemony, and cultural revolution. This Qu-Mao-Gramsci lineage will be discussed in detail later. For now, suffice it to suggest that the notion of a civil society, or public sphere, too, ought to be reevaluated in regard to the Chinese Revolution. The relationship between civil society and the state has undergone substantial transformation in China in comparison to Western Europe.

Moving toward the rural areas was concomitant with the twofold emphasis on cultural revolution mentioned earlier: that culture would become the principal political front of the revolution; and that it would foster a revolutionary class consciousness or new subjectivity in the making of the revolution. The philosopher Li Zehou formulated a thesis of "dual variation of the enlightenment and national salvation" to describe the Chinese Revolution.[4] The first role that culture would play vaguely corresponds to the notion of "national salvation," a metaphor for the politics of communist revolution, and the second to that of "enlightenment." While national salvation was certainly a high priority of the Chinese Revolution, however, the enlightenment project already assumed a new objective in the Revolution: to create a new revolutionary subjectivity. This was markedly different from that of the bourgeois enlightenment advocated by Liang Qichao and Cai Yuanpei.

Aesthetic discourse reflects many fundamental issues in the Chinese Revolution in cultural spheres. The formation of a Marxist aesthetics in China was related to at least three complex aspects of global modernity: the universalism embedded in Chinese cultural tradition; modern European humanist thought since the Enlightenment; and Marxist traditions around the world. The appeal of the aesthetic to Chinese lies first of all in its universal and universalizing claims. Its utopian dimension, too, is attractive. These aspects of the aesthetic strike a deep chord in China, which has its own tradition of universalism and utopianism in Confucianism, Taoism, and Chinese Buddhism. To be sure, Chinese universalism is ethnocentric, even though China hardly ever extended its ethnocentrism beyond its boundaries. This Chinese universalism crumbled with the advent of a modern European version that truly expanded its values and vision of universality across the entire world. Only a modern universalism could promise a real solution to the dilemma of Chinese universalists.

Not surprisingly, Chinese intellectuals turned toward European Enlightenment thought for new ways of reestablishing universality, viewing it as truly global and universal. They tried to free themselves from a narrowly defined, ethnocentric perspective, and genuinely believed that the European Enlightenment brought the hope of real universality for all humanity. This trend was well demonstrated in the thoughts of Liang, Cai, and Wang, representing emergent bourgeois liberalism and humanism in China. But Chinese liberal humanists remained largely idealistic. When translated into concrete actions, their attempts to mediate and reconcile the tensions of modernity were severely undermined because they were unable to find a tenable solution to the conflicts between the West and China. "Wholesale Westernization" would endanger China's own identity and sovereignty in the face of the intrusion of Western imperialism. Anti-Westernization in the name of preserving China's tradition, however, would obstruct modernization. The liberalist politics of moderation often appeared either unrealistic or irrelevant at the time of intense class conflict, and was vulnerable to political manipulation. In China, it was Chiang Kai-shek's autocratic and nationalist regime that prevailed, deploying the liberalists' universal utopianism merely as a masquerade for its profascist politics.

Marxism, by contrast, provided the Chinese intellectuals with an alternative solution to the predicament of modernity by way of a social and political revolution that would change China's social structure and culture. This change was meant to be systematic and fundamental, in keeping with the Marxist vision of a transformation of all societies in the world. Thus, Marxist aesthetics in China was crucially related to the Chinese Revolution in two senses: as a utopian discourse legitimating a socialist and communist universality, of which the Chinese Revolution was an integral part; and as a hegemonic discourse in constructing a new culture and revolutionary subjectivity. The dual mission of the aesthetic corresponded to the twofold character of the Chinese Revolution—it self-consciously constituted itself as part of a worldwide revolution and it took cultural revolution to be a main objective.

Two other crucial aspects further complicated the nature of the Chinese Revolution. The first has to do with urban Marxist intellectuals, who were champions and heirs of the May Fourth legacy, and pioneers of the Marxist movement in China. Lu Xun's aesthetic thought is arguably the most sophisticated of the urban Marxists. His aesthetic views are expressed primarily through his allegorical writings. Lu's overall thinking spared nothing in its unrelenting critique of culture, literature, the arts, or tradition, be they Chinese or foreign. It was also an "aesthetics of negativity," concerned mainly with the complex relationships of revolution, modernity, the arts, and politics. Except for his childhood, Lu spent his entire life in cosmopolises like Beijing and Shanghai. His career was devoted to critiquing a social order and cultural tradition that he saw as hopeless and decaying. Although he later accepted Marxism as his critical outlook, Lu hardly harbored optimism for the future. His negativity, therefore, distinguished him from other Chinese Marxists and non-Marxist, pro-Western liberalists alike.

Second and more important, the Chinese Revolution was a rural-centered, peasant rebellion. Insofar as urban Marxists were major practitioners of the May Fourth cultural revolution, their acceptance of Marxism as a radical enlightenment was a self-conscious choice. But the shift of the revolution from cities to impoverished rural areas was mostly the result of political expediency, and Chinese Marxists had little expectation and preparation for the transition. Moreover, it required formidable efforts to mobilize a largely uneducated and politically unmotivated peasant population into a revolutionary army, in lieu of a mature and powerful urban proletariat. A cultural revolution, therefore, was much needed in order to foster revolutionary class consciousness in the peasants. Since peasants were vital to the success of the revolution, its the so-called "line of the masses" became a central strategy.[5] The rural cultural revolution was inaugurated by Qu Qiubai. An urban Marxist intellectual himself, Qu's thought represented the difficult route that the aesthetic discourse took in the transition from the modern, coastal cosmopolises to China's rural hinterlands.

Allegory, Aesthetics of Negativity, and Antinomies of Revolution: The Legacy of Lu Xun Revisited

In the winter of 1940, at his famed Yan'an *yaodong* (cave house), Mao wrote "On New Democracy," his major programmatic treatise on the Chinese Revolution, in the thick of the anti-Japanese war. The essay focused almost exclusively on the issue of cultural revolution as a core of the revolutionary program. Mao also glorified Lu Xun as "the chief commander of China's cultural revolution," "not only a great man of letters but a great thinker and a great revolutionary."[6] While the "great revolutionary" epithet has always been controversial, because of the centrality of cultural revolution in China's modernity, Lu Xun's role must be carefully reexamined. It would be misleading to take "the chief commander" label literally, for Lu Xun was never a member of any political party or organization, let alone its leader. On the other hand, it would be futile to deny Lu Xun's importance to modern China's cultural scene. Further, Lu became a committed Marxist around the turn of the 1930s. This was a time of crisis for the revolution, after the revolutionary alliance between Guomindang and the CCP broke up, and Chiang Kai-shek began to round up and massacre his former communist allies in the "reign of white terror."

Lu Xun's conversion to Marxism was significant. As perhaps the most outspoken critical intellectual of the May Fourth movement, his turn suggested a decidedly left-wing, pro-Marxist transition among a majority of May Fourth intellectuals. Chiang Kai-shek's terror surprisingly galvanized communist sympathy among a substantial number of May Fourth intellectuals, in an extremely polarized, tension-filled political ambiance. Lu Xun's acceptance of Marxism also affected the revolution, in the sense that his influential work much enhanced the cultural struggles in the overall revolutionary movement. In Shanghai, a small yet highly energetic and dedicated group of left-wing writers gathered around Lu Xun. They and other factions of left-wing authors had miraculously effected a kind of "Marxist turn" in Shanghai's cultural and intellectual scene in the early 1930s, when Chiang Kai-shek virtually eliminated all communist activity in major cities and pushed CCP revolutionaries into the peripheral, impoverished rural regions of Jiangxi.

Interestingly, Shanghai's public sphere survived, in the cracks of the white terror's political domination. This was largely due to Chiang Kai-shek's inefficient and inept handling of urban affairs when Western colonies or concessions were involved. Within this fragmented and fragile public sphere, however, a Marxist cultural movement emerged and grew, masked by various aesthetic, theoretical, and scholarly pursuits. Its survival and growth was an incessant battle, first against Chiang Kai-shek's continued harassment, intimidation, and persecutions, and second amid numerous factional strifes and infighting. Nevertheless, this Marxist movement in the cities, primarily Shanghai, generated powerful cultural and political momentum, and offered a substantial troop of Marxist intellectuals, who later went to Yan'an to join the communist revolutionists during the Sino-Japanese War.[7]

It is certainly in the sense of Marxist transition that Mao praised Lu Xun's role lavishly. The Marxist cultural orientation in the cities and peasant guerrilla warfare in the rural areas were to become keystones of the Chinese Revolution and an alternative modernity. Qu was the first to bring the two together. He transferred left-wing intellectual and cultural insurgencies in the cities to the rural areas, launching an unprecedented cultural revolution among largely illiterate and subservient peasants. But Mao did not choose Qu as the idol of cultural revolution for obvious reasons. First of all, Qu's influence as a writer apparently did not match Lu

Xun's. Second, and perhaps more important, as chief leader of the CCP, Qu was responsible for the "leftist adventurism" that defeated the urban revolutionary insurgencies during Chiang Kai-shek's reign of white terror. Qu was ousted from his post as a result of this debacle, which cost nearly all the CCP forces in cities. Mao took this lesson to heart and opted instead for peasant uprising. Nonetheless, the idea and practice of cultural revolution remained firmly in Mao's mind. During the Yan'an period, after his political power was consolidated, Mao continued and much expanded Qu's experiments of the rural-centered cultural revolution.

Mao's admiration of Lu Xun, however, suppressed the immense tensions and contradictions inherent in the "Marxist turn" among the left-wing writers in Shanghai. Lu Xun's writings and activities incarnated the incongruities of this transition, and laid bare the deep-seated antinomies of cultural revolution in China. An understanding of Lu Xun's "aesthetics of negativity" is helpful in this respect.

Negativity, for Lu Xun had two primary meanings. First, it referred to his lifelong preoccupation with cultural critique in a negative vein. This critique was remarkably wide-ranging and profound: from China's traditional culture and "national character" to Western liberalism and individualism; and from Chiang Kai-shek's protofascism to sectarianism among left-wing writers. The most relentless critique was Lu Xun's "self-anatomy" of his inner conflicts, by which he hoped to use himself as a specimen for examining Chinese intellectuals. Second, Lu Xun's view of the relationship between literature and revolution was irredeemably negative and pessimistic, and often self-annihilating. His notion of their incommensurability amounted to a veritable negation of literature and arts in the revolutionary era. Given Lu Xun's career as primarily a dedicated man of letters, a preeminent public intellectual in the Sartrean sense, this presents a major paradox, or enigma, is his thinking.

Hardly anyone denies this predominant negative feature of Lu Xun's works and life, but its interpretation varies a great deal. PRC's "official" view in the past either dismissed Lu Xun's negativity and pessimism as inconsequential in his overall profile as a committed revolutionary fighter, or ascribed it to his earlier, non-Marxist phase.[8] Not surprisingly, Western scholars and non-Marxist critics tend to interpret those contradictions and negativity as signs of Lu Xun's reluctance to get involved politically, and halfhearted acceptance of, or distance from, Marxism. Internal paradoxes in his works are attributed to the archetypal conflict between individual self and society. In addition, Lu Xun's "moral ethos" is a favorite issue among scholars in the West; it is said to reflect the influences of traditional moral values invested in an intellectual identity at odds with political immorality and/or modernity itself.[9]

Issues of moral ethos, traditional values, and other factors contribute to Lu Xun's complex mind. Yet what of the complex and irreducible contradictions? One possibility is to see Lu Xun's aesthetics of negativity as the embodiment of the antinomies of cultural revolution itself. In other words, instead of harking back to the distinction between private and public, or the dichotomy between tradition and modernity, that Lu Xun forcefully critiqued, it is fruitful to examine his aesthetic views as expressions of the internal contradictions within a Marxist-oriented cultural revolution.

Some of Pierre Bourdieu's notions can help clarify questions concerning Lu Xun's Marxism. His "developmental phases" may be understood as changes and mutations in "fields of forces" or "social space." By the same token, the modernity/tradition dichotomy also underwent conceptual realignments. The moral ethos and traditional cultural predispositions are, on the other hand, the subjective "habitus."[10] One can view Lu Xun's acceptance of Marxism as a dialectical process—bringing his subjective dispositions and personal psychic structures into dynamic interplay with social conditions and structures—at a given historical conjuncture. Insofar as this particular moment in China's history broke down the unity or homology between the subjective and objective, private and public, Western and Chinese, past and present, Lu Xun was deeply affected. His thought was permeated with tensions and contradictions, and was inconsistent and fissured. Still, Lu Xun had a clear, sober, critical self-consciousness, and never lost sight of his responsibilities as an engaged intellectual to attempt to change society and improve humanity. His sense of history was also remarkable, anchoring his philosophical and literary reflections squarely within the context of modernity. Moreover, Lu Xun was by no means a narrow-minded nationalist, or as some critics have claimed, a traditional type of Chinese literati who was morally burdened by or obsessed with China. To the contrary, Lu Xun's cosmopolitanism was exceptional, just as his critique of ethnocentrism and sensitivity to the follies of cultural imperialism or any form of cultural superiority was most unsparing. In order to properly comprehend the complexity of Lu Xun's aesthetics, his works need to be situated within the internalized antinomies of the Chinese Revolution as well as the historical conjuncture of modernity—that is, beyond the existing interpretive framework that posits ahistorical, transcendental categories and sterile binary oppositions. Such kinds of interpretation may offer a self-contained, coherent explanation, but only at the expense of real historical contradictions and incoherence. Our rethinking of Lu Xun aims to sort out, through a cognitive labyrinth—namely, China's passage to modernity—multilayered and tension-filled discursive formations.

A reevaluation of Lu Xun's aesthetics raises serious theoretical and methodological questions about interpretation or interpretive strategies precisely because of the allegorical, metaphoric nature of his writings along with the centrality of cultural revolution in his thought. The "Marxist hermeneutic" that Fredric Jameson has conceived serves as a point of departure for a renewed and continued rethinking of interpretation as a theoretical issue.[11] Jameson proposes three concentric interpretive frameworks. First, "text" as a "symbolic act," an imaginary and aesthetic (and ideological) solution to real social contradictions. The individual text is read against political history as a subtext, fraught with social contradictions. Second, the framework of the "social" as a vast system of langue, or class discourse, in which a text is interpreted as a parole, or individual utterances embodying an ideologeme in antagonistic, oppositional relations to other ideological and discursive formations. Third, history itself, which Jameson designates as a complex ensemble of phenomena pertaining ultimately to given "modes of production" and "ideology of form." The most interesting point about this final interpretive horizon, or framework of history, is its definition of "cultural revolution" as "that moment in which the coexistence of various modes of production becomes visibly antagonistic, their contradictions moving to the very center of political, social, and historical life."[12]

Borrowing a slightly modified notion from Jameson, Lu Xun's aesthetics can be seen as a metacritical or self-reflexive "text," exemplifying all three dimensions enumerated above. Lu Xun's text is metacritical because while it can be scrutinized from Jameson's perspective, it simultaneously comments on Jameson's interpretive scheme, addressing crucial issues of cultural revolution. Additionally, Lu's text reveals a strong interconnection between the three "horizons," while Jameson emphasizes the separation and autonomy of each framework. Lu Xun's remarks on cultural revolution were allegorical and symbolic on the one hand, and shot through with a concrete critique of the class and political character of the aesthetic discourse on the other. This metacommentary was particularly clear in his *zawen* essays, a special genre that afforded Lu Xun the most effective way of analyzing and critiquing immediate political, social, and cultural issues in a polemical manner.[13] Lu Xun's works demonstrated a powerful self-consciousness of the contradictory, fragmentary nature of the issues he dealt with—a self-consciousness that grew significantly after Lu Xun's acceptance of Marxism. From then on, Lu Xun took Marxism not only as an ideological guide for his politics, but also as a scientific, epistemological guide for understanding the world. But Marxism did not guarantee a coherent answer to the problems Lu Xun encountered. Rather, it only sharpened Lu Xun's sense of contradictions and tensions, adding class struggle and revolution as two new aspects to his complex conception of modernity. This, in turn, intensified his own inner conflicts, well captured by his zawen or prose essays, which were sometimes highly contentious and tongue-in-cheek, and sometimes extremely enigmatic and esoteric. Their style and form can thus be characterized as allegorical.

The allegorical style makes an interpretation of Lu Xun's negative aesthetics quite difficult. Despite a sixteen-volume oeuvre, Lu never wrote a full-length monograph explicating aesthetic issues. Instead, he translated lengthy treatises and books on literary theories, authored by Russian Marxist philosophers Georgy V. Plekhanov and Anatoly V. Lunacharsky, and by Japanese scholar Kuriyagawa Hakuson, who had a strong Freudian bent.[14] The absence of long, systematic works of a theoretical nature may suggest that Lu Xun was not a philosopher or theorist. Or it may simply indicate that he was not inclined toward abstract philosophizing or theorizing. Either way, it is more interesting to explore the kind of aesthetic view that stems from his unsystematic, fragmentary, and sometimes idiosyncratic essays. This involves a critical reconstruction of Lu Xun's aesthetics from his writings, similar to the formidable, but fruitful task to reconstruct a distinct cultural theory from Gramsci's equally fragmented and bulky prison notebooks.

Jameson's allegorical reading of Lu Xun offers a good example. It not only tests the limit of Jameson's own Marxist hermeneutics, but also offers fertile ground for aesthetic interpretation. His interpretation is caught between a political, ideological critique and a purportedly nonpolitical reading. These two incompatible strands lay claim to the polysemic, ambiguous nature of allegory, which mirrors the very characteristic of the aesthetic itself. Jameson's reading of Lu Xun is original and refreshing. It occupies a central place in his important and controversial essay "Third World Literature in the Era of Multinational Capital," yet its significance is beyond that essay's arguments and critical framework.[15] Jameson contends that Lu Xun's allegorical texts nonetheless contain a more "literal" than "figural" condemnation of the cannibalistic and violent social reality, and that contrary to the "First World cultural tradition" that subjectivizes and psychologizes the sociopolitical reality, Lu Xun's work restores the political dimension in the most subjective, psychological, and private realms. He attributes the social and political dimensions of Lu Xun's work to allegory, which Jameson defines as "profoundly discontinuous, a matter of breaks and heterogeneities, of the multiple polysemia of the dream rather than the homogeneous representation of the symbol."[16] Jameson finds in Lu Xun's allegory an urgent sense of cultural revolution, desperately needed to change the mental inferiority and subservience of the people, or "subalternity" in a Gramscian sense.[17] It is true that Lu Xun advocated cultural revolution as a Marxist. He quoted Lenin to argue that without a change in attitudes and modes of behavior, the goal of revolution would never be accomplished.[18]

Since allegory can be read in a variety of ways, however, its interpretation can also be turned around. Thus, Jameson's reading of Lu Xun has been attacked. Critics reverse the dichotomies—between the political and psychological, the collective and individualist—that Jameson employs. Lu Xun's allegory, we are told, derives from a "fiercely individualist self" and "an isolated and alienated loner," rather than being constituted as a political statement of collective interests.[19] Such an ideological cliché can be ignored because it hardly says anything new, but one nevertheless needs to see Jameson's error in placing Lu Xun's work under the rubric of "national allegory" of a "Third World" kind vis-à-vis the "First World." In doing so, Jameson simply externalizes the internal contradictions of Western capitalist modernity, reminiscent of the Chinese proponents of a dichotomy between Chinese essence and the Western use or instrument, or ti-yong dualism. Although Jameson views the "Third World allegory" as a corrective to "First World" bourgeois ideologies, he somehow misplaces the real villain of the Western bourgeoisie in his drama onto a "Third World" stage. Aijaz Ahmad's rebuff of Jameson's "First-Worldism" is correct in that the latter's "sweeping hypothesis" that "all Third World texts are necessarily allegorical" is surprisingly undialectical.[20] Yet Ahmad says nothing about Lu Xun's works central to Jameson's thesis, nor does he acknowledge Jameson's penetrating analysis. Ahmad's diatribe, then, is partial and unbalanced. Furthermore, Ahmad is not self-conscious of his own prejudices and ignorance. Jameson's displacement of Lu Xun reveals his prejudices, too. Lu Xun's works are not simply "Third World texts," but those of a cosmopolitan, Marxist intellectual whose reflections capture the complex contradictions of modernity in general and the Chinese Revolution in particular. It makes better sense to place Lu Xun's works within the context of global modernity, without ascribing him to some predetermined geopolitical category, such as the "Third World."

Indeed, Lu Xun's allegory is better understood in comparison to Walter Benjamin's allegorical and metaphorical writings, which fuse Marxist materialism and messianic Judaism. Although they were contemporaries, there is little evidence that they knew each other's work or had any actual contact. Certainly, the cultural differences between the two are obvious. Nevertheless, Benjamin and Lu Xun wrote in a remarkably similar style or mode: fragmentary, nonsystematic, poetic, and idiosyncratic. This peculiar form inevitably affected their views of Marxism. Lu Xun's understanding was largely acquired through Russian Marxists such as Lenin, Leon Trotsky, and Plekhanov; he was generally unaware of contemporary works by German Marxists—with the exception of Karl Wittfogel, the incipient Frankfurt School was preoccupied with Western European problems, whose scope rarely extended to other continents. But as Martin Jay notes, Wittfogel's studies of Chinese society and the so-called "Asiatic mode of production" were not integrated into the Frankfurt School's main projects.[21] While Lu Xun's sources were rather deterministic and mechanical, his acceptance of Marxism à la Russian theorists was highly selective. He mainly focused on the ideas of class struggle and the class nature of culture, and hardly endorsed the deterministic and teleological views of the Russians, who invariably insisted that revolution followed a unilinear route to ultimate victory. In fact, Lu Xun's attitude toward the outcome of political revolution remained ambivalent and skeptical.

Benjamin, on the other hand, rejected Lukács's concept of totality in favor of a constantly shifting notion of "constellation," "wherein the relation between objects and the perspective of the viewer is always in a state of flux."[22] Benjamin's own thought, as critics point out, itself constituted a constellation, in which conflicting and contradictory ideas are in ceaseless flux. His notion of "art in the age of mechanical reproduction" involved a technological reductionism, while its valorization of technological reproduction remained inexorably utopian. He was undoubtedly sympathetic to the plight of the working class as a Marxist intellectual. Still, his skepticism and apathy toward organized revolution and political parties decidedly distanced him from any revolutionary movements for the liberation of the oppressed. Last but not least, Benjamin's radically subversive views of history informed by Marxist materialism remained nonetheless incompatible with his messianic will to redemption.[23]

Like his favorite modern poet Baudelaire, Benjamin also sought the "eternal and the immutable" among the "fleeting and the transient."[24] Allegory, then, provided him with endless possibilities for the transformation and reconciliation of contradictions. The allegorical mode allowed Benjamin to arrest the fleeting and transient—that is, his inner contradictions—into what he called "dialectics at standstill." Or, as Theodor Adorno observed, "to understand Benjamin properly one must feel behind his every sentence the conversion of extreme agitation into something static, indeed, the static notion of movement itself."[25] In Hannah Arendt's words, "metaphors are the means by which the oneness of the world is poetically brought about. . . . Without being a poet he thought poetically and therefore was bound to regard the metaphor as the greatest gift of language."[26]

Benjamin's metaphorical and static dialectics can also be applied to Lu Xun's prose poetry, *Wild Grass*. In this quite esoteric and modernist collection, the numerous imageries and metaphors of a "dead fire" and "ghost of rain" captured, in Lu Xun's own words, the "many contradictions" in his mind.[27] The Nietzschean pessimistic, nihilistic, and existential mood of despair and alienation in Lu Xun's work certainly manifested his profoundly negative views. Cast in an allegorical form like that of Benjamin's, Lu Xun's negativity was primarily aesthetic. Both men shared a sense of history. Lu Xun dubbed history a "cannibalistic banquet," a document inscribed with only two words, "eat man," while Benjamin called it a "document of barbarism." The main dilemma for an intellectual, then, is what to do with this barbaric and cannibalistic reality available through textual, archival forms.

Lu Xun attempted to grapple with this problem in his celebrated allegory of the "iron house":

> Imagine an iron house without windows, absolutely indestructible, with many people fast asleep inside who will shortly die of suffocation. But you know that since they will die in their sleep, they will not feel the pain of death. Now if you cry aloud to wake a few of the lighter sleepers, making those unfortunate few suffer the agony of irrevocable death, will you imagine that you are thereby doing them a favor?[28]

And likewise Benjamin, in his allegory about the fate of the "angel of history":

> His [the angel of history's] face is turned toward the past. Where we perceive a chain of events, he sees one single catastrophe which keeps piling wreckage upon wreckage and hurls it in front of his feet. The angel would like to stay, awaken the dead, and make whole what has been smashed. But a storm is blowing from Paradise; it has got caught in his wings with such violence that the angel can no longer close them. This storm irresistibly propels him into the future to which his back is turned, while the pile of debris before him grow skyward. This storm is what we call progress.[29]

While the sense of depression and pessimism is similar, the difference between the two is striking. Lu Xun's man crying out loud in the iron house is positively an impassioned activist of enlightenment, in the literal sense of the word. This man's distress stems from the sober awareness of the negative result of his action to waken up his fellow inmates; he is caught between action and inaction, both of which appear doomed. The contemplative angel, on the other hand, is torn between a desire for psychic wholeness, or unity of experience, and a reality that menaces to shatter his will altogether. Benjamin's Marxist outlook propelled him toward progress, but an acute sense of the detritus of history dragged him backward (or inward, depending on how you look at it), in an obsession with the past and memory.[30] Hence, for Benjamin, the privileged mode was allegory rather than symbol: the former signals a will to bring together object and spirit, while the latter presents an illusion of the perfect reconciliation or oneness of the two. Allegory, with its incongruence and heterogeneity, disconnects instantly, manifesting the contradictory nature of negative aesthetics. The aesthetics of negativity, in other words, finds its perfect mode of expression in allegory, for it is predicated on the aporia, or hiatus, of modernity, from which neither Lu Xun the activist nor Benjamin the apprehensive contemplator could escape.

Adorno's aesthetics of negativity also captured the aporia of modernity. Adorno, like Benjamin, was profoundly pessimistic. Comparing Adorno with Lu Xun is instructive, too. Both Adorno and Lu Xun had a strong sense of the practical link of their reflections to sociopolitical reality; both were cosmopolitan intellectuals. Adorno lived in the fascist state of Germany as well as the advanced capitalist society of the United States. Lu Xun spent most of his life in Shanghai, a major cosmopolis in Asia, where advanced Western cultural institutions coexisted with China's traditional social and cultural formations.[31] Perhaps most significantly, Adorno's involvement with Marxism was confined mostly to the academic and intellectual groups of the Frankfurt School, independent of the Communist Party and its organization. Adorno was never a Communist activist and was resistant to any kind of political manipulation. One finds a similar stance in Lu Xun's role in the League of Left-Wing Writers, where he adamantly opposed CCP interference with and control over the league. Lu Xun tried to protect and preserve the independent character of this organization in the public sphere, despite his Marxist views and personal friendship with many Communists, including Qu Qiubai.[32]

But Adorno's notion of negativity and Lu Xun's aesthetics were ultimately different in fundamental ways. For Adorno, negativity defined the essence of aesthetics in modernity. As Terry Eagleton observes, "the aporia of modernist culture lies in its plaintive, stricken attempt to turn autonomy (the free-standing nature of the aesthetic work) against autonomy (its functionless status as commodity on the market."[33] Adorno as a Marxist was not an advocate of art for art's sake; his aesthetic concern lay squarely with the social. In a consumption-and-exchange society and under an administered capitalism, however, the social function of the aesthetic was, in Adorno's view, attainable only through negativity. In other words, not until art becomes autonomous does it assume its social role of negative critique. Paradoxically, by negating its social ties, art becomes eminently social: "refraining from praxis, art becomes the schema of social praxis."[34] Apparently, Adorno's conception of negativity was premised on the assumption that the traditional social dependence of art, cou-

pled with modern consumer society's utilitarianism and instrumentalization, can only reproduce an affirmative and positive appearance of social
reality, one that is both false and untrue. Art in the sense of negative aesthetics, then, can rescue and restore its truth-bearing cognitive and ethical
functions by abandoning and severing its social ties and subservience,
with the eminently utopian hope that "what does not exist is promised because it appears."[35]

The thrust of Adorno's aesthetics of negativity stems from a number of
contradictions: between aesthetic experience in the Kantian sense of "disinterested satisfaction" and the social conditions of modern capitalism;
between the autonomy of art and culture, and the unity of sociality and
politics; and finally, between nonpraxis and praxis. This last contradiction
involves the more complex issues of polity and morality. The meaning of
praxis or practice is central to Marxist thinking, but remains controversial. Adorno, in fact, could never do away with "older," nineteenth-
century antinomies such as *l'art pour l'art* and *litterature engagée*. Instead, his negative aesthetics only intensified these contradictions, particularly in light of the Marxist objective of systemic social transformation.
In this respect, Li Zehou's critique of the Frankfurt School's displacement
of the Marxist notion of material practice with predominantly cultural
and idealist praxis is certainly valid, especially in view of the passive and
defeatist implications of Adorno's negative aesthetics, which tend to
cancel out even praxis itself.[36] Yet what happens if the scenario is completely reversed? What if the tendentious, revolutionary aesthetics, the
unity of the social and the aesthetic, and the active intervention or prac-
tice/praxis take precedence over the disinterested, the autonomous, and
the nonpraxis?

This is precisely what Lu Xun had in mind. To be sure, Adorno was adamantly opposed to the Stalinist political instrumentalization of culture,
just as he was vehemently against both the Nazi politicization of aesthetics and the liberal capitalist manipulation of the culture industry. Since
Adorno was only concerned with those aspects of modern consumer society that reified art objects and alienated humanity, he simply ignored the
dire consequences that would inevitably arise from a positive intervention
in revolutionary struggles. In principle, Adorno was against such intervention, as evidenced by his glaring apathy toward any active political engagement. Indeed, Adorno's Marxism became a prototype for garden variety post-Marxism today, a Marxism, in essence, without Marx's vital goal
of revolution.

Lu Xun, by contrast, was a revolutionary before he was a Marxist. In his
case, the negativity resides in the antinomies within class struggle and
revolution; his predicament was whether to insist on an independent cul-

tural critique in the urban public sphere as his critical space or submit to the dictates of political strategies in the revolution. With regard to class struggle, Lu Xun was unequivocal. He was resolute about the class character of aesthetic experience, and was always critical of attempts to deny class conflicts by recourse to a universal "human nature." He also stressed active engagement in social and political movements, against political nonparticipation. Lu Xun's battle with the so-called "third category" of political neutrality between radical socialism and Chiang Kai-shek was a famous example. Nowhere, Lu Xun declared, could such a "third way" stand on the intense battleground between revolutionary and counterrevolutionary forces.[37]

Lu Xun's attitudes toward revolution and the relationship between revolution and literature, however, were more ambivalent. The problems he faced were also complex, encompassing the relationship between cultural revolution and revolutionary culture, or between cultural critique and revolutionary propaganda. Political interference and manipulation were perhaps the most urgent problems both from within the revolutionary camps and without. Lu Xun's last years were largely spent in entrenched battles against both the CCP cultural cadres who wanted to put the League under their control, and Chiang Kai-shek's cultural police and spies who constantly harassed and menaced his life. Many of his close friends were imprisoned and executed by the Guomindang state, while many of his followers became estranged from the CCP cadres in the bitter disputes that broke out periodically over countless issues. Under such circumstances, Lu Xun's awareness of the everyday political struggle was heightened.

A substantial number of his polemical zawen essays were directed against right-wing ideologues, such as Hu Shi and Liang Shiqiu, and liberalist intellectuals and writers, like Zhu Guangqian and Shen Congwen. Insisting that "literature has a definite class character" and all writers "are unconsciously governed by class consciousness, even though they consider themselves 'free' or transcendent of class," Lu Xun was relentless in dismantling the myths of a classless human nature and the autonomous, transcendental character of aesthetic experience.[38] He tirelessly asserted the practical, social, and political functions of art against advocates of nonpractical, disinterested, and aesthetic contemplation. His critique of aesthetician Zhu Guangqian was a case in point. Influenced by Benedetto Croce and Kant, Zhu held liberal humanist views. Although he played a crucial role in the formation of contemporary Chinese aesthetic Marxism after his conversion to Marxism in the 1950s, in the 1930s, Zhu stood steadfastly by the humanism espoused by Liang Qichao, Wang Guowei, and Cai Yuanpei, among others. Zhu mainly promoted the Kantian disinterestedness of aesthetic contemplation and the autonomy of art. In fact, he could not transcend politics. His advocacy of disinterestedness can be construed as an implicit critique of the political abuses of literature and the arts, from both the Right and Left camps. Yet Lu Xun seized on Zhu's suppression of the historical and social contexts of classical Chinese poetry in praising its timeless serenity and beauty. Lu Xun critiqued Zhu's interpretive strategy of separation and exclusion. According to Lu Xun, Zhu only focused on those aspects of literary work that could buttress the critic's claims of aesthetic autonomy and transcendence, while eclipsing other crucial aspects and "external" sociopolitical contexts.[39] Zhu's "ultimate state" of aesthetic experience, namely transcendental serenity, was in Lu Xun's view merely an "illusory suspension" that would fall into an "ultimate impasse."[40] Ironically, an illusory suspension and ultimate impasse haunted Lu Xun as well, even though his own ultimate state—that is, the classless society promised by Marxist communist revolution—was diametrically opposed to Zhu's disinterested serenity and beauty.

Lu Xun was also involved in the 1932 "third category" literature debate. The main proponent of third category literature was Hu Qiuyuan, an original member of the league and a literary theorist well versed in Marxism. Hu upheld the need to maintain an independent, nonpartisan cultural critique, and the autonomy of literature, free from political intervention.[41] As Marston Anderson incisively observes, by promoting "a kind of disinterested *Kulturkritik*," and the separation and distancing of literature from the political arena, Hu's position "amounted to a vigorous defense of precisely those strains of May Fourth thought that theorists within the league, such as Qu Qiubai, wish[ed] to put to rest."[42] Strongly critical of the Western individualistic and elitist tendencies in May Fourth thought, Qu found Hu's denial of the class basis of literature unacceptable. Lu also mounted a critique of the third category.[43] Paradoxically, Hu and other third category critics, notably Su Wen, actually reaffirmed Lu Xun's worries about the precarious relationship between literature and revolution. Lu Xun's harsh rebuttal of the third category standpoint betrays incongruities in his attitudes toward revolution, politics, and art. It is symptomatic of his inner contradictions, torn between the May Fourth legacy of cultural critique and the political dictates of the revolution.

If Lu Xun's uncompromising stance against both liberal humanist autonomy and disinterestedness, and the third category critic's Kulturkritik was an indication of his firm commitment to revolutionary struggle on the cultural front, then his stubborn refusal to accede to the authority of the CCP in the league revealed the pessimistic dimension of his thought. Lu Xun's clash with the CCP erupted during the "Two Slogans" dispute in 1936. The CCP's main representative to the league was Zhou Yang, who was to become Mao's cultural chief after the founding of the PRC. In Lu

Xun's view, Zhou's promotion of the slogan "National Defense Literature" not only smacked of sectarianism, but also risked giving up the proletarian leadership in revolutionary cultural and literary movements.[44] To counter this, Hu Feng, on Lu Xun's instruction, coined the slogan "Mass Literature of National Revolutionary War" in order to forge an anti-Japanese united front among writers, while keeping the revolutionary leadership firmly in hand. It is indeed ironic that Lu Xun, who was never a CCP member, should reprove Zhou's betrayal of the revolutionary leadership. At the same time, it reveals Lu Xun's lifelong difficulty in equating revolutionary leadership simply with the party apparatus.[45] In the Two Slogans conflict, Hu was attacked by Zhou and other CCP members within the league. Angered by these rather nefarious assaults, Lu Xun came to Hu's defense. Lu's passionate statement, issued only a few weeks before his death, painted Hu as an honest, somewhat stubborn, revolutionist, while Zhou and his associates were condemned outright as opportunists. This was Lu Xun's strongest charge fired at his Communist comrades, and it remained a major embarrassment to the CCP cultural bureaucracy.[46] Hu was to pay dearly in the early 1950s. On the other hand, during the Cultural Revolution, Lu Xun's indictments became Jiang Qing's best tool to torture Zhou and his colleagues.

Lu Xun's negative aesthetics was also expressed in his misgivings over the relationship between literature and revolution, and between art and politics. In a speech at the Whampoa Military Academy on April 8, 1927, delivered only four days before the Guomindang and CCP split as well as Chiang Kai-shek's massacre of the Communists, Lu Xun admonished that works of art in an age of political upheaval were utterly powerless: "strong men don't talk—they just kill." "[D]uring a great revolution, literature disappears and there is silence."[47] He described a three-stage scenario in which literature remained consistently dubious and negative. It was irrelevant and useless in the prerevolutionary stage. During the revolution, it was simply superseded by revolutionary action. In the postrevolutionary period, literature would either assume a positive and affirmative role, eulogizing the triumph of the revolution, or wax hopelessly nostalgic for the old order and way of life.[48] Lu Xun submitted that postrevolutionary affirmative literature ought to be a "popular literature," produced by workers and peasants. But he was quick to note that such literature did not exist in China, at a time when the fate of the revolution was in peril.[49] Lu Xun, in fact, never considered the works produced by himself and his left-wing fellow writers to be "revolutionary literature." Although a substantial amount of his own short stories dealt with the lives of poor and oppressed peasants, he was preoccupied with uncovering the inner conflicts of intellectuals.

In another seminal speech delivered in December 1927, "The Divergent Roads of Art and Politics," Lu Xun offered his view on the questions of modernity, revolution, politics, and art in a succinct and plain fashion. He began by observing both the conflict and complementarity of art and politics:

> I have always felt that art and politics are often in mutual conflict. At first, art and revolution were not opposed to each other; they shared the same discontent with the status quo. Yet politics attempts to maintain the status quo, so it naturally stands in the opposite direction of art, which is discontented with reality. The art that was dissatisfied with reality, however, only emerged in the nineteenth century, and its history was rather short.[50]

Lu Xun had a clear historical sense, tracing the art/politics relationship from the eighteenth- and nineteenth-centuries bourgeois revolutions in the West to the twentieth-century Russian and Chinese Revolutions. He then discussed in considerable detail conflicts between the modern state and civil society. Lu Xun argued that in the process of capitalist modernization, "big countries swallowed numerous small countries," referring to the imperialist and colonialist expansions and invasions that brought about global modernity by force and violence:

> In the big countries, internal conditions became very complex, amalgamating diverse and heterogeneous ideas and problems. In the meantime, art thrived, causing constant conflicts with politics. Politics intended to maintain the status quo and to establish unity, whereas art propelled society toward evolution and gradual separation. Art brought forth ruptures to society, but only through ruptures could society progress. Since art is a thorn in the eyes of the politicians, it had to be eliminated. A lot of foreign writers could not stay in their own countries, and had to escape to other countries, and to be in exile one after another. This was the way of "exodus."[51]

Given the historical range and scope of his speech, this deceptively simple and pedestrian exposition (it was addressed to an audience of college students and faculty at Jinan University) encapsulated many of Lu Xun's concerns about modernity's internal contradictions, along with the historical and sociopolitical causes of exile for intellectuals. Lu Xun himself experienced a profound spiritual exile, amid a variety of adverse forces, from Guomindang foes to CCP friends alike. On a different occasion, Lu Xun made the desperate plea that "in order to liberate the children of each person, let the awakened men burden themselves with the weight of the past, and shoulder up the gate of darkness, giving unimpeded passage to their children so that they can rush to the bright, wide-open space and live happily thereafter as rational human beings."[52] For Lu Xun, the "gate of darkness" was real and literal, while the "bright, wide-open space" was far more remote and illusory.

Committed to the building of a classless future, Lu Xun nevertheless was too sober a realist to condone a positive, affirmative cultural life in a postrevolutionary society. In the same speech on art and politics, he advanced a depressing prediction on the postrevolutionary status of art and artists:

> After the revolution triumphs, there might be some leisure, and some would come out to flatter and extol revolution. But this will no longer be revolutionary literature. Flattering and extolling revolution is tantamount to glorifying those who have power; what does it have to do with revolution whatsoever? At this time, though, some sensitive and perceptive writers might feel again dissatisfied with reality, and want to speak out. Politicians agreed with what the artists said before the revolution succeeded. But after the revolution, they would again adopt the old ways, the ways that the revolution was opposed to. An artist could hardly be pleased by this, and the result [of this discontent] would inevitably be to be ousted, or to have his head chopped off. As I said before, to chop the artist's head off would be the best solution. This has generally been the trend of art in the world from the nineteenth century to the present.[53]

Lu Xun's gloomy picture was by no means based on pure speculation. He cited the suicides of the Russian avant-garde poet Yesenin after the Bolshevik Revolution, in addition to the example of China's Revolutionary Northern Expedition's efforts to wipe out the warlords. In the expedition, Lu Xun pointed out, "the writers stood on no ground," even "after being communized."[54]

Although Lu Xun hardly entertained romantic expectations about the glorious role of art in a postrevolutionary politics, this does not mean that he was reluctant to accept revolution and Marxism. Instead, Lu Xun's negative views toward revolution, politics, and art reflect the tensions and contradictions internalized within Marxist revolutionary movements. Despite his persistent self-denigration and rejection of the centrality of art in revolution, his own work constitutes an enduring legacy of revolutionary literature. In this respect, Lu Xun's negative critique is eminently aesthetic. His negative aesthetics should also be read dialectically and symptomatically. Lu Xun's skepticism, and fears about the suppression and absence of critical voices in the affirmative culture of a postrevolutionary society, raise serious questions. He implicitly raised the issue of providing a critical cultural space in which revolutionary consciousness and subjectivity could sustain themselves after the establishment of revolutionary hegemony. Lu Xun's aesthetics of negativity, then, contains valuable insights into an affirmative revolutionary hegemony. While acknowledging the fundamental differences between Lu Xun, Adorno, and Benjamin, one can still see their remarkably similar, and negative, views about the relationship of art and politics in modern revolutionary and postrevolutionary ages. Negativity is perhaps indispensable, given the prevailing affirmative nature of modern culture, whether it is produced in a consumer society or repressive state.

Critique of Europeanization and Formation of the National-Popular: Qu Qiubai's Theory and Practice

As both a major CCP leader and Marxist theorist, Qu Qiubai contributed significantly to Chinese Marxism in two ways: he critiqued the Europeanization of the May Fourth movement, and developed both a theory and practice of building a revolutionary national-popular culture. Moreover, his works laid crucial groundwork for the establishment of a revolutionary hegemony. Recently, a number of studies concerning Qu's historical role have been published in China. In the United States, Qu was the subject of Paul Pickowicz's intellectual biography, which provides a balanced account of the multifarious dimensions of his work and life, and points to fruitful areas of further exploration.[55] Yet Qu's contributions have been grossly undervalued, for different reasons. In the West, research on Qu falls primarily under the disciplinary division of modern Chinese history. This narrowly defined field of study hinders the broad evaluations and comparative studies that would link Qu with Marxists from other parts of the world. In China, by contrast, Qu's reevaluation has been conditioned by the political and ideological disputes surrounding the history of the CCP.

An interpretation of Qu's work involves the larger issue of rethinking China's revolutionary legacy with cultural revolution as its center. More specifically, any reassessment of Qu should take a multidimensional view that accounts for a complex set of areas, including the cultural, literary, and political. Qu played different roles in those arenas, and his roles as well as positions were often contradictory, particularly as a CCP political leader and literary theorist. Sometimes, the paradoxes are so great that one is tempted to accept Qu's own contention at face value: that he was essentially of a split and dual personality, or schizophrenic. Indeed, his whole revolutionary career was built on a series of dualities and splits, and thus, evaluations remain controversial.

Qu's life was certainly one of the most eventful and legendary of modern intellectuals and political leaders. Born in 1899 to a landlord-gentry family in decline, Qu's upbringing closely resembled Lu Xun's. Qu was an active student leader during the May Fourth movement, and one of the earliest Communists associated with Li Dazhao and Chen Duxiu. Unlike Lu Xun, however, who became a Marxist much later in life, Qu's career as a writer and critic began with his participation in Marxist movements. From 1920 to 1922, Qu spent nearly two years in the "land of hunger," Soviet Russia, as a journalist. His writings on the USSR and its leaders, including Lenin, whom he met on several occasions, aroused immediate excitement when they were published and had a lasting impact on China. On returning to China in 1923, Qu became involved in both the political and cultural spheres of the Communist movement. In 1927, when the Guomindang and CCP split, Qu assumed the CCP post of general secretary. As a political leader, Qu was allegedly responsible for the ultraleftist adventurism that organized urban insurgencies during Chiang Kai-shek's reign of terror. This episode, from 1927 to 1931, marked a low point in his career, as the CCP lost almost all its forces in the cities and was forced to retreat to the backward, impoverished rural regions. Qu was ousted from his position in 1931. Withdrawing from political activity, he went to Shanghai, occupying himself exclusively with cultural and literary issues. During this period, he wrote profusely on Marxist cultural and aesthetic theories, and literary criticism; in addition, he composed numerous zawen essays, and translated Russian Marxist literary theory and criticism. From 1934 to 1935, he again engaged in the political activities of the CCP in Jiangxi's revolutionary base areas, launching a rural cultural revolution and education movement. When the Red Army was compelled to abandon Jiangxi and embark on the epic Long March, Qu was left behind with some guerrilla troops, partly due to his deteriorating health and partly because the CCP leaders disliked him. Soon after the main Red Army departed, Qu was arrested, and in less than three months, Chiang Kai-shek ordered him to be shot, despite Cai Yuanpei's plea to save Qu's life. Before his execution at the age of thirty-six, Qu wrote a pessimistic and self-condemning final statement, "Superfluous Words," from his prison cell, summarizing his brief yet tumultuous life as totally "wasteful," "accidental," and "superficial."

Qu's life was anything but superfluous, as the salient aspects of his aesthetic and cultural thought reveals. To begin with, there is Qu's twofold critique of Europeanization: he insisted on a historical materialist notion of culture, and evaluated its failures and successes by the principle of class struggle. According to classical Marxist notions of history, Qu characterized European culture by several stages. He viewed modern bourgeois culture positively, crediting its "progressive" role in establishing modern capitalist societies in Western Europe. He also acknowledged the positive achievements of the May Fourth enlightenment and Cultural Revolution, which were both essentially under the influence of European bourgeois culture. Notions of class and class struggle were equally important to Qu, buttressing his most vigorous attacks on May Fourth thoughts. Qu's critique was aimed at the May Fourth movement's uncritical acceptance of Western bourgeois ideologies, and its subsequent degeneration into a blind promotion of Western bourgeois culture and its hegemony, divorced from the real interests of the working class as well as China's social reality. In fact, class emerged as the central motif in Qu's critique of the Western hegemony of modernity, which he saw as cutting across national, ethnic, and geopolitical boundaries.

In Edward Said's works, the critique of Western hegemony stems from a sociopolitical conjuncture in highly developed Western capitalism. In this advanced capitalist world, a commodified cultural production tends to both perpetuate and suppress the political distinction between the "West" and the "Orient." The Orient, moreover, refers almost exclusively to the Middle East or Arab world in Said's vocabulary. It is within a specific complex of the temporal-spatial context of modernity or postmodernity—distinguished by the fragmentation, diffusion, and dispersion of social life—that Said has conceptualized and critiqued "Orientalism" as the Western hegemonic representation of that very social reality of modernity. Not surprisingly, Said's conceptual tools are primarily derived from poststructuralist thought, particularly that of Foucault and Nietzsche. Said also draws heavily on Gramsci's notion of hegemony. These three theorists provide Said a nontotalizing, fragmenting, diffusing perspective with which to understand the phenomena of national, ethnic, racial, sexual, and geopolitical fragmentation and division underlying the cultural and knowledge production of Orientalism. Said, therefore, stresses the hegemonic strategy of Orientalism in terms of its "flexible *positional* superiority, which puts the Westerner in a whole series of possible relationships with the Orient without ever losing him the relative upper hand."[56] Additionally, Said argues that Orientalism operates not as a political subject matter, but to the contrary, as "a *distribution* of geopolitical awareness into aesthetic, scholarly, economic, sociological, historical and philological texts."[57] Despite the fact that Said is also critical of Foucault's notion of power, which he claims "obliterate[s] the role of classes, the role of economics, the role of insurgency and rebellion,"[58] Said's critique of Orientalism and Western hegemonic discourse is largely anchored in contemporary Western countries, the United States in particular. Flexible, transnational capitalism in the United States is crucially linked with ideas of fragmentation, dispersion, and dislocation, produced in cultural and aesthetic spheres. Gayatri Spivak, from a different angle, arrives at a similar and depressing conclusion. She contends that it is basically impossible for the subalterns—that is, disempowered, exploited, minority groups and communities—to speak for themselves in a cultural ambiance of "epistemic violence" that deprives the underprivileged of the ability to formulate their own class consciousness or collectivity, without reinscribing the bourgeois, hegemonic category of the sovereign subject.[59]

Unlike Said and Spivak, since Qu's critique of Europeanization was derived from the classical Marxist category of class and the historical stages of progress, he was able to grasp the historical totality at the conjuncture of fragmentation and dislocation. The social reality that Qu faced was certainly different from today's advanced capitalism in the West. Yet one can still see some structural similarities, in terms of social fragmentation and disintegration on the one hand, and centralization and totalization on the other. This historical dialectic is crucial for any understanding of real social momentum. At present, globalization constitutes a great historical paradox in all spheres of social life, with homogenization and unification side by side with fragmentation and diversification. In Qu's day, China lacked a strong, centralizing internal force, while the external, imperialist powers of Japan and the West never ceased to subjugate China under their total domination. But the distinction between internal and external is only relative to the global context of modernity. Qu always subsumed cultural and historical differences, and uneven developments, under the rubric of historical totality in his analyses and critiques.

In 1923, Qu attacked a reversed Orientalism, namely the polarization of Asian spirituality and Western materialism. This stance was advocated by "cultural essentialists" such as Liang Shuming and Zhang Junmai, and supported by Indian poet Rabindranath Tagore, who visited China that same year. Lurking behind this polarization was the older ti-yong dualism. Qu made it quite clear that "as there is no so-called East and West, hence there is no such problem as harmonizing the two."[60] Instead of cultural differences in the modern world, the single most universal contradiction was unquestionably class struggle. Only an organized political movement of the masses could solve this dilemma. Qu's critique of reversed Orientalism, however, showed a deterministic tendency. He insisted on "objective laws of history," as opposed to Tagore's "idealist" denial of them. Qu frequently invoked the classical Marxist teleological notion of irreversible and unsurpassable stages in history. He maintained that "Marxists differ from unscientific *narodniks* and anarchists in that they entertain no illusion at all of bypassing capitalism and arriving directly at socialism. There is only one way [to socialism], that is, to carry out class struggle on the basis of capitalism."[61]

Nearly a decade later, in 1931, as Qu launched his devastating critique of the Europeanization of the May Fourth tradition, he reflected on his earlier adherence to determinism. Qu introduced a complex, and often contradictory, viewpoint on culture and aesthetics, which eventually crystallized into a Marxist theory of cultural revolution. A fundamental contradiction in Qu's cultural theory involves the deterministic notion of historical stages and the concept of cultural revolution that unsettles it. Another incongruity is that while insisting on class and class struggle as universal phenomena irrespective of nations and race, Qu frequently emphasized cultural differences in refuting the inherent Europeanizing or Eurocentric presuppositions in many of the universalizing generalizations and abstractions.

Qu identified three stages in modern Chinese cultural and literary movements. The May Fourth era was the first stage, from 1915 to 1925, and the two-year interregnum lasting from 1925 to 1927, during which time the Guomindang and CCP formed a revolutionary coalition and then split, constituted the second. Qu argued that the predominant ideology in both stages belonged to European bourgeois ideas. Thus, May Fourth was primarily a bourgeois cultural movement.[62] Qu acknowledged the progressive side of May Fourth in its struggle against "feudalist tradition," but was quick to note the essentially negative character of this bourgeois cultural movement. He singled out the elitist and Europeanizing tendencies that placed the majority of May Fourth intellectuals "on the other side of a Great Wall."[63] He then sharply rebuked their alienation from China's reality: "They [the intellectuals] do not have a common language with working classes in China, and to the middle and lower ranks of the people, they are almost 'foreigners.' They live in 'their own country of intellectual youth,' and in the stationery shops of the European gentlemen."[64] In Qu's view, even in the second stage of the revolution and counterrevolution, the cultural spheres in cities continued to be dominated by a Western bourgeois cultural hegemony. The third stage, after the "Marxist turn" of left-wing writers, still left the impasse of Europeanization unresolved. In other words, even the acceptance of and conversion to Marxism among left-wing writers, in which Qu himself played a decisive role, was no guarantee of a real break with Western hegemony, a hegemony that separated the bourgeois-oriented May Fourth intellectuals from the working class.[65]

Qu was relentless in unmasking the May Fourth intellectuals' flexible positionality or "in-betweenness"; he claimed that they spoke a "hybrid" or "mule-like" language ("neither a horse, nor a donkey"), a "new classical language" blending archaic, aristocratic literary language with Europeanized idioms.[66] This allowed them to stay aloof from the social reality and common people. It also created a coterie for these intellectuals, setting them apart as "internal foreigners" whose cultural space was located in

Shanghai's Western colonial concessions.[67] Qu mercilessly chastised the pretentiousness of Europeanized intellectuals even when they converted to Marxism. In his view, Marxism itself could not redeem them from the self-imposed "epistemic violence" of the Western hegemonic discourse. For Marxism, Qu continued in his second stunning blast against Europeanization, appealed to the May Fourth intellectuals precisely because it was the latest fashion of Westernization. Marxism was accepted by the Europeanizers as an ideology of Western modernity, yet as a constituent of Western epistemic violence, it could only perpetuate China's social problems. The Marxist-oriented revolutionary and proletarian literature that "emerged from the May Fourth foundation," Qu argued, "simply offered the Europeanized gentry yet another sumptuous banquet to satisfy their new tastes, while the laboring people were still starving."[68] This was perhaps the most devastating critique of Chinese Marxist intellectuals made by a leading Chinese Marxist, especially as Qu's own Marxism was shaped by the May Fourth movement.

Of course, Qu's main episteme was the Marxist notion of class analysis, which offers little of the theoretical ambiguity and sophistication that characterize poststructuralism. The crucial concept of class, however, did not appear reductionist or dogmatic in Qu's exposition, but rather polysemic and often self-contradictory. In terms of the class basis of the May Fourth intellectuals, Qu observed:

> From May Fourth, 1919, to May Thirtieth, 1925, a diverse variety of "Bohemians" quickly aggregated in China's cities.[69] These petty bourgeois wanderers and intellectuals, like earlier outcasts from the literati-gentry classes, are products of the disintegration of China's feudalist, patriarchal society. They are victims of imperialists, warlords, and bureaucrats, as well as orphans, who were "thrown out" of the process of the lopsided development of the capitalist mode of production. However, as they became further urbanized, and shaped by modern trends,[70] their links with rural areas became further attenuated. They lost the sober realism of early generations, or in other words, they lost the down-to-earth, practical spirit of the honest peasants. Instead, they were deeply affected by the European fin de siècle ethos. These newly emerged intellectuals would often be the first to rush into the revolutionary upheavals because of their "passion," and yet often the first to defect, or to become decadent, or even traitors of revolution.[71]

Still traceable in this passage is the classical Marxist proposition that economic relations are the essential feature of class identity. But Qu also subtlely shifted his emphasis from objective social conditions to the subjective realm, or to the dispositions and ethos of intellectuals. This was meant to define more accurately the flexible and multiple social positions of the urban intellectuals, and to describe their shifting class identities, too—a conceptual move more evident in Qu's later work. It has several important ramifications. First, it stresses the intellectuals' self-education or ideological "self-remold," which was to become a central theme in Mao's project of cultural revolution. Second, it implies a shift in cultural revolution from urban to rural areas. It was expected that in the rural areas, dislocated and drifting intellectuals could stand on the solid ground of China's reality. Finally, by modifying and reformulating the idea of class struggle from economic and political spheres to the domains of culture and consciousness, Qu introduced to Chinese Marxism the idea of a revolution that would begin in cultural spheres, a revolution in which cultural change, as opposed to political or economic transformation, would be primary.

But the double reorientation of class struggle—from political to cultural, from urban to rural—has serious contradictions. One is the notion that class struggle and revolution would subsume ethnic, racial, and gender differences. There is also a tension in the emphasis on the dichotomies between Chinese and European, indigenous and exogenous culture. Despite the fact that Qu was himself an urban intellectual, and a prominent translator of foreign culture and literature, his critique of Europeanization nonetheless indicates an inclination to absolutize the differences between Chinese and European cultures, a premise at odds with the universalist assumptions of Marxism.[72] In addition, while he was sharply critical of the flexible positionality of the May Fourth intellectuals, Qu focused on subjective and cultural factors in the class identity of intellectuals, contradicting his own Marxist class analysis based primarily on political and economic affiliations. Indeed, Qu recoiled from a firm classical Marxist position that always emphasizes economic determination in social life in favor of a more fragmented and flexible position of subjective determination. His stance has some affinity with the postcolonialist idea of positionality, which grants the supremacy of subjective, psychological, or discursive determinants in class identity. Postcolonialism also reaffirms cultural, national, and ethnic differences over Marx's notion of class as a universal category. To some extent, Qu's critique of Europeanization shares this tendency with postcolonialism.

Li Zehou has commented on Qu's initial attempt to substitute the historical materialist principle of the mode of production with the dialectical materialist notion of class struggle in the domains of culture and consciousness. Li Zehou argues that Qu and Mao began to stray from the Marxist premises of material practice and mode of production, and embrace a cultural and ideological determinism. This gave rise to the central problematic of China's modernity: the fundamental contradiction between ideological, cultural revolution and material, economic reconstruction.[73]

A crucial distinction between Qu and today's postcolonialist academicians in the United States, however, is that the former's theorization was all translated into the concrete, material, social practices of insurgency and revolution, while the latter face an altogether different historical context in which social and political revolution has little, if any, relevance. But Chinese practices have political and social consequences that are not irrelevant to today's postcolonialism and other radical theories. Since the 1980s, storms have swept across the U.S. academic world in the social sciences and humanities, beginning with the introduction of French poststructuralism and deconstruction. Still, radical theories hardly have any impact beyond academic communities. Many, therefore, lament the loss of theory's critical and subversive edge in the prevailing careerist atmosphere of the capitalist intellectual market, while many more simply take it for granted as necessary professional training. Caught in this comfortable (in the sense of the material and social privileges that present-day Western academicians enjoy) predicament or interregnum, postcolonialist professors cannot help but operate within the First World academic enclave, with the assumption that it is impossible to break the pervasive Western hegemonic discourse or postcoloniality as their condition of existence.

Qu's time, of course, has nothing in common with today's American academic world. But looking back a step further, one sees connections between Qu's ideas and the political and theoretical resources of contemporary U.S. critical theory, postcolonialism in particular. Specifically, there are striking parallels to Antonio Gramsci's notion of hegemony and his cultural theory in general. Qu wanted to launch a proletarian, revolutionary, cultural movement that would solve the problem of the separation of intellectuals from working people, while simultaneously creating a new national and popular culture. Even Qu and Gramsci's concepts and terms are remarkably similar, and often identical. Qu highlighted the need to construct a proletarian popular literature and art that should also be national; Gramsci conceived of the notion of "national-popular" as a collective will, central to revolutionary hegemony. Qu arrived at the same conclusion concerning the role of culture in revolution.

These parallels are not surprising, once the theorists' respective historical contexts are compared. Qu, as we saw, made his most original and critical reflections on the May Fourth legacy and the future of the Chinese Revolution in the wake of urban proletarian insurrections, for which he was directly responsible as a CCP leader. The Communist revolution then had to confront the protofascist regime of Chiang Kai-shek, which had installed itself in power by a class alliance between the bureaucratic bourgeoisie and large landowners, and which enjoyed the crucial support of Western imperialist powers. The revolution in the cities was suppressed and had to shift its base to the impoverished rural areas; at the same time, the left-wing urban intelligentsia took a "Marxist turn" in the midst of the counterrevolutionary white terror. The urgent task for Qu, then, was to bring together the two revolutionary forces—the urban Marxist intellectuals and rural peasantry—under the hegemony of the proletariat. Gramsci confronted a similar sociopolitical conjuncture at roughly the same time. The ascendancy of the fascist regime in Italy was based on the successful alliance of what Gramsci called economic-corporate interest groups—namely, the northern industrial bourgeoisie and southern landowners, supported by petty bourgeois intellectuals. In a country divided by an industrialized north with a small proletariat and a backward, agrarian, "Third World" south with a large peasantry, Gramsci's strategic thinking from the perspective of a Communist leader was circumscribed by concrete historical conditions substantially analogous to those of Qu's China. The fascist consolidation of power ruled out immediate political revolution or the seizure of authority. Gramsci, therefore, saw the necessity of an interlude or interregnum, a transitional period in which the establishment of a Jacobinian coalition or united front of diverse classes and groups would be a crucial step toward the ultimate victory of socialism. In fact, the development of a national-popular will constituted the fundamental objective for constructing a revolutionary hegemony in Gramsci's tactics of socialist revolution.[74]

Qu shared the same concern, assigning supreme importance to cultural revolution. He urged that "we must link the popular cultural movement to the new literary revolution," and that the establishment of a new national-popular culture "was the central issue of the proletarian cultural movement." Moreover, the formation of a national-popular culture was, in Qu's opinion, "the concrete task of seeking the leadership in cultural revolution."[75] The expression *"lingdaoquan"* ("leadership") in Qu's use has strong affinities with Gramsci's "hegemony" in that both refer primarily to leadership in the cultural domain.

In addition, there are at least two other areas of overlap between Qu and Gramsci's views that merit attention. The first is the task of intellectual and moral reform that is closely linked to a national-popular cultural movement. For Qu, a rural cultural revolution was critical to dismantling the "Great Wall" that separated the urban intelligentsia from working people, who were essentially illiterate peasants. Intellectuals must merge with the people, transforming themselves from "bourgeois experts" into "proletarianized intellectuals" in the process of national-popular cultural revolution. They should also transmit knowledge to working people in order to help produce intellectuals from their midst.[76] Qu, however, did not assign a high priority to the ideological transformation of the intelligentsia; it was Mao who put "thought-reform" at the core of revolutionary hegemony and cultural revolution.

Gramsci, likewise, observed that "any formation of a national-popular collective will is impossible, unless the great mass of peasant farmers burst simultaneously into political life."[77] This, for Gramsci, was one of "two basic points," the other task consisting precisely of "intellectual and moral reform."[78] Such reform elicits intellectual potential or revolutionary consciousness from the fragmented, episodic, and inarticulate "subaltern groups," or peasants, or it activates the intellectual function of "all men," who in Gramsci's judgment, have the potential to be "intellectuals" and "philosophers."[79] Like Qu, Gramsci attempted to bridge the gap between intellectuals and working people that was created by a bourgeois cultural hegemony primarily vested in linguistic and aesthetic forms.

For this reason, a second area of convergence between Qu and Gramsci is the task of developing a new revolutionary language and aesthetic forms. The question of language, for Qu, lay at the heart of cultural revolution, since he was keenly aware of the ideological nature of discourse. He charged that the modern language revolution of 1915 failed to achieve its goal of integrating *wenyan* (classical, literary language) and *baihua* (vernacular) because of its Westernizing and bourgeois tendencies. The May Fourth cultural movement, according to Qu, only produced a *xin wenyan* (a new classical, literary language), a sterile hybrid of the archaic and foreign. This new literary language was far removed from the everyday, living vernacular of working people. A central vocation of the proletarian cultural revolution as a counterhegemonic movement was to create a new vernacular for the vast majority of the working class. This revolutionary language was conceived by Qu as essentially national, stemming from the popular arts of storytelling, puppet theater, folklore, local operas, and so on, which had been excluded from the canons of national cultural tradition by the ruling class and aristocratic cultural elite.[80] Hence, the creation of this new language amounted to a reconstruction of national-popular tradition vis-à-vis the double impediment of the archaic, aristocratic tradition and Western bourgeois culture.[81] Qu did not merely theorize in this respect. From his position of leadership in the Jiangxi revolutionary base areas, he was instrumental in developing a vernacular language and producing revolutionary popular aesthetic forms. Qu regarded these new linguistic and aesthetic forms as the core curriculum of a proletarian education. He also promoted the effort to Latinize the Chinese language, strongly believing that the difficult written script limited working people's access to knowledge and education. His enthusiasm for Latinizing indicates his universalist and modernist inclinations, despite the fact, as we have seen, that he was also a staunch critic of Europeanization in the May Fourth movement.

Gramsci's views on language and form corresponded to Qu's almost identically. He attributed the serious absence of a national-popular culture in Italy to the historical separation between intellectuals and the people that could be traced back to Renaissance humanism, or the dawn of Western modernity. Gramsci observed that in Italy, the Roman Empire, Catholic Church, and dominant literary languages of Latin and Tuscan coalesced to block the development of a vernacular, popular, national language and culture. It is significant that the construction and dissemination of a national language became the paradigm for Gramsci's project of national-popular culture: "Since the process of formation, spread and development of a unified national language occurs through a whole complex of molecular process, it helps to be aware of the entire process as a whole in order to be able to intervene actively in it with the best possible results."[82] Yet the creation of a national language was not to be achieved by switching roles in the cultural hierarchy, or in other words, by replacing official Latin (as used in the Catholic mass) with local dialects, philosophy with common sense, high culture with popular culture, intellectuals with the people. Instead, Gramsci conceived of a constructive educational alliance between the dominant and subordinate in order to establish an "organic unity between theory and practice, between intellectual strata and popular masses, between rulers and ruled."[83] The language barrier, for Gramsci, was a key impediment to the organic unity and alliance of intellectuals and the people, an impediment not merely restricted to Italy. Gramsci noted that in China, too, "there is the phenomenon of the script, an expression of the complete separation between the intellectuals and the people."[84]

In the shared aspects of Qu and Gramsci's thought, they both fundamentally altered the classical Marxist "economism." Qu accepted Lunacharsky's less deterministic interpretation of Marxism instead of Plekhanov's more rigid one. As to the base-superstructure relationship, Qu emphasized mutual interaction rather than unilateral determination. In his "Draft Postscript on Marxist Aesthetics," Qu stressed the significant role that culture and consciousness play in social revolution. He argued that under China's specific circumstances, revolutionary breakthrough might first occur in the superstructural realms, before social and economic transformations.[85] This was a modification of his earlier, deterministic notion of historical stages. Here, Qu rejected the need to construct a bourgeois culture in China as an inevitable step, promoting cultural revolution as a means to subvert and go beyond bourgeois cultural hegemony.[86] Qu remained evasive, however, on the relationship between the revolutionary party and cultural movement, although he had been a CCP leader for some time.[87] Instead, he endorsed Lu Xun's view on the relation between art and politics without reservation. In addition, in the confessional essay written before his execution, Qu described his "unfitness" for the role of political leader, portraying himself as a "literary intellectual" with a "weak, dual personality."[88]

For Gramsci, on the other hand, the issues and their solutions presented themselves in a different fashion. He focused his discussion of hegemony almost exclusively on bourgeois civil society, and in the realms of culture and consciousness. Gramsci is said to have sidestepped the pitfalls of "economism" or economic determinism by espousing a form of "culturalism." His notions of a nonclass-specific, flexible, and fragmenting "war of positions," "historical blocs," and "passive revolutions" prefigured the nonauthoritarian, new political alliances of heterogeneous social groups celebrated by current "post-Marxists" like Ernesto Laclau and Chantal Mouffe, as well as postcolonialist academics and various advocates of identity politics.[89] Yet, as David Forgacs incisively observes, the formations of new interclass alliances and strategies of hegemonic and counter-hegemonic struggles in the realms of culture and consciousness were basically transitional: "For Gramsci these problems were, after 1926, posed largely in theory, and they tended to be resolved in the notebooks within the formula of party centralism and the belief in the transitional nature of any form of interclassist alliance: in other words within a still essentially Leninist perspective of the single party and the replacement of parliament by soviets."[90]

While Gramsci's strategies remained primarily theoretical, Qu's theory and practice had serious consequences for the Chinese Revolution. Mao pushed Qu's ideas to the extreme, and eventually, their inherent contradictions burst out in the Great Cultural Revolution. Unlike Qu, Mao was a determinate, ruthless political leader. By his masterful strategy of armed guerrilla warfare as a scattered, fragmented, and molecular "war of positions," Mao won the revolution. And he ultimately put Qu's (and hypothetically Gramsci's) notion of cultural revolution to the test in the violent and brutal battlefields of both the revolutionary and postrevolutionary periods. As Paul Pickowicz describes it, "Mao said very little that had not been said already by Qu."[91] Qu inaugurated a decisive shift in Chinese Marxism from Shanghai to the rural areas, Jiangxi at first. Mao developed Qu's idea, elevating aesthetic discourse to the core of both the Chinese Revolution and Chinese Marxism.

CHAPTER 3

Hegemony and Counterhegemony: National

Form and "Subjective Fighting Spirit"

Mao Zedong characterized cultural revolution as an indispensable task of the Chinese Revolution: "to change the objective world and in the meantime change the subjective world."[1] The ascendency of culture (and the aesthetic as its most compressed expression) coincided with the formation of Chinese Marxism during the Sino-Japanese War (1937–1945). The role of culture reached another apex during the Cultural Revolution (1966–1976). Studies of communism in China and the Chinese Revolution mainly focus on the issues of rural revolution and peasant problems. The studies that do acknowledge the importance of culture tend to ascribe it to "voluntarism," "utopianism," "culturalism," and "subjectivism" in Mao's thought. These dimensions of Mao's thinking, in turn, are either attributed to China's unique cultural heritage, or the dialectical or subjective inclinations of Chinese Marxism, which emphasize struggles in the spheres of culture and consciousness.[2] Yet this fails to explain how culture became so central to the Chinese Revolution. This question is crucial, not only in order to understand the Chinese Revolution as an alternative modernity project, but also because it critically relates to problems of culture and cultural politics in the contemporary world. To subsume culture under the rubric of a political power struggle only sidesteps an inquiry into the dynamic interaction between the political and cultural spheres that typified the Chinese Revolution.

The concept of hegemony, particularly associated with the work of Gramsci, provides an alternative entry into the Chinese Revolution. As Raymond Williams puts it, hegemony "affects thinking about revolution in that it stresses not only the transfer of political and economic power, but the overthrow of a specific hegemony: that is to say an integral form of class rule which exists not only in political and economic institutions and relationships but also in active forms of experience and consciousness."[3]

But the explanatory power of hegemony, or a notion like "cultural politics," is limited. The Gramscian perspective of hegemony is based on epistemic presuppositions—such as separation and autonomy, civil society and state—that arise from capitalist modernity in the West, and therefore, cannot be applied to China without taking into account significant differences. Chinese Marxism did not merely emerge from Western capitalist modernity; by virtue of its self-conscious posture as an alternative, it also challenged many of the epistemological presuppositions of capitalist modernity.

Hegemony, nevertheless, can serve as a theoretical point of departure in a dialectical process. In other words, the historically specific problems of the Chinese Revolution can be reconstructed from the perspective of hegemony, even as the notion of hegemony is modified from a historical perspective. This process involves an attempt to historicize general or "universal" concepts, such as hegemony, to explore specific issues, and at the same time, contextualize those specific events and historical experiences that generate their own theoretical concepts and conceptual frameworks.

Hegemony and the Chinese Revolution

The Chinese Revolution was not only a local and nationalist movement, but also a significant part of an international revolutionary movement initiated by the Russian Revolution of 1917. Certainly, there were fundamental differences between the Chinese and Russian Revolutions. The Chinese Revolution was primarily a peasant one, centered in the backward rural areas. The Russian Revolution, on the other hand, was city-based, led by a revolutionary vanguard, that mobilized a well-organized urban proletariat. Cultural revolution was another difference. For Vladimir Lenin, revolution was primarily a political event, directed by a politically and ideologically sophisticated elite. But for the Chinese Communists, revolution was at once political, social, and cultural. Unlike the Russia of pre-revolutionary days, when objective conditions were considered ripe by the Leninist leadership, the Chinese Revolution had to generate its own revolutionary momentum. At the time, China was dominated by a powerful alliance of warlords and Western imperialists, and the existence of bourgeoisie and urban proletarians was negligible. This rendered China fragmented, decentralized, and tension filled, but also made a well-organized urban revolutionary insurgence impossible. Although the dominant political forces had practically no way to monitor the whole country, their formidable concentration of forces in the territories under their control—namely, the wealthy and relatively advanced coastal areas and major cities—was so great that the CCP was all but eliminated.

The Chinese Revolution, then, turned decisively to the peasants. The largely illiterate and unorganized peasants—labeled by Marx as petty bourgeoisie, a classification that the CCP leaders generally accepted—hardly qualified as a main force for revolution. Yet without a powerful urban proletarian class, peasants were the only possible masses for the task. Hence, the need for cultural revolution: to foster revolutionary class consciousness in the peasants and mobilize them into a revolutionary force. This was indeed crucial, for the whole fate of the revolution hinged on its success or failure. As we have seen, Qu Qiubai was the first to recognize the critical importance of this objective. He called on urban Marxist intellectuals to launch a cultural revolution in the countryside rather than the cities. Mao followed suit. He struggled to link urban intellectuals and peasants, not merely as a temporary alliance, but as a permanent and integrated revolutionary force. In both theory and practice, Mao also strove to establish a revolutionary leadership, or hegemony, amid the peasant masses. To win the hearts and minds of the peasants, of course, Mao had to rely on the national and popular culture belonging to the peasants themselves, embodied in a "national form." Mao's reflections on cultural revolution and hegemony contained novel antideterminist ideas in terms of both economics and history.

Mao saw the Chinese Revolution as "following the path of the Russians."[4] The Russian Revolution, by waging a socialist revolution in an economically backward country, broke the teleology envisaged by classical Marxism. This was both an inspiration and justification for the Chinese Communists, whose peasant revolution in a non-Western, agrarian society would constitute no less significant a breach than the Russian Revolution to Marxist teleology. Classical Marxists could only conceive of a socialist revolution in the highly industrialized, advanced capitalist countries of the West, and hardly ever thought of the non-West as a possible site for revolution. While Russia was almost at the periphery of Eurocentric thinking, to which Marx remained captive, China was positively removed, and Marx's only serious reflection on China was cast in a rather ambiguous double bind. Marx did not want to follow Hegel's ethnocentric notion to deny China a history outright, but he could not find a proper place in history for China, except in an indeterminate and vague "Asiatic mode of production."

In this respect, it is interesting to reexamine the differences between the Russian and Chinese Revolutions. The Russian Revolution was conceived by Lenin as the explosion of the intense contradictions within capitalist modernity, encapsulated by the thesis of "the weakest link." Essentially, Lenin argued, Russia constituted the weakest link in the Western capitalist system by virtue of its being the most economically and politically backward amid Western imperialism. At the same time, Russia had a Bolshevik Party that, in Lenin's judgment, was "far ahead of any Western 'socialist' party in consciousness and organization."[5] Russia's historical dialectic, being simultaneously at least a century behind the Western world in terms of capitalist development and way ahead in terms of revolutionary conditions, then produced a triumphant revolution. Louis Althusser considers this historical dialectic to be an "accumulation and exacerbation of historical contradictions."[6]

Mao also vividly described the impact of the "Russian road": "The salvoes of the October Revolution brought us Marxism and Leninism. The October Revolution helped progressives in China, and throughout the world, to adopt the proletarian world outlook as the instrument for studying a nation's destiny and considering anew their own problems. Follow the path of the Russians—that was their conclusion."[7] The Chinese Revolution, in spite of its many similarities with the Russian Revolution, was never understood by Mao as occurring within the capitalist world, but rather outside it. Indeed, it was a more thorough break with classical Marxist teleology and historical determinism than the Russian example.

Instead of following Lenin's strategy, Mao laid greater emphasis on the functions of ideology and theory in the making of revolution. "Marxism-Leninism," Mao contended, was a "proletarian world outlook."[8] Although Mao did consider historically uneven developments as the specific, objective condition for a revolution, over and over again, he reaffirmed Lenin's statement: "Without revolutionary theory there can be no revolutionary movement."[9]

As Arif Dirlik argues, the narrative embedded in Mao's theory of the Chinese Revolution grants priority to ideology and theory at the expense of an active role for revolutionary organizations.[10] Yet the supremacy of ideology, theory, and above all, cultural revolution in the Chinese Revolution cannot, as noted earlier, simply be dismissed as a voluntarism, subjectivism, or "culturalist predisposition" unique to Mao and Chinese Marxism. Mao's focus on culture and consciousness can be seen as a dialectical strategy of practice, and practice lies at the core of Mao's thinking. As Marx put it in his "Theses on Feuerbach," "The materialist doctrine that men are products of circumstances and upbringing, . . . forgets that it is men who change circumstances and that it is essential to educate the educator himself. . . . The coincidence of the changing of circumstances and of human activity can be conceived and rationally understood only as revolutionizing practice."[11] Mao's notion of cultural revolution, however, can be better grasped as an effort to cope with the intrinsic contradictions of revolution, especially the relationship between structure and agency. This relationship was extremely problematic for China, faced as it was with a fragmented, tension-filled sociopolitical reality, and equally dispersed and enfeebled political agencies or subjectivities. Bereft of revolutionary agency and subjectivity—a full-fledged urban proletariat and highly advanced revolutionary party—the Chinese Revolution from the outset had to grapple with the issues of consciousness and culture, creating its own revolutionary agency in the process of making revolution itself. Literature and arts thus became both instruments in the revolutionary struggle, and hegemonic expressions for the construction of a new culture and subjectivity. Serious contradictions arise in Mao's revolutionary strategies. Mao hardly spelled out a coherent and clearly articulated notion of subjectivity, crucial to a cultural revolution, while he increasingly leaned on instrumentalist politics in the cultural sphere.

As discussed earlier, there is a great deal of similarity between the Chinese Marxist project of cultural revolution and Gramsci's view of hegemony, since both were conceived as revolutionary strategies and tactics under comparable historical conditions. Arif Dirlik identifies at least four commonalities between Mao and Gramsci's thought: Mao's idea of a New Democracy appears similar to Gramsci's notion of hegemony; Mao's "sinification of Marxism" resembles Gramsci's idea of a national-popular culture; both emphasized the agrarian population in the formation of hegemony; and both had similar views on the role of intellectuals.[12] Indeed, Gramsci's Marxism instigates a fruitful dialogue when compared to Chinese Marxism, in addition to the significant encounters between contemporary Western Marxism and "Maoism" in the 1960s.

As an aside, Gramsci's concepts of "hegemony," "subalternity," and "organic intellectuals" are fashionable in contemporary cultural studies and postcolonialism. Such theoretical currency betrays a fundamental contradiction or paradox: Gramsci's concepts were formulated as practical strategies and tactics of revolution, while Western academic intellectuals on the Left currently are faced with a global capitalism in which not revolution, but commodification figures most prominently in social life. On the other hand, Chinese Marxist theories and practices have far more parallels with Gramsci's project than today's Western academics, particularly with respect to cultural revolution.

The relationship between Gramsci's Marxism and Chinese Marxism, however, is far more complicated than a "Maoist connection." Chinese Marxism is not monolithic, represented by Mao's thought alone. While Qu Qiubai's aesthetic and literary thoughts may have paved the way for Mao's rural cultural and aesthetic formations, Lu Xun and Hu Feng opened up another critical space for urban aesthetic formation and cultural critique. There are serious differences between the aesthetic and cultural views of Mao, Lu Xun, and Hu. Mao remained either silent or negligent on questions of a revolutionary subjectivity, civil society, and public sphere. Lu Xun and Qu gave serious reflection to these same issues. Hu devoted most of his effort to thinking about these problems and suggesting practical solutions. Although they shared a Marxist conceptual framework, it is essential to note their differences in order to understand the critical tensions within Chinese Marxism and the Chinese Revolution.

In the same vein, comparing the complexities within Chinese Marxism to Gramsci's theory can help illuminate the latter's contradictions, too. Gramsci remained inconsistent and ambiguous on the relationship between civil society and state, and that between a highly disciplined, unified revolutionary party and semi-independent, fragmented intellectuals and subaltern groups. These issues are basic precisely because they address conditions after the successful installation of a revolutionary hegemony—a hegemony that Gramsci hoped for, but was unable to bring about during his lifetime. Unlike the Chinese, Gramsci was a thinker of the defeat of revolution. Hence, he reflected a good deal on the conditions of interregnum, morbid disjuncture, and so forth. Such a posture may place him well within the ranks of modern aesthetic and academic Marxists in the West. The French poststructuralists and deconstructionists find Gramsci congenial as well, for they echo his sentiment on the failure of social revolution with their own experiences as radical social activists or revolutionaries during the Parisian "May Storms" of 1968.

Contemporary post-Marxist and postcolonialist critics in the West (in the United States in particular) are quick to seize on Gramsci's well-nigh anarcho-liberalist visions; the erratic, disorganized, fragmented nature of his subaltern politics; and his hegemonic and counterhegemonic formations. These ideas are said to fit squarely within contemporary Western civil society, where dispersed and fragmented social groups and intellectuals can formulate nontotalizing, antisystematic micropolitics or "identity politics," "politics of difference," and the like. Nevertheless, Gramsci's views on the most sensitive and practical problem, namely conditions in a postrevolutionary society after hegemony is established, are for the most part ignored.[13] Gramsci was not to blame if his ability to envision concrete issues and solutions in a socialist society was severely hampered by his own experience. The historical limit to Gramsci's thought, however, is not an excuse for the much romanticized notions of hegemony that postmodern and poststructuralist academics in the United States embrace. By ignoring the historical conditions that gave rise to his reflections, U.S. postcolonialists in the academy are blinded to the serious consequences and ramifications of Gramsci's thinking. Such consequences have been amply shown, intensely debated, and theorized by Chinese around and after Gramsci's time. Yet this Chinese legacy has largely been neglected by the intellectual Left in the West, with which postcolonialist academics in the States claim to be affiliated. Unlike Edward Said and Gayatri Spivak, who deploy Gramsci's assaults on bourgeois culture and hegemony in their own critique of the Western distortion or colonization of the knowledge of Arab or Indian cultures, a good number of China specialists in the West, and many scholars in China as well, now rush to debunk the Chinese revolutionary legacy and embrace ideologies of capitalism.

It is important to go back, therefore, as a way of going forward, as a way of creating a vision of alternatives to the Chinese experience. Chinese people actually practiced, by the millions and millions, a social, political, and cultural revolution that Gramsci had only thought about in the isolation of a fascist prison cell. Undoubtedly, he would have attempted to put his theories into practice given the opportunity. After all, Gramsci's theories were meant first and foremost to be utilized in revolutionary practice, rather than reduced to post-Marxist or postcolonialist intellectual exercises. It is essential, then, to explore the implications of cultural revolution and hegemony in the postrevolutionary society that the Chinese experience has abundantly demonstrated.

Cultural Revolution, Hegemony, and National Form: Mao Zedong's Cultural Theory

The Chinese Marxism that emerged from the process of *Makesizhuyi zhongguohua* ("sinification of Marxism" or "making Marxism Chinese") was not simply an outcome of what Mao called "the integration of the universal principles of Marxism with the concrete practices of the Chinese Revolution." By integration, Mao implied a kind of seamless synthesis, dissolving the vast differences between Marxism as a European thought and the given conditions in China. Chinese Marxism involved, as Arif Dirlik argues persuasively, a complex structural transformation or "vernacularization," conceived at the moment when the "globalization of Marxism outside Europe" took place, resulting in the dispersion, fragmentation, and ultimate universalization of Marxism.[14] Following Dirlik's analysis, the ways in which Mao theorized an alternative modernity, crucially linked to cultural revolution, can be examined.

Beyond the centrality of culture for Mao in addressing the problems of the Chinese Revolution and an alternative modernity, he was always concerned with the compelling tasks of the revolution, military strategies in particular. There was an indissociable connection and reciprocity between Mao's military strategies and his thought on cultural revolution and hegemony. Cultural revolution, carried out in a military fashion, was in Mao's mind the only effective means to ensure the success of a socialist alternative modernity. It is little wonder, then, that one of Mao's cardinal dictums during the Cultural Revolution (1966–1976) was the whole nation should learn from the People's Liberation Army, and that he was preoccupied during the war period with cultural revolution. Military rhetoric in Mao's discourse of cultural revolution is intrinsically linked with his belief in organized mass movements that can bring about the "mutation of contradiction" or "changes of relation of production":

> Revolutionary culture is a powerful revolutionary weapon for the broad masses of the people. It prepares the ground ideologically before the revolution comes and is an important, indeed essential, fighting front in the general revolutionary front during the revolution. People engaged in revolutionary cultural work are the commanders at various levels on this cultural front.[15]

Such a cultural movement, coupled with political and military movements, was of the utmost importance to the Chinese Revolution and an alternative modernity. Indeed, the cultural revolution constituted the very particularity or specificity of the Chinese Revolution. By the same token, an alternative modernity in China thus conceived and established requires that cultural revolution, or class struggle at the superstructural level, be ceaselessly reenacted, renewed, and reinforced.

The incipient formulation of cultural revolution can be found in Mao's philosophical texts, aimed at rationalizing and legitimizing the Chinese Revolution. As the titles of these two seminal works indicate—"On Contradiction" (1937) and "On Practice" (1937)—the Chinese Revolution was conceivable and feasible only by way of a revolutionary "practice" that capitalized on and provided solutions to the intense "contradictions" that China faced. Mao's notion of contradiction was the primary resource and inspiration for Louis Althusser's celebrated concept of "overdetermination," an attempt to overcome the Hegelian dilemma of idealist determinism and teleology.[16] For Althusser recognized the revolutionizing theses that Mao's conception of contradiction contains: the primacy of particularity, and the unevenness and mutability of contradiction. Althusser argues that a structural transformation occurs in the Marxist "inversion" of Hegelian philosophy, and the key term of the qualitative transformation from Hegelianism to Marxist dialectical materialism is the notion of "specificity" vis-à-vis the Hegelian concept of "universality." To arrive at a critique of the Hegelian notion that modernity is premised on universality, Althusser drew substantially on Mao's conception of the particularity or specificity of contradiction. For Mao, on the other hand, the most compelling and practical issue was to examine the particularity of the concrete circumstances in China through the perspective afforded by a universalist theory—that is, Marxism, produced at the moment of Western capitalist modernity.

Mao defined universality in both absolute and relative (relational) terms with respect to particularity, asserting a twofold proposition: the universality or absoluteness of contradiction implies the existence of contradiction in all spaces and times; and universality resides in particularity.[17] Universality, in effect, means the absoluteness of contradiction, which signifies nothing less than the particularity of contradiction at any given moment and location. Or to put it another way, Mao's universality is the absoluteness of particularity in terms of the temporal and spatial specificity or particularity of contradiction. The primacy and absoluteness that Mao accorded to particularity can also be illustrated by the conspicuous absence of an elaboration on universality as a metaphysical or ontological concept in Mao's texts. Rather, universality often appears in Mao's work as an epistemological or hermeneutic concept in comprehending and interpreting the temporal and spatial particularities of contradiction.[18] Mao devoted considerable attention to the complex processes of contradictions in which an alternative modernity is conceivable and possible within the overall contradiction of modernity. He developed the concepts of "the principal contradiction" and "the principal aspect of a contradiction," and expanded on the notion of the unevenness of contradiction. These ideas lay the strategic basis not only for the revolutionary, guerrilla wars of the peasants, but also for Mao's overall project of an alternative modernity.

Mao stressed that in any process of complex contradictions, one contradiction must be principal, and this has to be grasped by all means in order to solve problems—from winning a battle to achieving the goal of revolution.[19] The principal contradiction arises from uneven development, for in an overdetermined, complex process made up of a multiplicity of contradictions, the equilibrium is only temporary and relative, while "unevenness is basic."[20] "Nothing in this world develops absolutely evenly," said Mao. "We must oppose the theory of even development or the theory of equilibrium."[21] The unevenness of development has a vital correlation with the particularity or specificity of contradiction, and thus, strategic significance: uneven development, when applied to the historically concrete situation of China with respect to the capitalist West, indicates the temporally and spatially uneven and different objective conditions of modernity. The task of comprehending the principal contradiction—or in Althusser's term, "the structure in dominance"—prescribes the essential strategy of constructing an alternative modernity within the unevenly developed, general objective conditions of existence.

In "On Contradiction," the elaboration of the mutability of contradiction contains the basic proposition of cultural revolution as a way to bring about an alternative modernity. Mao introduced the issue of the mutability of contradiction in a discussion of the fundamental Marxist distinction base/superstructure and the determination of the economic. The decisive role of revolutionary theory and superstructure was the first clearly articulated theoretical rationalization for cultural revolution. Mao argued that

> When it is impossible for the productive forces to develop without a change in the relations of production, then the change in the relations of production plays the principal and decisive role. The creation and advocacy of revolutionary theory plays the principal and decisive role in those times of which Lenin said, "Without revolutionary theory there can be no revolutionary movement." . . . When the superstructure (politics, culture, etc.) obstructs the development of the economic base, political and cultural changes become principal and decisive.[22]

For Mao, the mutability of contradiction was an objective condition as important as that of the particularity and unevenness of contradiction (they were, in effect, coterminous in Mao's vocabulary). He even defined the concept of "identity" as precisely the mutability of contradiction: "in given conditions, each of the two contradictory aspects transforms itself into its opposite."[23] It is no coincidence that Mao's notion of identity has certain structural parallels with Adorno's notion of "nonidentity" in terms of the negativity by which contradictory aspects or opposites coexist. Furthermore, the mutability of contradiction in all processes of contradictions was considered by Mao as "absolute," and therefore universal, just as particularity and unevenness were absolute and universal.[24] Mao was unequivocal on the principal and decisive roles played by revolutionary theory and changes in the superstructure when the "conditions of time" were ripe for revolutionary action. In other words, Mao's resolution of the structure/agency dichotomy was a theoretically informed, activist notion of a "practice" that serves to bring about structural changes and mutations in its own condition of existence. Not unlike many Western Marxists, Mao believed that culture offered the foremost arena for practice. While still engaged in the heat of revolutionary wars to bring about "changes of relations of production"—that is, to seize the state power— Mao never lost sight of the crucial political roles of culture, ideology, and revolutionary theory (for Mao, unlike Althusser, Marxist revolutionary theory was synonymous with ideology itself, which had always been understood in a positive and "good" sense).

The problem of a mediation that could bring the universal theory of revolution, or Marxism, to bear on the concrete circumstances in a China fraught with unevenly developed and overlapped contradictions assumed centrality in Mao's thought, for it held the key to the "sinification of Marxism" as well as cultural revolution, both inextricably connected. Mao raised the issue of mediation via a "national form" in his first statement on the sinification of Marxism, "The Role of the Chinese Communist Party in the National War" (1938). From the outset, the formulation was registered in preeminently cultural and aesthetic terms.

> Another task of study is to study our historical heritage, and to summarize it critically by Marxist method. The several thousand years history of our great nation has its own laws of development, its own national characteristics, and its own treasures. . . . We are Marxist historicists, and we should not cut off history. We should summarize and inherit the valuable legacy from Confucious to Sun Yat-sen. Inheriting this legacy will then generate a method, which will significantly help in guiding the great movement of the present. Being Marxists, communists are internationalists, but Marxism can only be realized through a national form. There is no abstract Marxism, there is only concrete Marxism. By concrete Marxism we mean the Marxism with national form, and to apply Marxism to the concrete struggles in the concrete circumstances of China, rather than applying it in the abstract. For communists who are part of the great Chinese nation, tied to this nation by flesh and blood, to talk about Marxism apart from China's characteristics is merely abstract, vacuous Marxism. Therefore, the most urgent issue that the whole party must understand and resolve is the sinification of Marxism that will endow every manifestation of Marxism with a Chinese character, that is to say, applying it according to China's characteristics. Foreign "eight-legged essays" or stereotypes must be abolished, chanting of the vacuous and abstract tunes must be reduced, dogmatism must be put to rest. They must be replaced by the refreshing, lively Chinese styles and airs that are palatable to the tastes and ears of the common folks of China. To separate internationalist content from national form is the behavior of those who know nothing about internationalism.[25]

National form as mediation has a twofold objective: it is Mao's resolution of the transformation or concretization of Marxism; and it represents Chinese Marxism in both a discursive and political sense. It is constative and performative, simultaneously making statements and constituting practices of a specific kind.[26] The second objective is especially complex. It dictates that national form must represent itself as a concrete resolution, or vice versa, that the representation of a resolution constitutes the resolution itself. Alternatively stated, the resolution of the sinification of

Marxism lies in the representation of Marxism through a national form. Hence, a national form becomes the very substance or content of the sinification of Marxism.

National form thus understood contains a self-referential double movement. It entails a coalescence of intricate and diverse formations and determinations. It assumes the seemingly simple and straightforward task of mediating between a foreign theory or ideology, Marxism, and concrete Chinese circumstances. On closer scrutiny, however, this mediation involves at least three complicated clusters of contradictions and formations. First is the fundamental strategic and epistemological question of how to understand the objective condition of existence or concrete circumstances in China from a Marxist perspective, while modifying and adjusting the Marxist perspective itself according to the real condition of existence. Second is the problem of structure and agency as the focus of revolutionary theory and practice. National form, in this respect, must mediate and bring together the two major subjective forces or agents of the Chinese Revolution, namely the urban Marxist intellectuals and the largely illiterate and unselfconscious peasants or "subalterns." As such, it involves not only a definite evaluation and critique of the May Fourth legacy of enlightenment and cultural revolution, but also the "thought-reform" that was initially aimed at the urban intellectuals and later elevated to the core of cultural revolution.

Last but not least is the problem of representation, at two different but interrelated levels. The first is the political level of representation. In Marxian parlance, it is the notion of *Vertretung*; in Chinese, *daibiao* (substitution, proxy, "speaking for"). The question here is: Who can represent the peasants? Mao's notion of national form implies a strong skepticism about urban Marxist intellectuals as representatives of the peasants. Mao's solution was to virtually rule out the possibility of urban intellectuals serving as political representatives for the peasants. The second level entails discursive or cultural representation; *Darstellung* in German and *zaixian* in Chinese (re-presenting, signifying, staging). Mao's choice of the national, popular form—the "refreshing, lively Chinese styles and airs that are palatable to the tastes and ears of the common folks of China"— threatened to cancel out at a stroke the urban, cosmopolitan May Fourth legacy of enlightenment and cultural, literary revolution. At the same time, Mao paradoxically valorized the aesthetic, cultural form as the ultimate means of "making Marxism Chinese," reaffirming the quintessential May Fourth strategy of cultural revolution. This, of course, further complicates the problem of representation rather than solving it.

Mao's philosophical works on contradiction and practice offer a hermeneutical answer to the first epistemological problem of applying foreign theory to China's circumstances. Mao did this by "deconstructing" the Hegelian, totalizing notion of universality inherent in classical Marxism into dispersed, fragmented, and multiple particularities of contradictions. Furthermore, these contradictions are by Mao's account unevenly developed and can be transformed by theoretically informed, well-planned revolutionary practices. His hermeneutics takes the transformation of the superstructure, or cultural revolution and hegemony, as the solution of contradictions. The practical issue, then, is how to identify the specific features of revolutionary hegemony and strategies.

Mao laid out a blueprint for a "new culture" and its features in *On New Democracy* (1940). Although at the beginning of this text Mao obligingly acknowledged the classical Marxist precept that culture reflects political and economic life and the determination of the economic, he quickly launched into an elaborate discussion about the problems of revolution in political, ideological, and cultural spheres, leaving little room for economics.[27] Granted, the main topic of the text was culture; but this only reinforces the significance for Mao of culture in addressing the overall problems of the Chinese Revolution and modernity.

While a substantial portion of the text rationalizes and legitimizes the building of a new culture, or revolutionary hegemony, his exposition betrays a number of serious contradictions and inconsistencies. Mao justified the need for hegemony by referring to the historical materialist principle of periodization. He characterized the present—that is, the Sino-Japanese War period—as facing a fundamental antinomy: On the one hand, the time was not ripe for socialism, and hence, there remained the "objective mission" of "clearing the obstacles for the development of capitalism." Simply put, Mao argued that China should develop capitalism in preparation for socialism, which would be the next historical stage, but in the future. On the other hand, Mao insisted that such an essentially bourgeois revolution could not be led by the bourgeoisie. In addition, it should not lead to capitalism, but to a "new democratic society" controlled by a coalition of various revolutionary classes, in which "the proletariat participates in the leadership or takes up the leadership."[28] Such a description of the contradictory nature of the revolution actually unravels the contradiction in Mao's own thinking. At the same time that Mao accepted a deterministic and teleological notion of historical stages of development, he was strongly dissatisfied with historical determinism and looked for alternatives. He was clearly aware of the logic pitfalls and real consequences of rigidly conforming to historical determinism. Nevertheless, he was reluctant to admit that his refusal to accept historical determinism would undermine the basic precepts of classical Marxism, which is both Eurocentric and deterministic. Mao's own hesitation is evidenced by the later edition of this text, rendered in the 1960s' definitive *Selected Works*. In this edition, the phrase "the proletariat participates in the leadership" was deleted and a new sentence was added: "the revolution actually serving the purpose of clearing a still wider path for the development of socialism."[29] The new version stressed socialism instead of a new democratic society. Mao underscored the mutability of contradictions, which when translated into concrete historical terms, meant that the new democratic society, essentially the capitalist stage, could be sidestepped.

Another inconsistency lies in Mao's evaluation of the May Fourth movement, as well as his view of urban intellectuals. At the time of the Sino-Japanese War, a coalition between the CCP and Guomindang was formed. Mao's vision of a new democratic culture had to be strategically in accord with the principles of this anti-Japanese united front. The proposed new cultural formation was thus an amalgamation of the diverse cultures of the bourgeoisie, petty bourgeoisie, and working class in an attempt to serve the political and economic needs of the united front's anti-Japanese war.[30] Although this cultural hybrid was perceived by Mao as a political expediency, he by no means took the weight of the May Fourth legacy lightly in his considerations of the new culture. In fact, apart from bestowing the highest possible accolade, as we have seen, to Lu Xun, Mao conceded that in the May Fourth period, a revolution of the greatest (*jida*) significance took place in the domain of culture, particularly in the arts and humanities.[31]

Nevertheless, when it came to the question of leadership and representation in regard to the new culture, Mao quickly qualified his concept. He said that the new culture was a result of "Lu Xun's direction." Ironically, it turned out that Lu Xun's direction had little to do with the urban Marxist intellectuals and May Fourth enlightenment. Rather, the new democratic culture was defined by Mao as a "proletarian-led, popular, anti-imperialist and anti-feudalist culture"; it was a culture with national form and a new democratic content.[32] The three qualifications of the new culture were also related to the mediatory and representational power of a national form. The terms anti-imperialist and anti-feudalist were used by Mao to characterize the May Fourth enlightenment. Mao's Marxist version tried to counter the view of the May Fourth movement as an outbreak of the conflict between tradition and modernity. The other two terms, proletarian-led and popular, undoubtedly signified critical role changes for the subject and object, and the players and audience of cultural revolution. In other words, the leadership was no longer held by the urban Marxist intellectuals. It had now shifted to the "proletariat," which in Mao's vocabulary meant the CCP. Moreover, the term *renmin dazhong de wenhua* (popular culture, culture of the people, or culture of the masses) defined both the object and audience of the new culture as essentially the vast peasant population. The role of the popular masses, consisting mainly of peasants, had been steadily raised over and against the urban intellectuals. During the Cultural Revolution, intellectuals were denigrated as the "stinking No. 9," or the lowest of the social caste, like India's "untouchables."[33] Mao's coarse and harsh language indicates the extent to which he remained deeply distrustful of the urban Marxist intellectuals: "These comrades still have their asses on the side of the petty bourgeoisie, or, to put it more elegantly, their innermost souls are still in the kingdom of the petty bourgeoisie."[34] The new social hierarchy that *On New Democracy* implied contradicted Mao's erstwhile lavish glorification of the May Fourth legacy.[35]

From 1940 to 1942, Mao launched the Rectification Campaign, primarily in cultural and ideological spheres, in the CCP-controlled Yan'an area. The campaign was intended to boost the morale and revolutionary consciousness of the CCP forces. After the debacle in Jiangxi in 1935, the remnants of the nearly devastated Red Army had been forced to embark on a massive exodus, later known as the epic Long March (1935–1936). In the early 1940s, confronted with the formidable Japanese invaders and Guomindang blockage, the Communists were in profound political and military crises and retrenchments. At this critical juncture, rather than devising a major military and political movement like the Long March to rescue the CCP, Mao called on the entire Communist leadership to devote substantial efforts to tackling the problems of culture and ideology. This was partly because the CCP was relatively stronger than at the time of the Long March, so Mao did not need to panic. Yet Mao also realized the necessity of resolving internal conflicts within the CCP, and of unifying and solidifying the party along a definitive, authoritative ideological line. Toward this end, he delivered a series of speeches during the campaign, all of which became essential works of Mao's Chinese Marxism. Of these, the single most important and canonical text concerning art and aesthetics is titled *Talks at the Yan'an Forum on Literature and Art* (1942).

In his *Talks at the Yan'an Forum*, Mao argued that urban Marxist intellectuals should come to understand that their passage from Shanghai to Yan'an "involved not just two different localities but two different historical eras. One is a semifeudal, semicolonial society ruled by big landlords and the big bourgeoisie; the other is a revolutionary new democratic society under the leadership of the proletariat. To arrive in a revolutionary base area is to arrive in a dynasty (*chaodai*—translated by Bonnie McDougall as "period of rule"), unprecedented in thousands of years of Chinese history, a dynasty where workers, peasants, and soldiers, and the popular masses hold power."[36] Mao's worker-peasant-soldier dynasty with a revolutionary new culture sounds much like a Gramscian vision come true—

a new Jacobinian era of a "Modern Prince" where "national-popular collectives" hold sway. It would probably horrify Gramsci, however, that Mao's hegemony entailed a political hierarchization and stratification that subjected urban intellectuals to ceaseless coercion and manipulation in the name of "thought-reform," which was often synonymous with "self-incrimination." Mao's reversal of his own judgment of the revolutionary intellectuals and May Fourth legacy revealed a fundamental contradiction in his thought, with grave consequences. It generated intense internal strife and antagonism between the two essential forces of revolution, the peasant masses and urban Marxist intellectuals. In the same *Talks*, Mao made it clear that revolutionary victory hinges on both the "army with guns" and the "cultural army."[37] Yet Mao's anti-intellectual stance, particularly during the Cultural Revolution, severely undermined his project of building an alternative modernity. His hostility toward intellectuals also damaged the coalition between the two revolutionary armies. More than twenty years after Mao's death, a majority of today's Chinese intellectuals still cannot forgive him for the massive persecutions they experienced during his reign. Since Chinese intellectuals have provided the major contingent of cultural workers in the realms of media, education, literature, and the arts—the very sites of cultural representation—the tension between Mao and Chinese intellectuals highlights a critical aspect of the crises of representation under Mao's revolutionary hegemony.

Mao's concept of a national form epitomizes the predicament of a revolutionary hegemony that takes cultural, aesthetic, and formal changes as its essential paradigm. Mao was acutely aware of the Marxist dilemma of representation, particularly with regard to the peasant class. In *The Eighteenth Brumaire of Louis Bonaparte*, Marx spelled out his political semiotics succinctly by presenting the difficulties of the "small peasants" in forming class consciousness and representing themselves. Marx observed that insofar as the economic conditions of existence of the peasants put their interests and culture in hostile contrast to other classes, "they form a class." Concurrently, since the peasants cannot identify their interests by a "national union" and "political organization," "they do not form a class."[38] Hence, Marx continued

> they cannot represent themselves, they must be represented. Their representative must at the same time appear as their master, as an authority over them, as an unlimited governmental power that protects them against the other classes and sends them the rain and shine from above. The political influence of the small peasants, therefore, finds its final expression in the executive power subordinating society to itself.[39]

Mao recognized the dispersed, fragmented, and dislocated nature of the peasants as a class subject, but for him, the most compelling issue was how to reconcile and mediate the tensions between the urban intellectuals and peasants. He found his indisputable authority amid the peasant soldiers of the Red Army, who idolized and never challenged him.

As noted earlier, Mao sharply criticized the party's "eight-legged essays" as foreign and full of archaic cliché, echoing Qu Qiubai's assaults on the Europeanizing tendencies of urban intellectuals. He saw these essays (or in Qu's phrase, "new classical language") as the discourse of a petty bourgeois ideology. Mao wrote that since China housed a vast population of petty bourgeoisie, the CCP itself was surrounded by them, and he claimed that a substantial number of party members came from the petty bourgeois classes. His definition of the petty bourgeoisie, however, remained ambiguous and inconsistent. Sometimes, Mao categorized peasants as petty bourgeoisie; at other times, he set them aside as a unique "revolutionary class" parallel to the proletariat. But the unequivocal referent in the concept of the petty bourgeoisie was the urban intellectual, whether Marxist or not. The allegedly vast petty bourgeoisie population remained a gray area in Mao's mind. Nevertheless, it should be educated and transformed as a precondition of revolution. The reason was simple: the two revolutionary armies, the one with guns and the other with pens, could only come from the petty bourgeoisie. The purposes of cultural revolution and national form, therefore, were both ideological and hegemonic: ideological in the sense of reproducing and transmitting the signs, images, and representations of revolution; and hegemonic in the sense of constituting the ways of everyday life and routine practices of cultural institutions.

In this respect, Mao and Gramsci were similar in stressing the need to embrace the whole range of culture in everyday life. Yet they differed in other aspects, especially in the practical and political realms. Mao was ruthless in implementing ideological state apparatuses. Gramsci, of course, could not put his thought into action, and thus cannot be compared to Mao in this regard. But Gramsci remained rather evasive and ambivalent on the necessary strategies and machinery in institutionalizing revolutionary hegemony. Louis Althusser, whose "rediscovery" of Gramsci was significant for Western Marxism, is often blamed for conceptions of ideology and ideological state apparatuses that are much more rigid than Gramsci's hegemony. While Althusser said almost nothing about ideological state apparatuses in a postrevolutionary society, in the wake of the Chinese Cultural Revolution, he still desperately pleaded to the "grandeur and pathos" of Lenin, Gramsci, and Mao. Althusser called on the French and international working-class masses for an "ideological renewal of a cultural revolution" to be reflected in a "materiality of organizational structures," which "a materialist theory of ideology, State, Party, and politics" can help to reproduce.[40] Yet Althusser missed a crucial point in Mao's practice: an all-encompassing, all-inclusive hegemony in a post-revolutionary society cannot dispense with ideological state apparatuses. Such state machinery is repressive and coercive in the name of attaining consent; and manipulative and authoritarian in the name of democratic participation and social emancipation.

Indeed, Mao's views of cultural revolution and national form involved both innovative theoretical and practical strategies, and instrumentalist and ultimately oppressive measures. In short, toward the vast population of peasantry, Mao adopted the hegemonic strategy of attaining broad consent and participation; yet with regard to the urban intellectuals, he was at once persuasive and coercive, compelling them to conduct self-condemning and self-incriminating thought-reform.

The theoretical and practical efforts of Chinese Marxism in the cultural, aesthetic, and ideological spheres remain largely unknown to Western Marxism. Terry Eagleton, for instance, discusses the ideological nature of the aesthetic in a comprehensive work that encompasses major theoretical formulations. Still, the absence of Chinese Marxist cultural and aesthetic theories makes Eagleton's account not only incomplete, but also inaccurate.[41] Raymond Williams, however, came to recognize the serious implications of Mao's cultural theory. On Mao's efforts to resolve the tension between urban intellectuals and peasants through a national form, Williams notes

> an emphasis on the transformation of social relations between writers and the people. . . . Mao's alternative theoretical and practical emphasis is on *integration*: not only the integration of writers into popular life, but a move beyond the idea of specialist writer to new kinds of popular, including, collaborative, writing. The complexities of practice are again severe, but at least theoretically this is the germ of a radical restatement.[42]

Williams points to the theoretical value of integration or mediation of a national form in Mao's cultural and aesthetic theory, while acknowledging the "complexities of practice." Mao, of course, dealt with the questions of interaction, mediation, and representation primarily as practical issues, rather than theoretical ones. As Bonnie McDougall comments in her study of the *Talks*, Mao's "analysis of audience needs and the influence of audiences on writers remains one of the most important and innovative sections."[43] In effect, Mao's practical solution of artist representation constitutes an interesting concept of aesthetic reception or communication. His focus on aesthetic representation lies squarely on the side of reception or the response of the audience, which is in dynamic interaction with the process of artistic production. Mao's *Talks* delineated the contours of a prototheory of aesthetic production-reproduction-reception, comparable to the *Rezeptionästhetik*.[44]

In Mao's view, the mutual interaction and determination of aesthetic production-reproduction and reception were intimately bound up with a national form. Since literature and art must, Mao claimed, serve the broad masses as the audience, writers and artists must learn from the language as well as the "incipient forms" of the common folks—including wall newspapers, wall paintings, folk songs, folktales, and popular speeches— in order to educate the peasants.[45] This learning process was a twofold transformation: intellectuals shifted from petty bourgeois to proletarian positions, and the nonpopular, foreign forms they inherited from the May Fourth legacy evolved into the national, popular forms of the peasants. Furthermore, it was a critical process of "thought-reform": "The thoughts and emotions of our literary and artistic workers should become one with the thoughts and emotions of the masses of workers, peasants, and soldiers. And to obtain this unity, we should start by studying the language of the masses." As an immediate corollary, in order to become one with the masses, intellectuals must "make a firm decision to undergo a long and possibly painful process of trial and hardship."[46] For their works to be welcomed by the masses, it was imperative that intellectuals reform and transform their minds and standpoints, not by first studying Marxist works, but by learning from the lifestyles, languages, and speeches of the peasant masses.

As it turned out, popularization through a national form was not merely a process of aesthetic creation; it was first and foremost a process of political, ideological, and moral transformation—a process by which urban intellectuals could redeem their impure souls through immersion into peasant life. Mao often described the peasants in a moralizing manner: their "hands are dirty, feet soiled with caw dung." Yet Mao believed that their souls were much cleaner than those of the petty bourgeois intellectuals.[47] Mao's little fable of unclean intellectuals versus clean peasants practically sets him up as a Christlike, self-redeeming saint who can purify unclean souls.

Second, the process of production-reception as such was dynamic. The audience's horizon of expectations, in Mao's view, was a decisive factor in shaping the aesthetic experience of both creation and reception. Instead of acting as sheer passive receptors, by their response, the audience in effect determines the communicative efficacy of the aesthetic experience. In Hans Robert Jauss's scheme of things, communicative efficacy constitutes the "catharsis" of the aesthetic experience, merging both "poesis" as the productive side and "aesthesis" as the receptive side.[48] But for Jauss, the central locus of the catharsis is still "self-enjoyment," even if it is attained "through the enjoyment of the other."[49] In Mao's aesthetic of reception, however, the communicative efficacy stemmed unabashedly from the pragmatic purpose of serving a politics that promised the emancipation of all humankind. Mao contended that "we are revolutionary utilitarianists who adopt an extremely broad and long-range target." The difference between Mao and Jauss can be understood only by historicizing their theoretical formations in the context of their particular social and political junctures.

Finally, Mao's stance on aesthetic reception is related to his notion of aesthetic production and reproduction. His idea of reproduction appears to be less deterministic than the Leninist-Plekhanovist theory of artistic reflection. Yet, at the same time, Mao's formulation is susceptible to an instrumentalist manipulation. When the *Talks* were codified, together with his discussion of the specific tactics and policies of "partisan literature," into an incontestable tenet for all aesthetic creation and criticism, Mao's otherwise quite radical and liberational views of aesthetic reproduction became a virtual ideological and political straitjacket. His insights into the aesthetic productive process, however, are worth studying. Mao placed great emphasis on the artistic reproduction of preexisting "natural forms" of art and life, rather than on "direct" reflections of reality as such. Again, his stress was on the mediation of form through the mind of the individual author:

> Works of literature and art, as ideological forms regardless of their levels, are the outcome of the human mind reflecting and processing popular life. Revolutionary art is then the outcome of the mind of a revolutionary writer reflecting and processing popular life. Rich deposits of literature and art have always existed in popular life, which are the things in natural forms, crude but also most lively, most fertile, and most fundamental. They render all refined and processed literature and art pale in comparison; they are the sole and inexhaustible resources of all refined and processed works of art.[50]

Mao's identification of works of art as ideological forms corresponds to his definition of the "rich deposits of literature and art" in popular, everyday life as "natural forms." This is not a simple, transparent representation of real life as a mimesis of unmediated reality. Instead, it is a complicated process of semiotic "transcoding," a retextualization that transposes a prior textual form—the natural, crude form of popular arts and the mode of everyday life—into another ideological, textual form, which is also aesthetically more refined and polished. As Fredric Jameson puts it, the real or history "is inaccessible to us except in textual form, or, in other words, . . . it can be approached only by way of prior (re)textualization."[51]

But Mao's insistence on the political and ideological nature of the semiotic process of artistic creation and criticism soon became abstracted and separated from its immediate historical context. It was then reduced into a rather rigid doctrine, which perpetuated the dichotomy between politics and aesthetics, and prioritized political criteria over and above aesthetic ones. This can be seen in the extensive revisions of key statements in the *Talks*. For example, Mao originally stated:

> While both [the work of art in natural forms, and that which is refined and processed] are beautiful, the processed work is more organized, more concentrated, more characteristic, more idealistic, and therefore more universal than the literature and art in natural forms.[52]

This passage was later revised and codified as Mao's authoritative definition of the "essence of art":

> While both (life and art) are beautiful, life as reflected in works of literature and art can, and ought to be, on a higher plane, more intense, more concentrated, more typical, closer to the ideal, and therefore more universal than actual everyday life. Revolutionary literature and art should create a variety of characters out of real life and help the masses to propel history forward.[53]

Previous "forms of art" were substituted with "life" itself, which works of art must reflect faithfully; and the ideological and political mission of artwork was clearly spelled out: to "propel history forward." A theorization of the formal and semiotic complexities of aesthetic representation was then rendered into a neoclassicist, pro-Soviet "socialist realist" dogma. Mao's earlier argument underwent a substantial, structural transformation. Another important change was that Mao's remarks on specific strategies and tactics at the time of war were elevated into a "universal truth." The *Talks* were transformed into a sacred scripture by CCP ideologues and Mao himself. It further degenerated into a set of rigid, repressive, and manipulative rulings, that Hu Feng later defiantly and vividly characterized as "five daggers" hanging a hair's distance over the heads of writers and artists. Evidently, Mao made these changes mostly on his own, commencing with the codification of the *Talks* as the normative, regulatory policy statements and guidance for all production and criticism of literature and art in the postrevolutionary society.

Literary theorist and critic Hu Feng was probably the only individual who challenged Mao on almost all aspects of his ideas on art and aesthetics, from beginning to end—that is, from the time Mao articulated his views in the early 1940s, until Mao's death in 1976. Concentrating, as Hu did, on the crucial aesthetic issue of subjectivity, his battle with Mao was an important event within Marxist cultural and aesthetic circles. A discussion of subjectivity was singularly and symptomatically absent from Mao's theory of culture and aesthetics, and indeed, from all of his work. Instead of seeing Hu and Mao as absolute enemies, we may find that, in effect, Hu's views complemented Mao's in a theoretical sense, in that they unravelled many of the intrinsic contradictions and difficulties in Mao's notions.

The Aesthetic Experience of Subjectivity and Counterhegemony: The Case of Hu Feng Revisited

Prior to the establishment of the PRC, Hu was always at the center of controversies among China's left-wing literari. His writings, as Theodore Huters explains, "came increasingly to chronicle the internal dynamics of the leftist literary scene itself"; "there was to be no debate in literary circles after 1938 in which Hu Feng did not take an active role."[54] With the exception of Huters's study of Hu's role in the theoretical debates within Shanghai's League of Left-Wing Writers and his relationship to Lu Xun, analyses of Hu's ideas in English are sparse. The few explorations by China specialists almost invariably concentrate on the political implications of the anti–Hu Feng Campaign in 1955. These studies either ignore his contributions as a Marxist theorist or simply portray him as an anti-Communist, anti-Marxist political dissident, victimized by the totalitarian Communist regime.[55] In China, too, disputes over Hu remain largely political. As the titles of several recent Chinese studies suggest, Hu's theory remains "to be reassessed," or an "incomplete issue of inquiry."[56]

A reassessment of Hu entails formidable difficulties. Before and immediately after his death, reevaluation was shrouded by sensitive personal and political considerations, as many of his enemies and prosecutors were alive and in power. More than a decade later, near the turn of the century, Hu's work faces a different fate: oblivion and irrelevance. Under the current circumstances, in which the revolutionary legacy of modern China is being debunked and erased, Hu's name has steadily faded from China's cultural and intellectual arenas. Yet given the latest trend of "deradicalization" in China's intellectual circles as a strategy to promote ideologies of capitalist globalization, the preoccupation with cultural and aesthetic issues in Chinese Marxist thought, in which Hu's contribution is indispensable, ought to be understood as an alternative way of coming to grips with the problems of modernity. In this respect, Hu's ideas open up a critical space.

Moreover, the key question that Hu raised, namely subjectivity, has remained pivotal to Chinese Marxist thought. The early Chinese Marxists, like Li Dazhao and Qu Qiubai, hardly broached the topic. Except for persistent attacks on "subjectivism" that referred narrowly to specific, dogmatic, or empiricist attitudes of learning, as just noted, Mao never engaged with the issue of subjectivity in serious theoretical fashion. Hu introduced the issue with his view of a "subjective fighting spirit," formulated during the Sino-Japanese War. His concept aroused heated debate in the 1940s in both Yan'an and the Guomindang-controlled cities. After the PRC was established in 1940, Hu raised the issue again, ultimately sparking the anti–Hu Feng Campaign. Although Hu and his friends and sympathizers were silenced, the question of subjectivity was revived in the famous debates over aesthetics that began in 1956, only one year after the anti–Hu Feng Campaign, and continued until 1964. Still later, in the intense controversy in the 1980s over culture and modernity, known as "Culture Fever," subjectivity, or aesthetic subjectivity, again became central, encompassing all the major problems of China's modernity. Moreover, subjectivity has not only been a question of cultural and aesthetic formation, but has crucially been related to the problem of agency in a revolution as well. As such, the controversies about subjectivity bring to light many of the fundamental tensions and contradictions in both the Chinese Revolution and Chinese Marxist thought.

Born in 1902 to an impoverished peasant family in Hubei, Hu's early years resemble those of many Chinese leftist intellectuals and Communists. Through hard work and will, he made his way to Nanjing, and then Beijing, where he started his career as a left-wing political activist and literary critic. Hu joined the Chinese Communist Youth League in 1923; in 1926, he became an English literature major at Qinghua University. After the split between the CCP and Guomindang in 1927, Hu went to Japan. Here, he discovered lively literary and cultural movements, led by leftists and Marxists—a rare occurrence in modern Japanese history. Hu took an active part in most of the activities of the Japanese leftist writers. At the same time, he avidly read the works of Karl Marx and other German philosophers, in both the English and Japanese translations. In 1931, he became a member of the Japanese Communist Party as well as the Japanese branch of the Chinese League of Left-Wing Writers. Imprisoned for his leftist activities in Japan, Hu was deported to China in 1933, where he remained in Shanghai until the outbreak of the Sino-Japanese War. The Shanghai years distinguished Hu from other leftist and Communist writers. He assumed a number of leadership positions in the league, yet also clashed with the CCP cadre in that organization. And Hu developed a close friendship with Lu Xun.

During and after the well-known "Two Slogans Debate" of 1936 that marked Lu Xun's eventual split with the CCP leadership of the league, Hu became a self-conscious defender of his mentor's legacy or urban Marxist intellectual tradition as heir to the May Fourth enlightenment. Indeed, the rest of Hu's life and career can be characterized as an unyielding yet tragic battle on three fronts. First, he was faced in Shanghai with the formidable mainstream cultural establishments that combined bourgeois ideologies from the West with Confucian values and traditional practices. Then there was the political harassment and persecution of leftists and CCP sympathizers by the Chiang Kai-shek regime. Last but not least, Hu and his friends confronted the political manipulations of the CCP within the left-wing league, spearheaded by Zhou Yang. In the late 1930s and throughout the 1940s, Hu lived outside CCP-controlled areas, remaining in the cities under the Guomindang's rule. Through editing several literary journals and other editing and publishing activities, Hu Feng rallied a group of young leftist writers, and together, they voiced their protestations against the threefold domination of Japanese invaders, the Chiang Kai-shek regime, and CCP machinations.

After 1949, Hu realized all too soon the unfavorable prospect of working under the new CCP regime. His longtime nemesis, Zhou Yang, had become the powerful cultural chief of the CCP. Hu's "heretic" views and criticism of Mao's cultural policies had already drawn vehement attacks by CCP critics in the pre-PRC years. Now that the CCP was in power, Hu Feng would have to pay a high price. He and his friends were subjected to all kinds of discriminatory treatments and constantly harassed. Instead of recanting his "sin" of deviating from the CCP-dictated "political correctness," Hu wrote a book-length report (over 30,000 words) in 1954 to submit to the CCP leadership. In his *A Report on Literary and Artistic Practices since the Liberation,* he named the "five theoretical daggers" used by Zhou Yang and the like to threaten writers and artists. This proved to be the last straw. Mao, utterly outraged by Hu's defiance, passed the verdict himself by penning the famous (or infamous) editorials that ran in the *People's Daily* in 1955, condemning "Hu Feng's counterrevolutionary clique" as clandestine spies and agents for Guomindang and U.S. imperialists whose aims were allegedly to sabotage the new People's Republic.[57] This amounted to a verdict of high treason, meted out by China's utmost authority. Although Mao's indictment was later judged to be groundless, largely stemming from his personal fury, at the time Hu was doomed. The Anti–Hu Feng Campaign that swept China for almost the whole of 1955 was only a prelude to the more intense and massive Anti-Rightist Campaign of 1957, and the Great Cultural Revolution of 1966–1976, all started initially in the realms of literature and art.

Hu was imprisoned from 1955 to 1979, during which he suffered unimaginable pains. Toward the end of his confinement, his mental health deteriorated to the point of causing hallucinations and schizophrenia. On his release under a blanket "rehabilitation" policy that covered a large number of CCP officials and intellectuals jailed during the Cultural Revolution, Hu attempted to recover at home and in hospitals, finally dying in June 1985. He was cleared of all "unwarranted" criminal charges in the CCP Central Committee's 1980 review of his case. The review, nevertheless, retained the charges of promoting "anti-Marxist literary theory" and "sectarianism." A full-scale official "rehabilitation" only came posthumously, in 1988.[58]

Hu's ideas on revolution and resistance in subjective aesthetic experience were developed in the 1930s and 1940s. Subjectivity, for Hu, was key to realist representation, a mediation of political reality and lived experience. As such, it pertained to the question of cultural critique as a major objective of the May Fourth movement. He argued that subjectivity was crucial in the rejuvenation of Chinese culture, as well as in a critique of the Confucian tradition. Confucianism, in Hu's view, lacked a notion of the subject or subjectivity, and thereby subsumed individual consciousness under the rubrics of universal kinship and communality. Three aspects of Hu's thought deserve attention: his definition of the May Fourth legacy and "Lu Xun's direction" as enlightenment and cultural critique; his polemic on the issue of a national form; and his complex notion of aesthetic subjectivity.

The nature of the May Fourth legacy, or Lu Xun's direction, has remained controversial. Efforts to define this nearly one century long modern tradition have always been entangled in the political power struggles woven into the historical fabric of this very tradition. Interpreting this legacy is not merely a scholarly or intellectual inquiry; it bears directly on the legitimacy of modernization strategies, especially Marxist ones. Qu Qiubai and Mao offered their interpretations in order to construct a revolutionary hegemony and legitimize the Chinese Revolution. Lu Xun, however, said both too much and too little about this tradition. On the one hand, his writings can be read as unequivocal manifestations of the May Fourth enlightenment and its cultural revolution, insofar as his critique of the Confucian tradition remains the quintessential expression of May Fourth iconoclasm. On the other hand, his allegorical style and language reveal a profound ambivalence about the May Fourth legacy. His aesthetic negativity on the central issues of revolution, modernity, and politics implies strong skepticism and reservations about the May Fourth enlightenment. Yet when Hu interpreted and defended Lu Xun's direction, he could hardly justify his view as the only "faithful" reading of Lu Xun. Instead,

Hu had to reinscribe the critical issues, such as subjectivity, in Lu Xun's discourse as professedly "true." In so doing, Hu addressed a number of areas that Qu and Mao hardly examined, and Lu only vaguely suggested.

Hu's interpretation embodied an insistence on and defense of enlightenment and cultural critique. As an immediate corollary, Hu emphasized the role of urban intellectuals in the May Fourth cultural revolution. In the 1936 debates about "National Defense Literature," with Lu Xun and Hu on one side and CCP representatives on the other, Hu claimed that the new May Fourth literature, inspired by the realist literature of the West, was the only correct mode of expression to educate and mobilize the masses. In the ensuing debate about national forms, in 1939 and 1940, Hu again upheld the May Fourth legacy of realism. The proponents of national forms promulgated a populist and nationalist literature for the sake of war propaganda, whereas Hu was adamant on the absolute necessity of May Fourth realism in order to demystify traditional Confucian ideology and enlighten the masses (hua dazhong), rather than popularize (dazhong hua) ideas. As both Li Zehou and Liu Zaifu acknowledge, these disputes over national forms and May Fourth realism deal essentially with enlightenment and cultural critique.[59] According to Hu, the masses, composed mainly of illiterate peasants, should be educated and enlightened by intellectuals with revolutionary consciousness.

Contrary to Mao's view of "thought-reform" for educating urban intellectuals, Hu believed that urban Marxist and revolutionary intellectuals, represented by Lu Xun, were "progressive members of the people" who had historically been at the forefront of ideological struggles against imperialist-feudalist hegemony, and served as the "only bridge at the beginning, and a significant bridge now" between Marxist revolutionary thought and the Chinese people.[60] This assessment was made in *On the Path of Realism*, written in 1948 on the eve of the Communist victory. Hu drew extensively on Marx's work, *The German Ideology* in particular, in his evaluations of the May Fourth legacy and the role of urban Marxist intellectuals. As opposed to Mao's *Talks*, which focused on the audience, *On the Path of Realism* dealt with authorship and the intellectual agent as the core of a "realist aesthetics," or an aesthetic conception of subjectivity.

Utilizing on Marx's class analysis, Hu tried to identify urban intellectuals as "revolutionary masses." He argued that because of enormous social, economic, and political changes, most Chinese urban intellectuals had become dislocated and dispersed from their original petty bourgeois class status. The urban intellectuals, in Hu's view, had undergone a process of "proletarianization" analogous to that experienced by peasants uprooted from their land and deprived of any means of production except their physical labor. Intellectuals, too, had lost almost all their means and sources of support, and had to sell their labor as any other member of the proletarian working class.[61] Most important, Hu continued, this dramatic transformation of class status, unique to China's historical circumstances, prompted proletarianized intellectuals to enthusiastically embrace radical, revolutionary ideologies and rapidly formulate their revolutionary class consciousness. As one of the few Chinese Marxist theorists familiar with Lukács's work (Hu introduced Lukács to the Chinese and translated his "Narration or Description?" in the early 1940s), Hu's revision of Marx's notion of class was indebted to Lukács's idea of "class consciousness."[62] Hu's class analysis of Chinese intellectuals reversed almost completely the verdict of Qu and Mao. In short, Hu claimed that urban Marxist intellectuals were not petty bourgeoisie, but progressive members of the revolutionary working class. (Ironically, this working class identity was officially accorded by Deng Xiaoping to Chinese intellectuals nearly half a century later.) Having defined them thus, Hu then subtlely overturned Mao's thought-reform, suggesting that it was needed as a project of enlightenment against the "spiritual slavery" governing the subservient masses through traditional forms:

> Revolutionary culture and arts must share the burden of ideological struggle to awaken, to influence, and to reform individual persons, and to attract them into the great struggle [of revolution]. This is what we mean when we say that the purpose of ideological struggle is to destroy the ideological machinery of the dark forces, and to empower our practical struggles, through which the thought reform can be eventually accomplished.[63]

Hu's reformulation of thought-reform as a counterhegemonic "ideological struggle" is comparable to Gramsci's view of the role of intellectuals. Basically, Hu changed the meaning of thought-reform from an intellectual's self-education to cultural critique. Cultural critique, then, figured prominently in Hu's evaluations of the May Fourth tradition and the role of intellectuals. In this respect, it is interesting to recall the debate in 1932 between Lu Xun, Qu, and other league members and "the third-type literature" advocates represented by Hu Qiuyuan, who insisted on the mission of Kulturkritik. Hu Qiuyuan, a firm believer in Plekhanov at the time and well versed in Marxist literary thought, desperately defended the independent role of literature and art as social and cultural critiques vis-à-vis political instrumentalization. Hu Qiuyuan also unequivocally stressed both the political and class character of literature and art, which in his judgment was not derived from an instrumentalist and pragmatic function, but rather a semiautonomous, independent aesthetic dimension.[64] Grossly misunderstood and unfairly accused by Qu and Lu Xun, Hu

Qiuyuan actually had great respect for Lu Xun, using him as his role model in proposing an independent Kulturkritik. Hu Qiuyuan later became disillusioned with the left-wing cultural movement as well as Marxism, moving to Taiwan in 1949. In 1955, Hu Qiuyuan (not related to Hu Feng) spoke from Taiwan in passionate defense of Hu during the Anti–Hu Feng Campaign, indicating the affinity between his and Hu Feng's viewpoints.[65] Since Hu missed the 1932 debate with Hu Qiuyuan—he was still in Japan at that time—there is no way of knowing what he might have done.

Hu addressed the question of providing cultural spaces where independent, counterhegemonic cultural critiques could be conducted. His notion of an urban, cosmopolitan cultural space, however, was not conceived against the rural and local cultural formations. Instead, Hu pointed to the necessity of constructing heterogeneous and multiple cultural spaces on different levels. He contended that a local, rural cultural space was needed to resist Japanese invasion. This space should be constructed according to unevenly developed social and economic conditions. In other words, the construction of local and national cultures were only a means to an end— the anti-Japanese war, rather than the end itself. At the same time, Hu did not glorify cosmopolitan areas as the exclusive cultural center. Instead, he analyzed the material, institutional structures of urban civil society and suggested that they serve as the center of China's new cultural movement. He listed several key features of these "cultural centers," represented primarily by Shanghai. First, they best facilitated access to international cultural currents. In addition, they ensured adequate capital for the media and press, and advanced networks of distribution for publications. Third, they provided the economic condition of a capitalist mode of production, which allowed for the semiautonomous status of intellectuals, whose conglomeration in the modern cosmopolis was also closely related to the revolutionary movement that originated and was headquartered in the city. Finally, the state cultural institutions and apparatuses during the war period functioned as an effective means of coordination, assembling the diverse cultural institutions and organizations.[66] As a product of a modern capitalist mode of production, such cultural centers could not be highly centralized and homogeneous, but fragmented and dispersed, despite the contingency of a war that necessitated a certain centralization and streamlining. Hu queried: "Will there be any cultural center [under the circumstances of war]? The answer is affirmative. Cultural centers ought to exist, but should not have only one center, and may not only have the format of 'writer-publisher-reader' circuit."[67]

Hu's conception of "cultural centers" comes remarkably close to Gramsci's "civil society" as a democratic, mediated, structured relationship between people of diverse groups and interests, vis-à-vis the monolithic state. Gramsci's notion was formulated when the increasing penetration of Italy's fascist state threatened to collapse civil society altogether. As a leader in the Italian Communist Party, Gramsci saw the need to establish a revolutionary "civil society" in which "organic intellectuals" could speak for, and with, the subaltern classes. It is arguable that Gramsci was talking about the "modern state" in the sense of a democratic civil society, or in other words, that Gramsci conceived of the state as civil society.[68] Rather than valorizing Gramsci's notion as an innovative way to resurrect a bourgeois civil society cannibalized by a fascist state, however, it is more fruitful to note the inherent contradictions and predicament in his formulation. His reflections on the state's penetration and delimitation of the semiautonomous spheres of civil society, on the one side, and the party's role in fulfilling "in civil society the same function as the state carries out," on the other, uncover a profound incongruity and ambivalence in Gramsci's vision of revolutionary hegemony in a socialist state.[69]

The academic Left in the West today may simply ignore this contradiction, while celebrating Gramsci's nonauthoritarian, democratic notions of a "civil society" and "public sphere" that can recuperate bourgeois social formations. Yet Chinese Marxists such as Mao and Hu could not bypass the question of the state and civil society. They had to figure out a way to handle the structural relationship between them after the victory of the revolution. Mao's solution, not without its own contradictions, was quite straightforward: the state was the only social structure that could subsume civil society (Mao, in fact, never talked about civil society), because the so-called subaltern class, namely the peasant masses, would assume leadership of both the state and society when revolution succeeded. Hu, in contrast, saw the danger of such a monolithic state formation, and insisted on the necessary multiplicity and plurality of cultural centers in which rural, local, and popular cultural formations could flourish.

Hu's reflections on cultural centers and the May Fourth legacy address the issue of a public sphere in a postrevolutionary society. The May Fourth legacy, for Hu, was primarily the "awakened free will of the people" as embodied by Lu Xun. This "will of the people" confronted the "dark reality" of imperialist-feudalist domination and cultural hegemony. It also represented the "working people who were physically oppressed and spiritually poisoned, yet ever longing for resistance and for better, rational life."[70] Hu's key point was that the "awakened free will stemmed from the urban middle class, as a self-conscious revolt and resistance against both imperialism and feudalism. They consciously or unconsciously merged with the wills of the working classes. Such is the way that Lu Xun opened up the new cultural tradition through his revolutionary humanism and literary images."[71] Hu Feng asserted again and again that the May Fourth movement was a "revolution" led by "the revolutionary urban middle class," and its most valuable achievement was its *fengfuxing* (richness or diversity).[72] The notion of richness or diversity was formulated by Hu in 1948, specifically against the imminent political instrumentalization of culture. It became a desperate plea, echoed by Chinese intellectuals in the 1980s. The forty-year gap in between was marked by precisely the political instrumentalization that Hu opposed. Against such a historical background, Chinese intellectuals in the 1980s went a long way to reaffirm the value of "pluralism" within the May Fourth legacy.

The theoretical worth of Hu's thoughts on the May Fourth legacy lies essentially in its reconfiguration of the largely bourgeois civil society as a new social formation, merging the revolutionary urban middle class with the broad working class. This was Gramsci's hope, too. Hu emphasized richness and diversity, vis-à-vis Mao's instrumentalist view of domination and control, exposing a critical dimension in the issue of civil society. The accepted wisdom today is that China has no proper civil society, and indeed, has not become a really modernized country.

But the real question is not the existence or nonexistence of a civil society. Crucial are the internal tensions and contradictions in the process of establishing a new structural relationship between the state and society. Such a problem is by no means unique to China. Gramsci's work deals with exactly the same issue: that is, the construction of a revolutionary hegemony with a new relationship between civil society and the state in a socialist society. Yet Western academicians on the Left have remained silent on this most fundamental dilemma, suggesting that defeatism still prevails within a significant part of their ranks.

Hu's polemic on a national form was also intimately connected to his view of the May Fourth legacy. His concept of a national form was primarily concerned with the issue of aesthetic representation, rather than the question of political mediation. Hu never separated aesthetic "form" from either a political or ideological "content," but looked instead at the immanent ideological content of the aesthetic form itself. Hu's discussion of a national form probed the complex nature of aesthetic form and representation, without referring to structuralist and formalist concepts—indeed, there is no evidence to suggest that Hu had read any Russian formalist works. (Mao, as noted earlier, also developed a complex view of aesthetic mediation and representation through aesthetic forms.)

In early 1940, shortly after Mao announced his idea of the "sinification of Marxism" through a national form, Hu wrote *On the Question of National Form*. A major work in his oeuvre, this book was ostensibly Hu's polemic in the debate over national form that occurred within the left-wing cultural circles in Chongqing, then the provisional war capital of China.

Hu was certainly well aware of the political and ideological subtext of the debate, initiated by Guo Moruo. Guo, a May Fourth–veteran writer, had become a Mao sycophant. He played an active role in almost all the political campaigns against intellectuals, and therefore, was detested privately by many writers and artists. Guo's collaborator in the debate was Xiang Linbing, a novice among CCP-controlled literari who showed strong enthusiasm for promoting Mao's ideas in the Guomindang areas. Rather than debating with Guo, whose work was largely manifesto-like, Hu took issue with Xiang, who wrote lengthy articles of a theoretical nature. Hu thought that Xiang's view was simplistic and misleading. Xiang contended that traditional folk and popular cultures were the only resources for a national form. Moreover, Xiang denounced the radical and revolutionary literature and arts of the May Fourth period, accusing them of being foreign, derivative, and elitist. Xiang actually reiterated, in a rather undialectical fashion, many of the charges made by Qu Qiubai in the early 1930s.

Hu's strategy was to concentrate on the aesthetic aspect of form, within concrete political and ideological contexts. He reinforced his argument by quoting Lukács: "new styles, new methods of presenting reality never come into existence because of inherent dialectics of artistic forms ... every new style comes into existence out of life, and is the inevitable product of social development."[73] Hu concluded that "form is the essential element of content; the organizing power of form stems from the cognitive methods of comprehending reality. Hence the way to penetrate the content [of reality] is by grasping the nature of form. 'National form' by its very nature is the way that May Fourth realist tradition develops itself *self-consciously* under the new historical conditions."[74] National form, which traced its ideological lineage to May Fourth realism, could not be canceled out in a stroke, nor was it viable or desirable to simply go back to the pristine traditional forms of folk and popular culture.

Contrary to Qu and Mao—who both tended to romanticize traditional, national, and popular forms—Hu pointed out their negative aspects, regarding them as part of feudalist hegemony. Hu mounted a forceful critique of the hegemonic character of "feudalist traditional culture," in which "popular culture" and "national forms" were major constituents. He contended that popular, peasant cultural forms—such as folklore, local operas, folktales, and popular tales and songs—reflected the ideologies of the feudalist ruling class, and disseminated feudalist values that "simultaneously sparked with the wisdom and artistic representations of the popular life."[75] Thus, precisely because of this, national forms had to be relentlessly dismantled and transformed. In Gramsci's terms, these were the forms by which the ruling class "manages to win the active consent of those over whom it rules."[76] Critique and transformation of traditional, "feudalist" hegemony was in Hu's mind the most important objective and major achievement of the May Fourth enlightenment and cultural revolution.

Hu believed that the May Fourth movement was, among other things, an unprecedented revolution of aesthetic forms. The "formal revolution of May Fourth" initiated a powerful critique of the rural and "feudalist" culture of the peasants. Hu argued against a populist romanticization of the national popular culture. He wrote that "one cannot forget to weave into the aesthetic experience of the peasants a nonpeasant red line," and that nothing can be accomplished with regard to either national liberation or a transformation of national forms "if one simply capitulates to the aesthetic experience of the peasants, or to naturally grown folk forms, on the ground that the peasants constitute a majority of the population, and therefore they must have a 'determinant role' in aesthetic production."[77]

The "red line" would not come from the peasantry, according to Hu, but from May Fourth realism, which provided a formal mediation of subjective practice and objective conditions because it inherited and integrated the best of revolutionary literature and arts across the world. Hu, in effect, reversed Mao's notions on the sinification of Marxism and national forms. He asserted the mutual determination and constitution of form and content to critique Mao:

> Realism is the principal guideline by which the reality of our nation can be comprehended. Hence, we must penetrate into concrete, living facets of the real life [through realism]. The former [realism] is the method to grasp the object; the latter [real life] is the object to be grasped. The former is dissolved into the latter, thereby transforming the international into the national; the latter is strung together through the former, thereby transforming the national into the international. If "new democratic content" is constituted by the mediation of the former [realism] through the latter [real life], then "national form" itself is constituted by the mediation of the latter [real life] through the former [realism].[78]

Without the mediation of a realism that "embodies the scientific worldview [Marxism] . . . through specific artistic representations," Hu claimed, national form itself can neither represent nor mediate a new democratic content. In other words, a national form must be generated (mediated) by the realist aesthetics that represents the revolutionary, scientific worldview of Marxism about China's reality. Hu's argument was premised on the assumption of the mediatory mechanism of ideology and aesthetic representation, on which Mao's proposition of the sinification of Marxism was also based. The difference between Hu and Mao, then, lies in the question of realism as aesthetic representation. Mao simply sidestepped the is-

sue by assuming the mediatory function of the national form in its traditional, natural, or pristine condition. A national form, in Mao's view, need
not be mediated by international, revolutionary ideology or theory
through realism. As we know, Mao disliked the cosmopolitan May Fourth
realist literature. But the key issue is not so much Mao's personal feelings
or biases, as his contradictory position on the question of subjectivity or
agency in both revolution and its representation. In Mao's scheme of
things, the mediation of a national form was presumably carried out by the
CCP itself as the revolutionary agent who alone possessed the truth of
Marxism. Subjectivity did not need to be constituted or mediated; it was
simply at one with the CCP. Ultimately, it resided with Mao, as the supreme subject to which all others were subjected. Hegemonic features of
what Hu called feudalism embedded in the traditional national forms, on
the other hand, did not seem to bother Mao at all. Rather, the intellectual
agent, central to the aesthetic and ideological mediations of May Fourth
realism, appeared to Mao as the object, rather than the subject, of the process of thought-reform under the tutelage of the CCP cadres and revolutionary peasant masses. In this respect, the significance of Hu's tireless
insistence on the aesthetic mediation of realism becomes evident, particularly in light of his emphasis, described below, on a subjective fighting
spirit as the core of realist aesthetics.

   The debate about subjectivity in 1945 was a continuation of previous
ones over national form and realism. Questions in the earlier debates over
national forms and Western influences, enlightenment and popularization, crystallized into a philosophical discussion of subject-object relationships in the new debate, which mainly took place in the Guomindang-
controlled area three years after Mao's *Talks* codified Chinese Marxist
literary criticism. In January 1945, Shu Wu's article "On Subjectivity" and
Hu's "Situating Ourselves in the Struggle for Democracy" were published
in the literary journal *Xiwang* (Hope) in Chongqing. Hu was editor of the
journal. The publication of these two articles ignited a heated dialogue.
Hu's "subjective idealist" views were then under fierce attack by CCP critics. In a report given at the 1949 Congress of Chinese Cultural Workers
held in Beijing, Mao Dun, a veteran May Fourth writer, summarized the
disagreement:

> They [Hu and his colleagues] on the one hand stressed the defects of
> the people, because of feudalist rule, and took as their fundamental
> task to combat these defects. . . . But their views are in fact petty bour-
> geois fantasies that depart from the real life of the people. Discussions
> of literary subjectivity must therefore deal with the problem of a writ-
> er's ideological standpoint and attitude, as raised in Comrade Mao Ze-

dong's *Yan'an Talks*. If a writer cannot totally abandon his petty bourgeois standpoint in order to become one with the people, then the issue of literary popularization cannot be fully resolved.[79]

By 1949, Mao Dun, once the main proponent of May Fourth realism and an accomplished novelist, had given up creative writings and assumed the official post of cultural minister in the new PRC government. As Mao Zedong's major cultural bureaucrat, Mao Dun had to recant the "petty bourgeois flaws" of the May Fourth realist tradition. But Hu refused to bow down, even though Mao Dun's statement amounted to official disapproval. Hu was perhaps a little too naive to accept the fact that, above all, what mattered was political and ideological conformity or unconformity, not scholarly and intellectual debates. The debate about subjectivity was finally "settled" in 1955 with the Anti–Hu Feng Campaign. Disagreements over aesthetic and philosophical questions were labeled by Mao Zedong himself as acts of political sabotage and dissent, subject to China's criminal law.

Hu's theory of a subjective fighting spirit was mainly concerned with the problems of form and representation in realism, rooted in the nineteenth-century European literary movements, and transported and practiced by May Fourth writers. By concentrating on the relationship between subjective experience, or class consciousness, and representation, his theory encompassed the critical dilemmas of ideology and hegemony, body and desire, domination and resistance. A subjective fighting spirit, for Hu, served as a powerful weapon to combat both the "subjective formulaism" (*gongshi zhuyi*, or a dogmatic adherence to literary "formulas") and "objectivism" then in vogue. The Japanese invasion and subsequent national crisis prompted a spiritual and emotional upheaval among Chinese writers. In Hu's view, a subjectivism prevailed. Yet instead of leading to a truthful representation of social reality, subjectivism only helped produce formulaic, stereotyped literary work. In deriving its inspiration from abstract idealism and romantic sentimentalism, this subjectivism remained divorced from the concrete world and individual lived experience. The ethos of national defense and political imperative was so overwhelming, however, that the writer "felt himself completely given over to the demands of the time, and found solace in a state of selflessness."[80] Objectivism thus dominated literary work, which prevented writers from recognizing the broader issues of the war by engrossing them in daily events.

It turned out that objectivism was used as a coded term, like "naturalism" in Lukács's vocabulary. It actually referred to the narrow-minded, partisan, and utilitarian views of art held by CCP propaganda bureaucrats.

Hu contended that both subjective formulaism and objectivism were but two sides of the same coin. Only a subjective fighting spirit, he argued, can lead to realism: "The unity or combination of subjective spirit and objective truth has produced a militant new literature. We call it realism."[81] There is an eminent Hegelian overtone in Hu's emphasis on the unity of the subjective and objective in an individual's consciousness as a way to grasp the totality of meaning. The subjective fighting spirit, hence, bears a striking resemblance to Lukács's class consciousness. Lukács insisted that proletarian class consciousness was the only way to overcome alienation and reification through comprehending social reality as a historical totality. Hu, by comparison, regarded a subjective fighting spirit as the only means to understand social reality and realize the potential of working people. This twofold objective can only be accomplished by realist literary representation. It is no coincidence that Lukács, too, took the literary form of narrative as the most privileged means of fulfilling revolutionary class consciousness.[82]

Realism served as a powerful ideological critique and counterhegemonic strategy. In his seminal essay of 1944, "Situating Ourselves in the Struggle for Democracy," Hu highlighted the combative character of the creative process by which an authentic work of realism is produced. Hu called this process the "interfusion" of the "subject" with the "object," a term synonymous with social life itself in Hu's vocabulary.[83] The interfusion of the author's self with the object-other, by which subjectivity is constituted, was made possible only through revolutionary practice. This revolutionary practice included "opposing fascism and feudalism, lashing out at all forms and measures of slavish ethics, unearthing the potential power of the people, and articulating the people's desire and struggle for liberation."[84] Key to the successful constitution of revolutionary subjectivity was the power to combat the "spiritual slavery" of the masses and uncover their revolutionary potential:

> Although their [the people's] desires or struggles of life embody the demand of history, they take on myriad and malleable forms, and they marched on complicated and tortuous paths. Although spiritually they were given over to liberation, the scars of thousands of years of spiritual slavery are always rooted and scattered in their mind. If the writer does not want to drown himself in the ocean of such a sensuous existence, when engaging himself deeply into it, he has to foster a critical power in combating the content of their life.[85]

Hu located spiritual slavery at the internal, unconscious level of "sensuous existence," as an ensemble of cultural constituencies of domination, forged through consensus rather than imposed by coercion. His idea of spiritual slavery is comparable, in some measure, to Gramsci's notion of hegemony. Under similar circumstances of war and revolution, both Gramsci and Hu saw revolutionary practice as the path toward humankind's liberation. The subjective fighting spirit thus takes on a counterhegemonic character, in the sense that its task is to combat embedded and internalized cultural values installed over thousands of years by the holders of power. This is precisely the primal objective of the May Fourth cultural critique, to which the Li Zehous and Liu Zaifus of the 1980s were to return with a deep sense of belatedness and vengeance.

A subjectivity of resistance in Hu's view stemmed from sensuous, bodily experiences, rather than rational abstractions. In the same 1944 article, Hu portrayed the formation of revolutionary subjectivity as a "struggle of one bloody mark after one scourge." The passion and affliction incurred in the course of artistic creation was "not simply the reaction to pressures of the time or the burden of life, but the internal process of conscious expansion, accompanied by the pain of the body."[86] Literary representation, or realism, was entwined with this bodily experience, and made possible only through the "passionate expansion," spiritual "embrace," and "penetration" of this powerful subjective experience, will, and feeling into its object of representation. In a Hegelian synthesis of the subject-object relationship, Hu described artistic creation as

> stemming from the struggle with the real life of flesh and blood. The real life of flesh and blood, of course, means the sensuous object.... The struggle with the real life of flesh and blood is a process of embodying and absorbing the object, as well as a process of overcoming and critiquing the object.... The critique ... must grasp the social significance of the object from its concrete, lively, and sensuous experience, and instill into this experience the author's positive, affirmative, or negative viewpoint.[87]

In *On the Path of Realism* (1948), Hu argued for a close link between subjectivity, sensuous experience, and reality: "The Real as such is simply the glowing and painful historical content, in which flows the people's burden, awakening, potentiality, and desire and longing for life; ... the author must internalize this historical content into his own subjective demand."[88] The internalization of the historical content or objective condition was called by Hu the fusion of the subjective and objective, too. It was attainable exclusively through the aesthetic form of realism. Form, for Hu, was the true bearer of the author's subjectivity: "Form is the rational expression of the objective reality *unified with the author's subjectivity*."[89]

In Hu's theory of a subjective fighting spirit, the dialectic of domination and resistance can be resolved by transforming the people's desire and potential for liberation from the state "in-itself" into the state "for-itself."[90] Hu associated this spiritual transformation with the literary form. As discussed earlier, he also considered traditional national forms to be carriers of feudalist hegemony, or spiritual slavery. Therefore, the transformation of people's minds and uncovering of revolutionary potential can only be realized by adopting the new forms of May Fourth realism: "When feudalist culture (popular culture) still exerted its power through the 'sluggishness of history,' the urban class emerged in China as a powerful material force, and this class led a great literary revolution."[91]

Hu's subjectivity in literary creation is essentially a social agency of revolution and resistance. It is thus a historical construct, but one lacking the metaphysical presuppositions of a self-regulating, self-determining, autonomous, and sovereign subject. Rather, it is a dislocated, divided, and dispersed formation of a subject-in-conflict. It does not draw its vital sustenance from serene, distanced, disinterested, and transcendental aesthetic contemplation in a Kantian fashion. Instead, it emanates from the bodily, sensuous experiences of everyday life, analogous to the aesthetic experience of a carnival, as Mikhail Bakhtin suggested.

Hu and Bakhtin did not know each other's work, yet their similarities are not coincidental. Bakhtin, after all, can be regarded as a thinker of cultural revolution at the moment of intense social and cultural upheavals. His "architectonics of answerability" provide a theory of aesthetic subjectivity. In addition, Bakhtin's concept of the "carnival" effectively captures the aesthetic experience of the bodily, sensuous, everyday life of the common people at the time of revolution and transformation.[92] Bakhtin's architectonics of subjectivity is closely related to aesthetic experience. The dialogue between author and hero, self and other, is Bakhtin's aesthetic conception of subjectivity. In his architectonics of self, Bakhtin conceived of a process of communication and dialogue between the self and other by which one's subjectivity was constituted. The subjects of communication and dialogue are all concrete, individual sensuous beings in an uninterrupted chain of events or processes: existence is "the unique and unified event of being."[93] Aesthetic experience, in Bakhtin's view, provided the synthesis and unity of art and life through *otvetstvennost* (answerability/responsibility), referring to the intersubjective dialogues between author-self and hero-other from which subjectivity is constituted.[94]

It is also in the sense of intersubjective interaction that Bakhtin talked about Fyodor Mikhaylovich Dostoyevsky's "polyphonic novel." The thrust of the polyphony is the process of the formation of self-consciousness through dialogues between the self and other. In other words, it describes the process by which subjectivity is constituted during a period of cultural ruptures and transformations. The historical condition for a new subjectivity was one of profound social crisis and cultural discontinuity, a historical turning point and threshold: "The most favorable soil for [the polyphonic novel] was . . . in Russia, where capitalism set in almost catastrophically."[95] This is precisely the moment of cultural change whereby social conflicts become most intense and various cultural formations clash. After the collapse of the unifying and centralizing discourse of myth, all different cultural systems enter into an animated contention and interpenetration, vying for the power of language. Heteroglossia, or the diversity and multiplicity of languages and discourses, becomes the very emblem of cultural change. Under such historical circumstances, the subject (self) gains an acute awareness of the voices of others, and the necessity to establish one's own subjectivity and identity.

Bakhtin's notion of the carnival can be construed as an aesthetic of cultural revolution based on "the material bodily principle": "The material bodily principle is contained not in the biological individual, not in the bourgeois ego, but in the people, a people who are constantly growing and renewed."[96] The carnival as an aesthetic of the sensuous and concrete, as Ken Hirschkop puts it, suggested "a collective democracy, grounded in civil society, in which the abstract identity of the citizen or subject is replaced by that of one who eats, drinks, procreates and labors."[97]

Hu's theory of a subjective fighting spirit, too, deals primarily with the question of authorship as the revolutionary agent. Despite the Hegelian idiom employed in his writings, Hu's notions of the subject, aesthetic experience, and reality are in fact quite un-Hegelian, and close to Bakhtin's concepts. Hu was adamantly opposed to the instrumentalist view that the author serves merely as a "tool," a "dead, 'material' container" that allows the object to flow in and out spontaneously. Rather, he saw the author as a "sensuous activity" or an "event," and contended that the "process of aesthetic production for the realist is the process or event of his own life itself."[98] It is, like the Bakhtinian "event of being," a struggle of flesh and blood by which the subject (author) experiences, penetrates, and interfuses with the living content of the object (hero-reader). This turned out to be a dynamic intersubjective battle through bodily, sensuous experiences and interpenetrations "at the time of insanity," in a carnivalesque explosion or subversion of feudalist hierarchies and hegemony, "in order to strive for the future without insanity."[99]

Hu might share some Hegelian vocabulary, and certainly the notion of realism as aesthetic mediation and representation, with Lukács, but they also parted company on the decisive issues of objectivity and subjectivity. Lukács's passion for totality dictated his concept of realist representation as an attempt to achieve complete "objectivity." It was ultimately susceptible to determinism and instrumentalism, as shown, indeed, by Lukács's later endorsement of the Stalinist principle of "socialist realism." (Bakhtin, as we know, was sharply critical of Lukács's Hegelianism.) Hu's aversion to instrumentalism was evident in his strong reservation about Lukács's aesthetics.

Hu's dynamic and dialogical notion of the intersubjective "penetration" and "fusion" of the subject (author) and object (hero-reader) not only parallels Bakhtin's *Rezeptionästhetik* but also shares some common ground with the contemporary. Hu's insistence on the intense "battles" and "struggles" between the author and hero-reader points to an active process of aesthetic production-reception by which the horizon of expectation of the reader is radically altered and transformed. Such a dynamic aesthetics bears certain features of "avant-gardism" not unlike progressive, revolutionary avant-garde aesthetics in the West.[100]

At the same time, Hu's notion of aesthetic production has much in common with Mao's, despite the fact that the terms and language in their otherwise similar conceptions often appear inverted: Mao favored the working-class audience and distrusted the intellectual writer, while Hu saw a much more active role for the author in the intersubjective exchange and embrace between the subject and object. The similarities and differences between Mao and Hu on these issues certainly have much broader implications beyond the purely political and aesthetic; they are indicative of the internal tensions and contradictions within Chinese Marxist cultural thought on the crucial questions of hegemony and the relationship of politics and culture. Hu's views are largely counterhegemonic, and can thus serve as a means of "symptomatic reading" that may decipher the flaws and inner contradictions of Mao's theory and practice.

In an essay written during the Cultural Reflection of the 1980s, Li Zehou hailed Hu as one of the foremost Chinese Marxist thinkers who promulgated enlightenment as an absolute task for Chinese social revolution and transformation.[101] Li, however, also pointed out the failure of Hu's theory to exert a major influence on Chinese cultural and literary scenes. In a comparison of Hu's theory and Mao's *Talks*, Li concedes that Mao "talked about literature and the arts from a sociopolitical perspective, which is higher than the laws of literature and the arts per se."[102] Mao's view, therefore, triumphed, dominating the Chinese cultural scene for nearly four decades.

CHAPTER 4

Aesthetics, Ideology, and Cultural

Reconstruction

On the eve of the final victory of the revolutionary war, Mao enumerated the forthcoming goals and strategies of the Chinese Revolution by suggesting a spatial shift. He remarked that, from 1927 to 1949, the CCP's work had always been in the village or countryside, but now "the center of gravity of the party's work has shifted from the village to the city."[1] Mao, of course, did not mention the earlier spatial relocation, or reterritorialization, around 1927 from the city to the countryside. This deliberate silence on the first crucial shift is, as we have seen, symptomatic of a major contradiction in Mao's thought. He privileged "revolutionary theory" and consciousness, and at the same time, discounted and ignored the very sources and agents of this theory, namely the May Fourth enlightenment and its cultural revolution, and urban Marxist intellectuals. The tension between urban and rural within the revolutionary forces, after the new spatial and territorial change, intensified, compounded by new contradictions. Of all the contradictions, the twofold goal of consolidating revolutionary hegemony and reconstructing China's society—from economic infrastructure to political and cultural institutions—presented the greatest challenge. Building a revolutionary hegemony required that cultural revolution be ceaselessly continued and renewed. Yet continued revolution inevitably entailed destabilization and disruption of the routine, institutional practices necessary for the construction and maintenance of the country's economic and social structures. On the other hand, the tasks of consolidation and reconstruction dictated the establishment of an ideological orthodoxy or ideological state apparatuses to ensure the normativity and regularity of social life. These two conflicting goals remained central to China's project of an alternative modernity.

In any event, Mao's cultural and ideological policies, which straddled the fundamental tension between revolution and reconstruction, quickly led to the massive politicization of aesthetics and culture, as well as the aestheticization of politics. The ceaseless revolution along with political and ideological struggles in the cultural sphere, now in hindsight, seriously hindered economic development. Mao's political instrumentalization was responsible for oppressive campaigns in cultural and aesthetic spheres. Still, Mao also unintentionally allowed counterhegemonic formations to emerge. This was not due to Mao's policy of "letting hundred flowers blooming and hundred schools contending," which appeared to encourage differences in cultural styles and forms. His critics now accuse Mao of deploying the "blooming and contention" policy as a trap to sort out antisocialist elements. In fact, this policy was a precursor to the Anti-Rightist Campaign of 1957, in which hundreds and thousands of writers and artists were victimized. But Mao's revolutionary hegemony promoted the democratic participation and intervention of the masses, while asserting state control and coercion. Mao urged intellectuals to engage in theoretical debates, simultaneously seeking ways to manipulate them. Thus, the Chinese cultural scene under Mao cannot be understood as simply the repression of a totalitarian regime and dissent of intellectuals, like the way that cultural life in the former Soviet blocs was usually characterized in the West.

Of all the campaigns and debates in post-1949 China's cultural arena, the one from 1957 to 1964 concerning aesthetics deserves attention. The debate dealt with basic issues in Marxist theories of culture, focusing on the crucial problematics of subjectivity, practice, and ideology. Starting from different political and historical conjunctures, the views of Chinese aesthetic Marxists converge in interesting ways with those of Western Marxists, the Frankfurt School in particular. Perhaps the most valuable dimension is that the Chinese aesthetic Marxists searched for a constructive alternative, based on a non-Western, socialist historical experience. Social and cultural reconstruction was central in the aesthetic debates. This reconstruction can be seen, first of all, as an effort to reconfigure and reterritorialize cultural space in a socialist, postrevolutionary society. Mao, the state cultural apparatuses, and the theorists and writers whose stances differed from the hegemonic "orthodoxy," all contributed to the project of cultural reconstruction.

Revolution and Reconstruction: New Territories and Constellations

Although the revolution shifted spatially and politically from the war against the Chiang Kai-shek regime to building a new society, revolution itself still dominated Mao's thought. Mao warned his CCP cadres that after the "enemies with guns were wiped out there will still be enemies without guns."[2] This preoccupation continued until Mao's death. Instead of real battlegrounds with bloodshed, the site in which Mao's wars against new enemies were fought was primarily culture. Mao's vision of the new war was reminiscent of his early identification of two revolutionary armies, one with guns and the other with pens. The new "enemy with pens" was a logical deduction of Mao's own revolutionary strategy—enemies might well adopt a similar tactic to undermine the revolution, just as the revolutionary army with pens had done to its enemies. Yet more was at stake there. Mao's identification of new enemies was not unrelated to his suspicion of the revolutionary army itself. The Cultural Revolution uncovered two major enemies: the new "bureaucratic class" or "capitalist roaders" within the CCP; and writers, artists, and academics, who were labeled "bourgeois intellectuals."

There had been, of course, dissent and protest against Mao's view of culture and society, and his cultural and intellectual policies. Many at first resisted Mao's views and policies simply because they were in principle opposed to Marxism. Those anti-Marxist voices soon were silenced. Many more intellectuals accepted Marxism as the only tenable solution to China's modernity, either through forced thought-reform or by their own choice—a significant number of Chinese intellectuals turned toward the CCP out of sheer disillusionment with Chiang Kai-shek's corrupt and inept regime. Contrary to the accepted view of China studies in the West that characterizes the political and ideological struggles in the PRC as largely waged between anti-Communists and the CCP, a majority of cultural and ideological discourses in post-1949 China were concerned with the problem of constructing a socialist alternative to capitalism. Granted, antisocialist, pro-Western capitalist forces have always existed in China. But ironically, their role has been exaggerated by Mao's ideological state apparatuses, the Western media, and China studies alike. Historically speaking, both Mao and the enemies of the CCP in the West were governed by the ideological closure of the cold war. But cold war ideologies only perpetuate self-righteous myths about the relationship between the self and other in absolute, dichotomous terms. Such a sterile binary opposition of pro- and anti-Communism hardly allows for insight into the complex dynamics within China's cultural sphere, and the internal tensions and differences within Marxist perimeters.

Another issue is the relationship between Western and Chinese Marxism. During the social and cultural upheavals of the 1960s that swept the globe, Mao's views heavily influenced Western leftist movements. The voices of Chinese "aesthetic Marxists," however, barely reached beyond China itself, remaining unknown to Western Marxists. It is thus valuable to compare Chinese "aesthetic Marxism" and Western Marxism as a means of understanding the historical development of modern Marxist cultural theories. Chinese aesthetic Marxism and Western Marxism have both created a theoretical space for critical interventions by empowering cultural politics. While European and North American cultural politics have fostered an oppositional vision focused on the problems of domination and resistance, manipulation and self-government, consent and coercion in a modern capitalist society, aesthetic Marxism in China served the twofold mission of criticizing the intrinsic contradictions within revolutionary hegemony and offering a constructive vision of culture in a postrevolutionary society. Aesthetics provides a focal point in contemporary Marxist discussions of culture, cutting across social and geographical boundaries. Chinese aesthetic Marxism, therefore, should be placed within the context of global cultural critique.

When comparing Chinese Marxist debates about aesthetics and Western Marxist aesthetic theories, another factor is the nature of aesthetic discourse and cultural critique. Should the aesthetic only serve the negative function of critique? It makes sense for Marxists in the advanced capitalism of Western Europe and North America to insist on the negative, critical function of the aesthetic. Yet the Chinese aesthetic Marxists contended, in a different context, that the aesthetic holds out a constructive promise in a socialist society. Furthermore, this Chinese constructive view of the aesthetic is not merely a local and particular vision. By virtue of the fact that Chinese aesthetic Marxism is engaged in a Marxist discourse that is universalist and utopian, the constructive, rather than negative function that they see in the aesthetic pertains to Marxist utopianism and universalism. It can be argued that a utopian vision lies at the heart of Western Marxist projects, however negative and critical they may appear. In contemporary China, a Marxist cultural politics is faced with the task of critiquing Mao's instrumentalization and politicization of culture and aesthetics, as well as China's local, national, and classical tradition. This Marxism will have to address the consequences of the global capitalism that deeply penetrates China today. The Deng and post-Deng era has greatly exacerbated the ideological tensions and contradictions in China, and any Marxist critique cannot but confront Deng's legacy as well as post-Deng cultural and ideological contradictions.

But there is also the positive, constructive aspect of the aesthetic. To be sure, this positive notion is eminently utopian. The positive, constructive utopian aspiration that Chinese aesthetic Marxism upholds deserves serious consideration. It had functioned effectively as a theoretical paradigm shaping much of the ferment in China in the 1980s. Moreover, as a humanist vision, it has a critical relevance to Marxism and socialism in general. With former Soviet and East European socialism becoming things of the past, and Mao's revolutionary utopianism in China having ended in a dreadful debacle, radically discredited by his pragmatic successors, Marxist utopianism indeed faces a deep crisis. Consequently, Western Marxists have become further entrenched in ideological critique or self-questioning. A negative mood now prevails in the Left academic circles of Western Europe and North America. Compounded by right-wing attacks on so-called "political correctness," hopes of positive and constructive alternatives seem even more remote. The negativity, in short, so dominant within the Western intellectual scene, evokes a turn-of-the-century déjà vu, with postmodernist doxa as both its symptom and diagnosis.

In such a critical ambience, the Chinese Marxists's insistence on a constructive Marxist cultural theory appears outdated and almost irrelevant. Granted, today, a negative critique is much needed to unravel and confront the oppression, injustice, and inequality that continue to plague the globe. But a negative consequence of being too negatively critical is perhaps an obsession with poststructuralist linguistic aporia that may obscure real differences in a nondiscursive world, where notions of constructive subjectivity, or even "essence," can have an urgently needed impact.[3]

There are other complications in the Chinese case. To a Western audience, Chinese aesthetic Marxists may not only sound derivative, but also outmoded: as discussed earlier, they were inspired by classical German philosophy and the writings of Marx, and their theoretical discourse is suffused with terms such as the "essence of beauty," "humanization of nature," "ultimate fulfillment of man's essence," and so forth. These phrases are generally discounted as "metaphysical" and "essentialist" among today's academics in the United States and Western Europe who are interested in Marxism and cultural critique. The other problem with Chinese aesthetic Marxists is that their language is by and large abstract and philosophical, referring more to German and continental European thought than things specifically Chinese. This creates yet another obstacle for China studies in the West. For a China specialist, the aesthetic debate would seem rather uninviting, like an officially sanctioned, ideological rehearsal of Marxist-Leninist doctrines hardly useful for analyses of the political reality in China.[4]

Another complex issue is the influence of Maoism. For the Western Left (and Right as well), Maoism seems to be the ultimate incarnation of Chinese Marxism. Mao's theory and practice of a cultural revolution attracted Marcuse, Sartre, Althusser, and French leftists associated with the journal *Tel Quel*. As Fredric Jameson puts it, in their efforts to resurrect a revolutionary legacy in the cultural terrain, "the rumors of Maoism that reached the Western Left during this period seemed to provide fresh theoretical and political ammunition for this particular struggle."[5] Western Marxist appropriation of Maoism is an intriguing question in itself, and deserves at least a book-length study. By focusing only on "Maoist rumors," Western Marxists nevertheless missed an opportunity to communicate with the alternative forces within Chinese Marxism. Now that Mao's thought is generally accused of being an "Oriental despotic" version of totalitarianism, Western Marxists's "flirtation with Maoism" has fueled the Right in Western Europe and North America in assaulting the Western Left.[6]

An excessively negative and fragmented intellectual Left in the West today may recognize the value of, rather than turn its back on, any alternative thinking. Such alternative thought may dramatically differ in some areas from the Western Left. But if difference is what the Western Left looks for, it may find it beneficial to attend to the alternative thinking that Chinese aesthetic Marxism offers. Chinese aesthetic Marxism emphasizes both historical totality and local specificity, and is both critical and constructive. It tries to retain a utopian vision, while urging practical participation and intervention in constructing a democratic society. For all its limits and contradictions, Chinese aesthetic Marxism raises significant issues concerning the function of cultural criticism and the role of intellectuals. What we as academic intellectuals can do is fundamentally critical, but we cannot merely stop at that. Chinese aesthetic Marxists have constituted a critical intervention into cultural issues. Their efforts are analogous to what Edward Said would call an "act of insurgency" with real and practical consequences in the world.[7] Apart from this critical aspect, their positive and constructive vision also reveals a different dimension of the aesthetic. Ultimately, we must ask ourselves: What can be done next, after all is deconstructed, demystified, and decentered? Chinese aesthetic Marxism may not present a viable answer, but it continues to raise such questions, no matter how troubling and vexing.

Aesthetics in modern China is closely related to the creation of a revolutionary hegemony. Mao, as previously discussed, took the establishment of hegemony and cultural revolution to be the main tasks of the Chinese Revolution. But in doing so, Mao politicized and instrumentalized the aesthetic, stripping away its function as an affective, subjective domain of culture within which hegemony operates by diffusing its values and gaining consensus from the ruled. Aesthetics itself, then, becomes alienated under Mao's collapsing of political apparatuses and ideological means, resulting in the wholesale aestheticization of politics as well as politicization of aesthetics.

Raymond Williams observes that Mao's cultural revolution was a "sustained (and of course confused) attempt, in People's China, to define new priorities and alter actual and foreseen political relations, trying to make new forms of popular power within and where necessary against the received shapes of a socialist economic order."[8] In a sense, Mao's vision was counterhegemonic, against the "received shapes" of Soviet-style social-ism. At the beginning, Mao self-consciously differentiated the goals of the Chinese Revolution from the Russian model. Cultural revolution and peasant guerrilla warfare were conceived by Mao as the antideterministic alternative way of China's modernity and revolution. This put Mao's revolutionary strategies at odds with both Marx's historical determinism and Leninist revolution.

Yet Mao was not immune to determinism. In making a strategic plan for the Chinese Revolution in the 1940s, he oscillated between going through a "capitalist stage" as a first step, and waging a revolution in culture and consciousness to move directly into socialism. By 1949, Mao's tactics were vindicated by the seizure of state power through peasant guerrilla warfare. Since historical conditions in China took a decisive turn at this point, Mao did not really change much of his strategies. Despite his acute awareness of the historical transition, and his own pleas for strategic transformation, Mao had yet to switch gears, so to speak, moving from war maneuvers to the planning of economic and social reconstruction. Indeed, Mao never really abandoned his military tactic and perspective during his reign, even though the main objectives changed fundamentally from violent destruction to peaceful construction after the PRC was established. Of course, the new China was then still surrounded by hostile forces from within and without. Taiwan was taken over by Chiang Kai-shek, supported by the United States in its post–World War II strategy of containment against Communism. In the first year of the new regime, one of Mao's central objectives was to conquer the island, but the Korean War broke out. The ensuing blockage of the Taiwan Strait by the U.S. Seventh Fleet, and Chiang Kai-shek's clamor for reconquering the mainland, all helped to intensify the panic and fear that the new regime experienced. Under these circumstances, the need to fight the "enemies with guns" continued, while the struggle against the "enemies without guns," by Mao's calculation, had to start in the cities immediately on the "cultural front," to fully conquer the whole country and solidify its victory. A certain amount of determinism was necessary, in a strategic sense, to tackle the compelling practical issues. Translated into practical measures, determinism simply meant the determined and ruthless suppression of political opposition. Mao and his colleagues shared much in common with Harry S. Truman and Joseph McCarthy, in the sense that their thinking was anchored squarely in an antagonistic, dichotomous mode. Binarism was directly linked with cold war ideology, and it was first a bloody battle of life and death before it was anything discursive or rhetorical. The cold war marked a turning point in modernity (or an alternative modernity), during which dichotomous thought saw its apex across the globe.

We need, however, to differentiate various kinds of determinism. There is a conceptual, epistemological determinism by which long-term historical strategies and visions are charted and conceived. It can be said that Hegelianism and classical Marxism belong in this category. Perhaps in a basic sense, European Enlightenment rationality, and much of the ideas of modernity, are shaped or strongly affected by some form of determinism, be it scientific, historical, or even ontological. On the other hand, there is a strategic, tactical type of determinism. It always arises from specific needs and expediencies, and is almost invariably practical or pragmatic. It may not have any profound philosophical ground, and is always amenable to revision and modification. Especially at the conjuncture of intense crises, such as wars and societal disorder, ruthless measures are taken, which appear in a rather rigid deterministic fashion. In the modern world, there are at least two interrelated yet different kinds of determinism: a "conceptual determinism," or determinism as a matter of principle; and a "strategic determinism," or determinism as a matter of contingency. In reality, these two determinisms are difficult to distinguish and mutually transferable. Still, the qualitative transformation of one kind of determinism to another often starts with quantitative changes. Such a transformation is discernible in Mao's strategies.

Mao first conceived of cultural revolution as an alternative to historical determinism. Hence, it can be argued, antideterminism was a principal thread in Mao's thought on cultural revolution and an alternative modernity. Yet Mao took pragmatic, contingent measures to implement cultural revolution and engage in struggles against the "enemies without guns." During the complex and overdetermined course of cultural revolution—that is, from the Anti–Hu Feng Campaign, to the "blooming and contending" movement, to the Anti-Rightist Campaign, and finally, to the Great Proletarian Cultural Revolution—a fundamental, qualitative transformation took place. To carry out revolution and struggles in the cultural sphere, Mao sought ways to politicize and instrumentalize cultural and aesthetic discourses, and to subject intellectuals to incessant coercive thought-reform, self-incriminations, and persecutions. Those deterministic, pragmatic strategies, devised paradoxically under Mao's greater and quite antideterminist vision of cultural revolution, eventually changed into a "conceptual determinism." It was evident that Mao, in his later years, tended to ontologize cultural revolution, or class struggle in superstructures, into an absolute "objective law." A cultural and ideological determinism began to take shape in the formative years of the PRC, reaching its zenith in the Cultural Revolution period.[9]

The ascendancy of this cultural and ideological determinism was conditioned by at least three principal factors. First, it involved strategic needs in the creation of a revolutionary hegemony, in which culture played a decisive role. Second, the revolutionary legacy itself, which always placed cultural revolution at the core of its mission, had substantial bearings on Mao's attempts to ontologize culture or cultural revolution. Last but not least, Mao's attempt was essentially a pragmatic move to address concrete political and social issues at a specific conjuncture. Cultural revolution, as we have seen, was first conceived by Mao as an antideterministic, alternative way of achieving socialism. But when it became necessary to establish ideological orthodoxy to ensure normativity and regularity, Mao was inclined to favor cultural and ideological revolution. On the other hand, Mao had little, if any, experience and knowledge in economic matters, and he remained suspicious of economism throughout his life. After the PRC was solidified, Mao still considered revolution to be a top priority over economic reconstruction.

It is crucial to note that "modernization," contrary to popular opinion, did not at first occupy a prominent spot in Mao's discourse; it was developed as such only after the Eighth Congress of the CCP in September 1956, which set the development of productive forces or economic modernization as its main priority.[10] Mao, however, insisted on the primacy of political struggle in the overall project of modernity (revolution and reconstruction). Cultural revolution was, in Mao's view, a political revolution, and thus, an integral component of an alternative modernity. In this respect, Perry Anderson was thus wrong to consider Mao's cultural revolution a mere "metaphor" or simply "psychological and moral conversions."[11]

In one of his major philosophical works, "On Correctly Handling Contradictions among the People," delivered in February 1957 only a few months after the Eighth Congress of the CCP, Mao wrote that after the establishment of a socialist mode of production, class struggle would not necessarily come to an end. Instead, it might intensify because of the existence of bourgeois cultures and ideologies within the capitalist world system, which surrounded China. This was the first significant statement about the need for cultural and ideological revolution in a socialist state. It also provided the raison d'être for the Cultural Revolution. In Mao's view, cultural revolution and class struggle in both political and ideological spheres will last a long time, affecting the future development of Marxism itself:

> The class struggle between the proletariat and the bourgeoisie in the ideological sphere will still be protracted, tortuous, and even violent at times. The proletariat wants to transform the world according to its own worldview, and so does the bourgeoisie. In this regard, the question of whether socialism or capitalism will win in the battle between

them has not yet really been settled. Whether among the entire population or among the intellectuals, Marxists remain a minority. Therefore, Marxism still has to develop through struggle. That Marxism can only develop through struggle holds true not only for the past and present, but will also inevitably hold true in the future.[12]

According to Mao, after 1949, the revolution had changed its space and content, from the countryside to cities, from wars to cultural and ideological struggles. What remained constant and indeed permanent was revolution itself. A logical conclusion obtained that cultural revolution, or any kind of revolution, was discovered as an objective law rather than a political, strategic move. In his "Notes on the Soviet Textbook of *Political Economy*," written between 1961 and 1962, Mao sharply criticized the Soviet schoolbook's neglect of superstructure and ideological class struggle, and identified political and cultural revolution as a "general, objective law":

> All revolutionary history has proven that it is not true that transformation of the backward relations of production can take place only after the new productive forces have been sufficiently developed. Our revolution started from propagating Marxism-Leninism. It created the new social sentiment for the revolution. Only by overthrowing the backward superstructures through revolution was the elimination of old relations of production made possible.[13]

And also:

> It is a general law that first the social sentiment be created for the seizure of state power, then the problem of the rights of ownership can be solved, and the great development of productive forces will follow. There are differences between proletarian revolution and bourgeois revolution (in that there was no socialist relations of production prior to proletarian revolution, yet the preliminary capitalist relations of production already grew from feudal societies), but basically these revolutions are identical [in terms of the general law].[14]

As an objective law, class struggle in cultural and ideological spheres not only took precedence over economic reconstruction, but also dictated the whole of social life. Consequently, incessant ideological campaigns and thought-reforms were waged in order to adhere to class struggle as an objective law. One result of these campaigns was that the facile boundary between state and civil society was altogether collapsed. Mao mobilized millions and millions of Chinese citizens to actively and voluntarily participate in the campaigns against bureaucratic state apparatuses. Such an antibureaucracy movement was launched for the sake of defending socialist democratic participation. Coupled with a national, popular cultural hegemony that internalized its values in the minds of the people in their everyday lives, Mao's strategy of class struggle under socialism was remarkably effective. The Anti-Rightist Campaign and Cultural Revolution both adopted such hegemonic strategies to install and internalize socialist values on a wide scale. The pedagogical technologies went hand in hand with ruthless measures of coercion, control, and manipulation. Paradoxically, Mao's antibureaucratic, democratic, and educational movements frequently produced a militant mob rule that deprived ordinary citizens of basic individual, democratic rights. Mass movements in China turned out to reinforce, rather than reduce, the oppressive power of state apparatuses. In order to avoid escalating tensions and animosities between the rulers and the ruled, the cultural hegemony was to provide moral subsistence for the precarious cadre system and its mass support network. In other words, both the ruling party members and the ruled masses had to rely on an ideological-moral ecosystem in order to sustain the ceaseless struggles against the structure itself. Under such circumstances, it is instructive to reevaluate the counterhegemonic formations made by Hu Feng and by other Chinese aesthetic Marxists, who identified and challenged Mao's political tactics that mistakenly took an ontological view of class struggle as an objective law.

In his famous report on China's cultural spheres in 1954, Hu pointed out the dangers of instrumentalizing culture. He listed, as mentioned earlier, "five theoretical daggers" stifling different voices, and homogenizing artistic styles and forms: the "perfect Communist worldview" as the precondition for artistic creation; the focus on the "life of workers, peasants, and soldiers" as the sole resources of aesthetic representation, excluding other aspects of social life; "thought-reform" as a precondition for artistic creation; the exclusive privileging of traditional, national forms vis-à-vis international, cosmopolitan culture; and finally, the "prior determination of the subject matter."[15] The thrust of Hu's view was that the party should not determine and dictate artistic creations and cultural work, which must have their own, relatively autonomous space. Hu contended that a Communist worldview, thought reform, and national form were the necessary, but not sufficient, let alone absolute, conditions for aesthetic work. He insisted on the "aesthetic principles of realism," synonymous to his subjective fighting spirit. This aesthetic principle should be sustained in order to avoid the party's interference in cultural and aesthetic spheres. In short, according to Hu, questions of cultural space and subjectivity were intimately tied up with a healthy socialist cultural environment or public sphere. Unfortunately, Hu's valuable insights were misinterpreted by Mao as an act of subversion. In 1954, Mao simply stamped out Hu and his friends and sympathizers using brutal suppression. It should be noted that Mao's paranoia was a direct response to the cold war atmosphere. The Korean War had only ended a year earlier, in 1953; China was still besieged by hostile Western powers and Chiang Kai-shek's forces in Taiwan. Mao, in turn, was ruthless. Since Mao considered literature and arts to be vital to his revolutionary hegemony, an explicit challenge from someone claiming Marxist and revolutionary positions would appear especially pernicious. But as a major consequence of the Anti–Hu Feng Campaign, cultural and aesthetic work in China have been subject ever since to instrumentalization and politicization under strained conditions.[16]

Rethinking the Subject: The Aesthetic Debate

The aesthetic debate (1956–1964) should be understood within the context of the complex process of establishing a socialist hegemony and modernizing the economy. First of all, the debate was to serve the objective of disseminating Marxism in China's intellectual circles. Second, the emphases in the debate on cultural reconstruction, practice in material life, and the utopian vision of a "humanized nature" were linked to the project of modernization. In order to ensure a socialist hegemony, Mao launched continued campaigns to promote Marxism, and criticize "bourgeois and feudalist" ideas. Aesthetics proved to be a resilient spot within China's cultural arena, then filled with tension. As a field of inquiry, aesthetics is inextricably connected to literature and the arts. Yet its discourse is more philosophical than practical, and thus, it is distanced from literary and art criticism. This distance, however tenuous and fragile in China's volatile circumstances, made aesthetic discussions less vulnerable to political interference. Moreover, aesthetics in China has been associated with the May Fourth legacy, and its German origin also has special appeal to Chinese revolutionaries due to its relationship with Marxism. At first, Mao and his cultural bureaucrats saw the need to engage in a Marxist critique of aesthetics as a predominantly "bourgeois" discourse. And for the sake of studying Marxism, discussions of Marxist aesthetic theories were encouraged.

The debate was triggered by a self-critical essay from China's leading aesthetician, Zhu Guangqian, on his "idealist aesthetics." Zhu, then a professor of English at Peking University, had been an influential scholar since the 1920s. Also known as K. C. Chu, Zhu was born in 1897 to a traditional scholar's family in Tongcheng, Anhui Province, where the famous Tongcheng School of neoclassical prose originated. He studied English at the University of Hong Kong. In 1925, he went to Europe, first to the University of Edinburgh and then to France, where he studied at the Sorbonne and the University of Strasbourg. Zhu received his Ph.D. in 1933 from the University of Strasbourg. That same year, the University of Strasbourg Press published Zhu's *The Tragic Psychology*, based on his dissertation, and he returned to China to teach at Peking University, Sichuan University, and Wuhan University respectively. In 1949, he went back to Peking University, where he taught until his death in 1986.

In "The Reactionary Aspects of My Literary Thoughts," published in 1956 in the widely circulated journal *Wenyi bao* (Literary gazette), Zhu criticized his own "subjective idealist views" on aesthetics, hoping to "break with old, bourgeois ideas and to build new Marxist views."[17] Zhu had been China's foremost advocate of Western modern aesthetics, especially Benedetto Croce's intuitive-expressive theory. His first encounter with Croce, as he put it, "enabled me to see Kant, Hegel, Schopenhauer, Nietzsche, and Bergson through a Crocian lens."[18]

Still, it was Kantian aesthetics that provided the larger framework in which Zhu, like most other Chinese intellectuals in a variety of time periods, apprehended modern Western aesthetic theories. Kantianism bridged classical, Enlightenment, and modernist aesthetics in Europe, and featured prominently in the Chinese aesthetic Marxists's call to reconstruct subjectivity in Chinese culture in the 1980s. This era, in turn, had its roots in much earlier cultural discussions, including the May Fourth enlightenment and the 1950s and 1960s' debates over aesthetics. But writers and critics in the Republican period had hardly ever interrogated Western modernism on philosophical and theoretical levels. In this respect, Zhu's assiduous efforts in the 1930s and 1940s, first to introduce modern Western aesthetics and then to incorporate them creatively into China's aesthetic tradition, broke new ground for the eventual convergence of Marxist cultural theory, Chinese tradition, and Western modernism. His encounter with Western aesthetics, though described in the 1956 essay in a negative vein in accord with the official discourse, actually verifies Zhu's vanguard position vis-à-vis Western modernist aesthetics, and thus, it is worth pursuing here at greater length.

Croce, Zhu maintained, "comes closer to Kant than to Hegel in his aesthetics," because "Kant . . . first formulated the notions such as 'disinterestedness,' 'purposiveness without purposes' as well as 'pure form,'" and Croce stretched Kantian aesthetics to a "reactionary extreme to defend formalist arts of the bourgeoisie in decline."[19] Zhu had adopted Croce's theory of intuition-expression in two ways. To begin with, rather than focusing on Croce's language-oriented theory of symbolic representation of both logical and intuitive conception, Zhu mainly appropriated the Kantian implications of Croce's formulation of aesthetic experience as a detached, autonomous, and pure imaginary process. This, in fact, reflected

Zhu's concern with the problems of modernity, captured by Kantian and post-Kantian aesthetic theories precisely as self-conscious separation and the autonomy of the arts from other spheres of life. Second, Croce's emphasis on the expressive and psychological dimensions of aesthetic experience, as well as the lyrical mode as the quintessential expression of emotion, seemed to indicate a possible point of convergence for modern Western and classical Chinese aesthetics. Taking Croce's position as a cue, Zhu incorporated a variety of modern Western aesthetic theories, from Kant's "disinterested contemplation" to Arthur Schopenhauer's notion of aesthetic experience as "forgetfulness," with the Chinese Taoist notion of "forgetting both self and matter" as the ultimate goal of aesthetic contemplation. In particular, Zhu was drawn to the psychological theories of "aesthetic distance" represented by English psychologist Bullough, as well as Lipps's theory of *Einfühlung* or empathy. Trained as a psychologist, Zhu was well versed in Freudian psychoanalysis; indeed, he was among the first Chinese to study it systematically. Unimpressed by its central belief in an isolated individual psyche, and repelled by its parochialism, he was also one of the first Chinese to criticize Freudianism.

Although there is undeniably a modernist tendency in Zhu's aesthetic theory, his earliest work exhibited a fundamental ambivalence. On the one hand, he was attracted to Kantian-Crocian notions of the autonomy of the arts as distinct concepts of modernity. Committed to the task of "contending for an independent space for literature and arts," he also voiced criticism of the Confucian pragmatic and didactic tradition that used literature as a vehicle for conveying political and ideological messages.[20] Interestingly, Zhu was critical of the tendency of modern Chinese enlightenment intellectuals to perpetuate rather than undermine Confucian cultural determinism. On the other hand, he was troubled by the Western modernist separation of art from life and the valorization of the aesthetic. Zhu sought to complement what he took to be the Western modernist notion of the autonomy of art by emphasizing the "identity of self and matter" in aesthetic experience; to do so, he drew from Chinese classical Taoist aesthetics. "Identity" for Zhu was not simply a moment of Einfühlung in aesthetic contemplation, although he toyed with the correspondence between Lipp's theory and Taoist aesthetics. Rather, Zhu's invocation of identity signaled his ambivalence toward Western modernist aesthetics. In this regard, what he held to be incongruous was the modernist notion of disinterestedness, specifically in light of China's political reality, one devastated by violence and saturated with corruption.

Zhu insisted that his main disagreement with Croce was the latter's formalist propensity to totally separate aesthetic judgment from cognitive and moral political activities.[21] By focusing on identity in aesthetic judgment, Zhu demonstrated his uneasiness with the Western modernist aesthetics of the autonomy and separation of the arts and reality. After Zhu accepted Marxism in the 1950s, he modified and extended, rather than entirely abandoning, his earlier theory by substituting the dialectic notion of "unity" for the more static one of "identity." When measured against Adorno's celebrated concept of "nonidentity," Zhu's distance with Western modernism becomes apparent. Though Adorno's nonidentity cannot simply be equated with the modernist notion of aesthetic autonomy, his insistence on nonidentity as a central concept is closely linked to his modernist theory of aesthetic experience as a site of resistance to capitalist conceptual domination. Adorno's view is as much a critical response to, as a product of Western modernist movements. His nonidentity and Zhu's unity mark a major difference between the Frankfurt School and Chinese aesthetic Marxism, to which we shall return.

Contrary to the rather misleading essentialist language that he often used in his theoretical writing, Zhu's notion of identity is not a metaphysical category postulating an invariable "essence of beauty" where mind and matter are identified. Instead, the essence of beauty in Zhu's view was totally relational: "Beauty does not lie in the matter, nor in the mind; rather, it lies in the relationship between mind and matter. But unlike Kantian assumption and the common sense that conceives such a relationship in terms of matter as a stimulus and mind as reaction, it is the mind's expression of emotion through the image of the matter. . . . Beauty must be created by mind and soul."[22] Irrespective of its Crocian implications, Zhu's formulation of the aesthetic (or "beauty") touches on a crucial problematic: the subject-object relationship in aesthetic judgment. Even as he renounced his own "bourgeois idealism" in 1956, Zhu continued to argue that his relational concept of the aesthetic was "basically correct" because "to solve the question of the aesthetic, a unity of the subject and object must be achieved."[23] His defense of this position immediately elicited criticism, which charged that his attempt at a Marxist notion of "the unity of subject and object" was but a reassertion of his previous "subjective and idealist" stance derived from Kantian-Crocian idealism. To this, Zhu made a quick response, using notions acquired from Marx's *Economic and Philosophic Manuscripts of 1844* to further his new concept of the aesthetic. The exchanges between Zhu and other critics on the problem of the essence of beauty, which is in effect an issue of the subject-object relationship in the aesthetic experience, kindled a controversy that was to last for eight years. More important, this dispute evolved into a theoretical debate that somehow, ironically, fulfilled Zhu's earlier pre-Marxist wish to create an "independent cultural space," this time in a Marxist symbolic world.

From the outset, the debate was a testimony to the resilience and ambiguity of its topic: aesthetics. It not only effectively reopened a key subject of the May Fourth enlightenment cultural critique, but also generated a series of theoretical positions for an emergent aesthetic Marxism. Subtly, the debate continued and developed Hu Feng's view of a subjective fighting spirit. It also initiated in China for the first time discussions of Marx's *1844 Manuscripts*, which constitutes nothing less than a foundational text for much of Western Marxism as well as Chinese humanist Marxist thought that, in the beginning of the 1980s, stormed China's cultural scene with its powerful critique of "alienation" and "reification" in socialist society. Further, for aesthetic Marxists, the debate helped establish a positive and constructive vision of the future, especially Li Zehou's theory of aesthetic subjectivity as a major force in the cultural ferment of the 1980s. Li first surfaced when he criticized Zhu in the debate of the 1950s. It was, in fact, Li who brought the *1844 Manuscripts* to the attention of Chinese intellectuals during that formative debate.

Subjectivity, or the subject-object relationship, is of central importance to modern aesthetics, for it encapsulates the basic tension inherent in modernity. Since Marxism claims to have found the only viable solution to this tension, it becomes especially imperative for modern Marxists to reaffirm their positions on this subject-object relationship. In this regard, Chinese Marxists have been conspicuously incoherent and nonchalant. Early Marxist intellectuals of the May Fourth cultural enlightenment, like Li Dazhao and Chen Duxiu, held that their first obligation was to wage a social revolution that would reverse China's backwardness, thus bringing it in line with the evolution of history as a progressive telos.[24] Since the core concept of Marxist revolution—class struggle—requires a revolutionary agent—the working class—the earlier Chinese Marxists tended to posit a metasubjectivity or collective subject of revolution without differentiating the individual subject from the social collectivity. Nor did they bother to attend to the philosophical distinctions of subjectivity-objectivity, which involve an ensemble of epistemological and ontological questions of mind and matter, universality and particularity, structure and agency, and so forth.

Mao overdeveloped the Chinese Marxist orientation of class struggle at the expense of other Marxist categories, especially Marx's philosophical reflections on subjectivity. Mao's concept of class struggle identified the popular "masses" as the primary revolutionary force in lieu of the genuine proletariat that only existed, according to classic Marxist definition, within a capitalist mode of production. But Mao was no populist in a strictly political sense. Antielitist predisposition notwithstanding, Mao tended to default to Leninist vanguardism and centralized party politics when the question of an ultimate political authority was raised. In essence, he took it for granted that the CCP and its cadres formed the decisive revolutionary agent or subject. Still, Mao oscillated between a notion of

revolution that stressed "subjective initiative" and "self-conscious ability" (winning him the name of "voluntarist"), and an objectivist view that
held Marxism to be the universal, truthful "objective law."[25] Mao's philosophical essays, "On Contradiction" and "On Practice," tended to ontologize "contradiction" as the universal and objective law generating and
governing the totality of the world, from society to nature. Objectivity
therefore, becomes synonymous with the universal law of contradiction
in Mao's thought. The subjectivity of the revolutionary agent who must
initiate practice was curiously conflated with the a priori, objective truth
of contradiction.[26]

Objectivity was further codified into a pervasive ideological system legitimizing Mao's political rule after the founding of the People's Republic.
Mao's cultural bureaucrats made objectivity a socialist-realist aesthetic
principle, while denouncing subjectivity as a bourgeois and idealist concept. In spite of Mao's efforts to bring about democratic participation by
the masses, a hierarchy emerged in the cultural institutions and ideological state apparatuses that created crudely political exigencies, subordinat-
ing culture to politics. Mao not only remained oblivious to the conceptual
ambiguity of the relation between subjectivity and objectivity, he also ignored the intricacies of subject formation in revolutionary practice. That
is, despite his emphasis on thought-reform to foster revolutionary consciousness, Mao had little understanding of, and less interest in, the complex fabric of the individual psyche that enables an individual consciousness to negotiate with social determinations.

Hu Feng did venture deeply into the psychic realm, which he perceived
to be a crucial site of resistance. His formulation of a subjective fighting
spirit attempted to capture the relationship of subjective experience or
class consciousness, on the one side, to representation on the other. Specifically, in the late 1940s, he contended that to represent social reality and
revolution, a realism rooted in a subjective fighting spirit was necessary.
In the 1940s, Hu broached the issue of subjectivity in revolutionary practice and aesthetic representation. Renounced by Mao as a "bourgeois idealist" and "counterrevolutionary" in the 1950s, the thorny question Hu
raised still remains, especially in the field of aesthetics: who, after all, can
judge what is beautiful? If one ascribes to the reflection theory, which assumes that "objective reality" determines the "beautiful" and human
consciousness only reflects beauty in objective reality, the answer surely
squares well with the principle of "socialist realism" that fetishizes objectivity and disavows subjectivity. This was precisely the position taken by
many critics of Zhu in the Chinese debate. But the discussion never resolved the problem of *who* had the final authority for knowing the objective reality, let alone judging that most evasive and ambiguous thing
called beauty. Mao simply displaced the question by assuming an a priori

revolutionary metasubjectivity embodied by the party, with indisputable authority, because it alone understands objective, universal laws. Although arguably sufficient in a political sense, this tautology is nonsense insofar as literature and the arts are not the equivalent of objective reality. They are artifacts that must necessarily be created by a subject—a writer or artist—who can hardly be equated with a metasubject like the party. Hu's theory worked to unravel the constitutive aspect of subjectivity in both cultural and aesthetic realms, thereby pointing to a space different from political and economic sectors. Moreover, foregrounding the category of the subjective itself revealed the inherent paradox in Mao's simultaneous valorization of objectivity as a universal law and his insistence on the metasubjectivity of the Communist Party.

In the subsequent debates of the 1950s and 1960s, Zhu's formulation of the "unity of subjectivity and objectivity in aesthetic experience" sparked further interest in examining culture and aesthetics as independent and autonomous spheres, and had far-reaching philosophical and ideological ramifications. The notion problematized the Maoist hierarchy of objectivity and subjectivity, and threatened to unmask many other critical lacunae in the revolutionary hegemony. In addition, by identifying aesthetic subjectivity as the ultimate Marxist ideal, the Chinese debate reaffirmed the constructive dimension of Marxism in the cultural realm. Zhu formulated four theses on the unity of the subjective and objective. First, beauty is a false concept that perpetuates the mechanical materialist conflation of beauty with objective reality, and should therefore be redefined as the beautiful or an aesthetic experience, which signifies the subject-object dialectic. Next, because aesthetic experience is derived primarily from the creative and imaginary work of art and literature, the characteristics of art and literature should be central to aesthetic inquiry. In the third place, just as art and literature are ideological forms, aesthetic experience by its very nature is ideological. As an ideological form, aesthetic experience is subjective, but like ideology, it is determined objectively by social conditions. (This is a version of Zhu's earlier thesis of the unity of the subjective and objective.) Finally, the main task of aesthetic inquiry is "practice," through which the unity of the subjective and objective are potentially materialized.

By forcefully promoting aesthetic experience as the true aesthetic issue, Zhu underscored the problematic nature of subjectivity, and consequently, was accused of harboring a "remnant bourgeois idealism." The most prominent of his critics, Cai Yi and Li Zehou, engaged in extensive debates with him on the subject-object relationship. Cai (1906–1992), a veteran Marxist aesthetician who adhered to Lenin's reflection theory, insisted on the existence of beauty as an objective entity in the material, natural world, and on the concept of aesthetic experience as only a reflection or recognition of the "essence" of the "objective law of beauty." Cai defined this as the "law of typicality": what is beautiful is what is typical in nature. He never equivocated on the absolute primacy of objectivity in aesthetics, and continuously opposed Marx's *1844 Manuscripts* for its "residual bourgeois humanism and subjectivism." Of course, Cai found Zhu's theory objectionable in principle because, in his view, the assertion of aesthetic experience as such connoted "bourgeois subjective idealism."[27]

Li Zehou, then a fledgling young philosopher, criticized Zhu from a more complex perspective. Li was born in 1930 in Hunan (Mao's home province). From 1950 to 1954, he studied in Peking University's philosophy department, and in 1955, accepted a position at the Institute of Philosophy, Chinese Academy of Sciences. Li first distinguished himself in the aesthetic debate of 1956. His reputation rose rapidly after the Cultural Revolution with the publication of *Critique of Critical Philosophy: A Study of Kant* in 1979. In the 1980s, Li became a major figure in China's intellectual milieu, especially during the "Culture Fever" of the late 1980s. He enjoyed a fame among young Chinese intellectuals that resembled Sartre's in France. After the June 1989 Tian'anmen event, Li's works were banned by the Chinese government, and he was forced into exile in the United States, where he still lives today. Although Li remained moderate throughout the 1989 upheaval, the ideological authorities suspected his work of providing stimulus for the students, and marshaled ideological assaults against his "heretic" views.

In the debate of the 1950s, Li argued for the primacy of objectivity with no less passion than Cai, but his description of the objective was far more subtle. Briefly, Li's objectivity refers to social existence, which determines the objective nature of beauty. Li contended that because objectivity means the "sociality of beauty," Zhu was wrong to identify the social aspects of beauty as subjective. Furthermore, Li criticized Cai's metaphysical proposition attributing to beauty an essentialist "natural property" as simply collapsing the natural object with beauty, a social phenomenon. Li's view of "objective social existence" is primarily relational and structural: beauty as a social phenomenon must be objective, since social being is determined by structures of social relationships that lie beyond human consciousness and feelings, which is "physically intangible and imperceptible but objectively existent."[28] This para-structuralist position has certain parallels with Althusser's theory. Althusser regarded history as a structural totality, an absent, objective cause. This resembles Li's idea of social being as objective existence. It must be noted that there was no actual contact between Li and Althusser at the time that they reflected on these questions, although Althusser had a great interest in Chinese Marxist cultural theory—primarily through Mao's work. Althusser, on the other hand, became known in China only in the 1980s.

Zhu tirelessly defended his own view of aesthetic subjectivity. He defined subject and object as epistemological rather than ontological categories, and then critiqued the radical separation of the two in what he called "metaphysical thinking."

> In terms of knowledge of the external world, man is the "subject" and the external world the "object" [*keti/duixiang*]. From the subject's point of view it is "subjective," while from the object's point of view it is "objective." Hence, consciousness and general psychological phenomena are subjective, and the external world to which consciousness relates itself is objective. It is undeniable that there is an apparent opposition between the subjective and objective, but to see the two as absolutely opposed and separate is metaphysical thinking. . . . *The subjective also has an objective basis and objective effect.* On the other hand, is there any objectivity [*keguan*] that has nothing to do with subjectivity? Having nothing to do with subjectivity means having nothing to do with humankind, and even if one assumes that it exists, it is out of our concern here. *Insofar as it becomes an object* [*duixiang*] *of our discussion, it then turns into an object* [*duixiang*] *of our knowledge and practice.* And as such it must be the object [duixiang] of a subject. It is an oxymoron to say "object [duixiang] without subject" or "subject without object [duixiang]." One can say that knowledge means that objective existence determines subjective consciousness, and practice means that subjective consciousness affects objective existence. This is precisely what Marx means, as we analyzed before, by "objectification [*duixiang hua*] of man" or "humanization of nature," as the unity of the subjective [*zhuguan*] and objective [keguan].[29]

Philosophically, what is at issue is the conceptual ambiguity and polysemic indecisiveness both of the concepts and related terms of subject/object, subjectivity/objectivity, and subjective/objective. In Chinese, there are two words for object: keti and duixiang. As a noun, keti refers to the object as matter, the external world, nature, the opposite of mind and consciousness. It is a modern term for the philosophical concept of object. In classical Chinese philosophy, no equivalent term can be found, except the more specific notion of *wu* (matter, thing, material).[30] But the related adjective keguan (objective), as well as the noun *keguanxing* (objectivity), also refer to that which is general and universal, including specifically social totality. This was Li's meaning, one that was sharply criticized by Zhu for collapsing two different realms—society and nature—into one single concept. The other Chinese term for object, duixiang, refers to the object of a subject's knowledge, and therefore, is more epistemological and phenomenological than ontological. Zhu grappled strenuously with the slippage of the concepts in his argument, for he believed that the resolution to the aesthetic problematic lay in the subject-object relation.

Adorno, in a different context, tackled a similar set of ambiguities. In his seminal essay "Subject-Object," Adorno called attention to precisely that dialectic relationship between subject and object that cannot be resolved at one stroke by privileging one over the other. He regarded Western thought's separation of subject and object as "both real and illusory. True, because in the cognitive realm it serves to express the real separation, the dichotomy of the human condition, a coercive development. False, because the resulting separation must not be hypostatized, not magically transformed into an invariant."[31] This preoccupation with the dialectical tension between subject and object led to Adorno's critical principle of negative dialectics, or the "nonidentity" of subject and object. While insisting on "the preponderance of the object" irreducible to an active subjectivity, Adorno cautioned in *Negative Dialectics* that "it is not the purpose of critical thought to place the object on the orphaned royal throne once occupied by the subject. On that throne the object would be nothing but an idol. The purpose of critical thought is to abolish the hierarchy."[32] In "Subject-Object," Adorno contended that "since primacy of the object requires reflection of the subject and subjective reflection, subjectivity— as distinct from primitive materialism, which really does not permit dialectics—becomes a moment that lasts."[33]

It is in this same sense that Zhu talked about the "unity of the subjective and objective" in which the moment of subjectivity is ineradicable. Moreover, Zhu similarly wished "to abolish the hierarchy": "The error that [Chinese] aestheticians presently commit is to *absolutize the object while kicking out the subject at one stroke*." This error, he added, stems from "eradicating the unity of the opposites between the objective and subjective, for superstitiously fearing the subjective and absolutizing the objective. The redundant and scholastic reasoning, like a mouse jabbing inside an ox horn, is predestined to be metaphysical in its method. This is why aesthetics at present comes to a dead end. It is time to decide on a road for aesthetics."[34] Zhu's message is unmistakable and took courage to articulate it at that specific time, when the sheer mention of subjectivity would be not merely "politically incorrect" but dangerous. Set against Herbert Marcuse's more assertive statements, Zhu's words may appear rather unassuming, yet the sentiment is quite close:

> Even in its most distinguished representatives Marxist aesthetics has shared in the devaluation of subjectivity. . . . And in contrast to the rather dialectical formulations of Marx and Engels, the [base-

superstructure] conception has been made into a rigid schema, a schematization that has had devastating consequences for aesthetics. The schema implies a normative notion of the material base as the true reality and a political devaluation of nonmaterial forces particularly of the individual consciousness and their political function.[35]

While Marcuse maintained that "liberating subjectivity constitutes itself in the inner history of the individuals—their own history, which is not identical with their social existence,"[36] emphasizing the irreconcilable schism between the subject and object, Zhu envisioned greater links, or unity, between the two by way of practice.

Zhu's notion of unity should not be confused with identity. On the contrary, Zhu's proposition of the "unity of subject and object" was articulated against, albeit indirectly, the theory of "identity of thought and existence" then triumphant in the major controversy over the identity issue so prominent in China's philosophical circles, which occurred roughly at the same time as the aesthetic debate. In 1958, the philosopher Yang Xianzhen criticized the *Soviet Concise Dictionary of Philosophy*'s confusion of two kinds of identity as Marxist conceptions: the identity of thought and existence, and the identity of contradictions. Yang contended that the notion of identity of thought and existence was derived from Hegelian idealism, while the identity of contradictions was dialectical materialist. His view was rebuked by Ai Siqi, a veteran philosopher and close associate of Mao from the Yan'an period, who insisted that the concept of identity was materialist. The heated exchange between Yang and Ai developed into a major debate in the Chinese academy. In 1960, Mao felt it necessary to intervene, declaring that a rejection of the identity of thought and existence would inevitably lead to Kantian dualism. Accordingly, Yang was attacked as a "revisionist" and "right-wing opportunist." The philosophical dispute amounted to nothing less than an assessment of Mao's "Great Leap Forward" Campaign of the late 1950s, which ended up a scandalous fiasco. Behind the notion of identity of thought and existence, Yang saw a voluntaristic impulse that precipitated Mao's "grand revolutionary praxis." Although apparently defending Mao's concept of contradiction, which the Soviet *Dictionary* attacks, Yang in fact took the question of identity as an opportunity to criticize Maoism. Yang again came under assault in the mid-1960s, and later during the Cultural Revolution. Yang's other philosophical thesis, *he er wei yi* (two combines into one), an aphoristic way of saying "dialectical unity of the opposites," was labeled a "recipe for class conciliation," and denounced as anti-Maoist, for Mao's thesis was *yi fen wei er* (one divides into two), which served as a philosophical justification for permanent class struggle.[37]

Adorno, as mentioned earlier, relentlessly rejected the identity theory, but his rejection was occasioned by the historical conditions of modern capitalism. The sociohistorical underpinning of the identity theory may be the exchange value in capitalist society, which generates the facile sameness or identity of radically different things. As Fredric Jameson argues, Adorno's notion of nonidentity must be understood in connection with the form of the economy: nonidentity as a refutation of money as an exchange value that erases critical differences in social relations.[38] By the same token, the Chinese debates, especially Yang's notion of nonidentity, were politically motivated. In a 1960 response to Cai's criticism, Zhu maintained that the philosophical debate over identity of thought and existence "touched on the fundamental philosophical problem. Once this problem is solved, then the difference between metaphysical and dialectical modes of thinking becomes clear. In the meantime, it will solve the subquestion of whether beauty stems from the unity of subject and object under the general question [of the identity of thought and existence]."[39]

Although Zhu's notion of unity may give the impression of being aligned with the identity theory, in fact, the crucial difference between the unity of subject and object and the identity of thought and existence lies in the latter's cancellation of the difference between thought and existence, and the former's insistence on the indispensable *difference* between subject and object in aesthetic experience. Hence, Zhu was prescient in his unremitting refusal to absolutize and essentialize beauty as objective existence, and his tireless assertion of the *relational* nature of beauty and the beautiful. On the other hand, Zhu's position comes closer to Yang's notion of "two combines into one," in the sense that the unity of subject and object posits a conciliatory and creative resolution of differences and oppositions through aesthetic mediation and negotiation of tensions and contradictions. Such a concern for mediation, rather than confrontation, indeed underlaid Yang's thesis, formulated during the apex of Maoist praxis of "class struggle." Yang's notion appeared more abstract than Zhu's, for the appeal of the latter's aesthetic mediation and reconciliation of conflicts lies precisely in its sensuous concreteness and particularity. But ironically, the concreteness of sensuousness and the emotional efficacy of the aesthetic can also be used for the opposite purposes of inciting struggles and confrontations, as shown, indeed, by the intense aestheticization of politics during Mao's reign. It boiled down to the issue of aesthetic representation as a political and ideological practice; but what exactly constitutes the structural relationship between aesthetics and practice?

Practice as a Trope of Cultural Reconstruction

The question of practice emerged in the heated arguments about subject-object relation. Following the *1844 Manuscripts*, Chinese Marxists generally considered practice a key link that mediated the subject and object. Most telling, in this respect, is Li's shift of positions from an earlier insistence on objectivity to his later passionate plea for a construction of aesthetic subjectivity. The notion that "aesthetic subjectivity" constituted a redefinition of the intellectual self as well as the deployment of an autonomous and self-determining subject was formulated in response to the profound intellectual crisis that followed the Cultural Revolution; yet this shift was not really an abrupt break with Li's earlier stance. The foundational position of practice featured prominently in Li's work from the beginning. The young Li, though an ardent advocate of objectivity, was never committed to an essentialist view like Cai's. Instead, his parastructuralist notion of objective social existence understood subjectivity as indispensable social agency. Like Gramsci, who argued that objectivity always means "humanly objective," or "universally subjective,"[40] Li's shift of positions on subjectivity is grounded in historical considerations. In his 1956 essay "On Aesthetic Experience, Beauty, and the Arts," Li introduced the *1844 Manuscripts* to Chinese intellectuals, arguing that it was a crucial work in Marxist cultural and aesthetic theory.

The *Manuscripts* contained Marx's main concepts of history and the future of communism. Since its publication in 1933, it has had a fundamental impact on modern Marxism. The controversies around the *Manuscripts* in the West marked the major difference between a "humanist" and "nonhumanist" Marxism. For humanist Marxism, the representatives include Lukács, the Frankfurt School philosophers, and Sartre, among others. Althusser, in contrast, is considered to have championed the nonhumanist or "antihumanist" trend in modern Marxism. Western Marxists, with perhaps the exception of Althusser, hailed the *Manuscripts* as a major monument of Marxism. But in the Stalinist Soviet Union, it had always been treated as a premature work of the young Marx with a residual bourgeois humanism (an opinion shared by Althusser, but for different purposes). Following the Soviet view, Chinese Marxist scholars had paid scant attention to this work, even though the first Chinese translation came out as early as 1940.[41]

Mao had said nothing about the *Manuscripts*, but the general negative view of the CCP's ideological apparatuses was articulated by Zhou Yang in 1963, then the minister of the CCP's propaganda department. Zhou identified Western humanist Marxist reappropriation of the notion of "alienation" in the *Manuscripts* as "revisionist," observing that they "counterpose the young Marx to the mature, proletarian, and revolutionary Marx. In particular they make use of certain views on 'alienation' expressed by Marx in his early *Economic and Philosophic Manuscripts of 1844* to depict him as an exponent of the bourgeois theory of human nature. . . . The humanism advocated by the modern revisionists is intimately tied up with the contemporary humanism of the reactionary bourgeoisie of the West."[42] In his 1956 essay, however, Li did not echo the Western humanist reclaim of alienation. Instead, he focused on young Marx's idea of a "humanized nature," and made this notion the foundation of his Chinese Marxist aesthetics. This link between subjectivity and practice makes possible a constructive view of culture and society, which though itself a utopian vision, is nevertheless quite distinct from Maoist radical revolutionary utopianism.

Li's utopianism is similar in some pertinent ways to that of the Frankfurt School. Adorno inscribed a utopian hope in a certain subjective experience that he essentially defined in aesthetic terms: "Approaching knowledge of the object is the act in which the subject rends the veil it is weaving around the object. It can do this only where, fearlessly passive, it entrusts itself to its own experience. . . . The subject is the object's agent, not its constituent; this fact has consequences for the relation of theory and practice."[43] While implying that the individual subjective experience can resist the domination of rationalist discourse by sensuous receptivity, Adorno was never certain about how "the relation of theory and practice" could be affected by an experience that remains "fearlessly passive." As Martin Jay reminds us, Adorno's aesthetic experience "is hardly a formula for political activism."[44] Adorno, of course, was not at all optimistic in his projection of a utopia, for the profound pessimism encapsulated in his axiomatic phrase, "To write poetry after Auschwitz is barbaric," seriously contorts his vision. But despite his stubborn refusal to flesh out a utopian alternative to present-day society, Adorno offered a glimpse in his moment of "peace": "In its proper place, even epistemologically, the relationship of subject and object would lie in the realization of peace among men as well as between men and their Other. Peace is the state of distinctness without domination with the distinct participating in each other."[45] Although "distinctness without domination" lies at the heart of Adorno's utopia, utopia as such can hardly be materialized in the real world, at least in Adorno's view.

Like most Western Marxists, Adorno was preoccupied with the issues of alienation and reification. He feared more than anything the domination of subject over object, or vice versa, and accordingly, opposed any attempt to suppress heterogeneity in the name of identity. His hostility toward the privileging of production in "vulgar Marxism" has to be seen in conjunction with his efforts to resist the subject's domination over nature, and restore irreducible differences and heterogeneity in the material world. Admittedly, Adorno's celebrated posture of perpetually playing off difference against identity makes him eminently amenable to poststructuralist thinking generally and deconstructionism in particular. While the trenchant critique of Western culture and capitalist domination that Adorno and poststructuralists have mounted is certainly valuable, how plausible is the possibility of utopian peace in the real world after the deconstruction of all values, by theory at least, if not by physical force? Nor is Marcuse's assertion of art as a radical revolutionary praxis any more viable. Marcuse's affirmation of aesthetic remembrance as the revolutionary agent simply recasts Adorno's concern that "all reification is a forgetting" in a Hegelian foreclosure, taking remembrance as the reinternalization or retrieval of a lost subjectivity vis-à-vis an externalized objective world. In other words, Marcuse is reluctant to go beyond the subjective realm and ground artistic creativity in material practice.

In this regard, Li's critique of the Frankfurt School's "idealist" notion of praxis is well taken. The Frankfurt School philosophers' tenacious refusal to grant material practice any constructive or positive status in critical theory, as well as their persistent denigration of "productivist" vulgar Marxism, is in sharp contrast to Chinese Marxism. Chinese views of practice and practical subjectivity, on the other hand, are imbued with an optimism about the projected future of a humanized nature. Chinese Marxist thinking claims that material and creative practices enable human beings both to objectify their essential powers—to fully realize their potential—and humanize the natural world, signifying the unity of subject (humankind) and object (nature).

Chinese aesthetic Marxism's reinvention of practice does not start from Mao's famous notion of practice integrating theory with action. Ideologically, Mao's view has been influential, particularly his emphasis on the integration of Marxist theory and Chinese practice, which has functioned as a principal means of legitimation for the sinification of Marxism. Thanks to the very ambiguity of Mao's usage, practice also became a powerful weapon for the pragmatic leaders of post-Mao China when they turned to debunking Maoist doctrines in 1978 under the slogan "practice as the sole criterion for evaluating truth." There is plenty of room for the argument forwarded more recently that Mao's view lacks theoretical coherence in light of the Western Marxist notion of praxis.[46] But aesthetic Marxists like Li find that Mao's notion of practice leans too far in the direction of the voluntarist and idealist views of praxis that characterize Western Marxism. In the context of post-Mao rethinking, Li has sharply criticized both Maoist radicalism, responsible for the catastrophes of the Great Leap Forward and Cultural Revolution, and a Western Marxism that privileges cultural praxis over material production or practice.

Even in the debates of the 1950s and 1960s, Zhu and Li remained adamant that praxis and practice were different entities, and that the latter was the historical materialist core notion on which Marxist aesthetics could be erected. In Zhu's argument, Marxist aesthetics can be extrapolated from the first of Marx's 1845 "Theses on Feuerbach." Marx, Zhu contended, regarded practice as the link, or unity, between subjective activity and objective reality, in the sense that "the thing, reality, sensuousness" must be understood as "human sensuous activity, practice."[47] Critical to aesthetic theory, practice should be grasped as "human sensuous activity," for aesthetic experience must be defined as the concrete, sensuous experience of human beings. But Zhu was not content with the obvious connection between aesthetics and sensuousness. Practice as the cornerstone of Marxist aesthetics was explicit in the *1844 Manuscripts*, where Marx made one of his few remarks on the "laws of beauty":

> In creating an *objective world* by his practical activity, in *working-up* inorganic nature, man [*sic*] proves himself a conscious species being, i.e. as a being that treats the species as its own essential being, or that treats itself as a species being. Admittedly animals also produce. . . . It produces one-sidedly, whilst man produces universally. It produces only under the dominion of immediate physical need, whilst man produces even when he is free from physical need and only truly produces in freedom therefrom. An animal produces only itself, whilst man reproduces the whole of nature. . . . An animal forms things in accordance with the standard and the need of the species to which it belongs, whilst man knows how to produce in accordance with the standard of every species, and knows how to apply everywhere the inherent standard to the object. Man therefore also forms things in accordance with the laws of beauty.[48]

Zhu believed that the two theses—namely, "man produces universally" and "man . . . forms things in accordance with the laws of beauty"—are indissolubly one. This is not simply because the laws of beauty imply a creative labor, or objective material practice, that produces in freedom and in universal terms. Indeed, the Schillerian overtone of freedom and universality in Marx's passage was accentuated by the Chinese aesthetic Marxists in the 1980s, especially Li; but in the 1950s and 1960s, the emphasis was rather on a material practice that humanizes nature. Marx stated that "for not only the five senses but also the so-called spiritual senses, the practical senses (will, love, etc.), in a word, *human* sense—the humanity of the senses—comes into being by virtue of its object, by virtue of *humanized* nature."[49] In his 1960 essay on Marxist practical aesthetics, Zhu detected in the concept of a humanized nature a vital connection between artistic creativity and material labor:

> No matter whether it is creativity of labor or artistic creativity, there is only one principle: "humanized nature" or the "objectified essen-

tial powers of man." There is also only one fundamental experience: one experiences joy and pleasure when one sees the object as one's own "work," which embodies one's essence as a social being, or one's "essential powers." . . . *Productive labor is humanity's grasp of the world in practical spirits, and it is thus humanity's grasp of the world in artistic ways.*"[50]

Zhu saw aesthetic and material production as mutually dependent. The elimination of "alienated labor" enables an aesthetic state of playful and joyful productive labor. Zhu, therefore, considered Marx's concept of alienation essential to aesthetics, for it "not only unmasks the reasons of the decaying tendency of the bourgeois culture but also points to the great prospect of the general culture in communist society after alienation of labor is abolished."[51] Zhu's notion of aesthetic practice seems to be reaffirmed by Terry Eagleton's interpretation of Marx's aesthetics as a materialist rethinking of the body: to the extent that the humanized *senses* of the body as naturally given constitute the paramount aesthetic experience, the material practice of labor is aesthetic in terms of somatic pleasure or bodily experience.[52] But Zhu's concern was not so much with bodily and sensuous experiences as with cultural and aesthetic work itself. His conception of cultural and aesthetic work as part of a Marxian notion of practice can be construed as a trope for cultural construction, which as a distinct kind of practice of artists, must be valued in the same way as the material practices of workers and peasants. Unlike Mao, whose notion of practice primarily consisted of class struggle and revolution, Zhu's was essentially constructive. In this respect, he remained consistent with his conviction to create an independent cultural space. He tried to theorize how to create and construct a new aesthetic experience and sensibility that would be at one with the practices of unalienated material production in a socialist society. It marked a substantial departure from Zhu's earlier position, which took aesthetic experience as disinterested contemplation.

On this score, however, Zhu has been severely criticized by Li in particular. Li argues that there are two distinct categories of practice—material and spiritual—that cannot be confused, and humanized nature does not simply mean human senses; it refers, first and foremost, to the objective material world as the precondition of the human existence.[53] Li tirelessly insisted on the fundamental distinction between and precedence of objective, material practice over intellectual and artistic ones:

When I talk about "humanized nature," I am referring to the productive labor of making and using tools or the concrete material activity that changes the objective world. I think this is the real origin of beauty. . . . It is not the individuals "essential powers" of feelings, consciousness, thoughts, wills, etc., that create beauty; on the contrary, it is the essential powers of the *sociohistorical* practice of the *totality of humankind* that create beauty.[54]

From this basic definition of practice as concrete material activity, Li elaborates on his constructive philosophy, claiming that in order to transcend the idealist enclave, the primacy of material production must be preserved as the absolute precondition of the aesthetic state, or humanized nature. In other words, to humanize nature means to change the objective material world through material practice, or the development of productive forces. Or, as Marx stated in the *Grundrisse*, this entails "the highest development of the forces of production, hence also the richest development of individuals."[55] Marx's productivist and anthropomorphic views have been rejected by many Western Marxists in the face of the troubled relationship between human beings and the ecological environment consequent on modernization. But for Li, the distinction has to be made between a productivist notion or economic determinism and material practice itself. For Western Marxists, in contrast, alienation and reification constitute the central categories in their *critique* of capitalism. The antagonistic aspects of the relation between human beings and nature are perceived as part of capitalist alienation. Freud's notion of the irreconcilable hiatus between cultural constraints and natural instincts adds another dimension to the antagonism between humankind and nature.

These differing positions confirm that even such widely accepted wisdom in the West is also historically conditioned and partial; it cannot exhaust all other alternatives, either conceptual or real. Insofar as Marx's notion of a humanized nature is eschewed by Western Marxism for its outmoded productivist tendency, a constructive view of practice as a utopian vision is unlikely to emerge. Terry Eagleton, for example, concedes that Marxism remains "the single most creative aspect of the aesthetic tradition," and yet, he cautions against the "premature aestheticization" of aesthetic experience that Marx's "romantic humanist" views may entail, and against "premature utopianism," which is either "desirable but unfeasible" or "inevitable but not necessarily desirable."[56] Eagleton's concern, however, arises out of a specific understanding of "material practice" in Marx's aesthetic view that somehow constricts its rich meaning to the body and senses as a material realm. Mostly preoccupied with the problems of representation and communication, Eagleton offers only a hazy identification of Marx's economic categories with the aesthetic ones. If, as in Eagleton's theorization, aesthetic experience and utopianism remain locked within the conceptual and/or sensuous realms of culture, a positive utopianism that does not risk being self-complacently illusory is hardly possible. Moreover, Eagleton's remark that "many of Marx's most vital economic categories are implicitly aesthetic" seems to conflate Marx's conceptualization of the economic with the economic itself.[57]

But it should be added that Li's emphasis on material practice as the precondition of aesthetic fulfillment is not simply productivist. His somewhat crude early positions developed and expanded over the years into a psychologically oriented theory of aesthetic subjectivity. In one of his major philosophical works, *Critique of the Critical Philosophy: A Study of Kant*, which tries to connect historical materialist categories and Kant's reflections on human rationality and subjectivity, Li expatiates on his "aesthetics of practical subjectivity":

> Marx's "humanized nature" . . . means productive labor as the fundamental social practice of mankind [*sic*]. . . . Man becomes the master of nature . . . through active social practice that unifies the oppositions of man and nature concretely and historically. Only then, the real unity of contradictions, between man and nature, truth and virtue, sensuousness and rationality, laws and purposes, necessity and freedom, becomes possible. . . . Rationality can thus become sedimented or congealed into sensuousness, form into content, and the form of nature then becomes the form of freedom—which is also beauty.[58]

Drawing on Kant and Jean Piaget, Li here conceives of a grand historical process of material practice that transforms humanity from its natural form to a "form of freedom," an internalized or sedimented rationality embodied by a creative subjectivity. How exactly the material practice of productive labor transforms humans into beings fully developed both in sensuousness and rationality is never clearly described, and the overemphasis on rationality inherent in Li's theory is certainly problematic. Yet what emerges from Li's theory are the contours of a constructive utopianism of freedom and beauty that lies not in nonmaterial forms of thought but concrete material practice. That is, Li envisions a positive and constructive alternative "post-Marxism," distinct from the various negative and pessimistic post-Marxisms and Western Marxism. Because Marxism—from Marx and Engels, through Lenin, Trotsky, and Mao, all the way to Lukács and Gramsci—has always been a "theory of revolution and a theory of critique," Li asserts an urgent need to "creatively transform Marxism from a critical philosophy and revolutionary theory to a *constructive* philosophy. It is precisely for such a reason that my philosophy has nothing to do with the entire Marxist theory of class struggle and proletarian dictatorship, and that mine is a 'Post-Marxism.'"[59]

Li's insistence on the primacy of material production as practice also contradicts his overall vision of aesthetic subjectivity, which takes culture, rather than material production or economic development, as its central site of reconstruction. The aesthetic also serves cognitive and heuristic functions in Li's project of reforming education and psychology. In this respect, his ambitious project coincides with Zhu's. But their differences are quite revealing, too. Li was primarily concerned about the Cultural Revolution's impediment to economic development. In the 1980s, Li criticized Mao's "idealist tendency" by privileging dialectical materialism over historical materialism. Yet in the 1950s and 1960s, when he might well have sensed the danger of excessive stress on cultural revolution at the expense of economic development, he could only express his disagreement obliquely by critiquing idealist tendencies in other scholars, such as Zhu. Zhu, on the other hand, envisioned the need for an independent and autonomous cultural space as the most pressing issue. Both Li and Zhu grasped the contradictions in Mao's revolutionary hegemony, but from different angles. Both the neglect of economic development and the politicization of culture and aesthetics were equally serious problems that undermined the project of China's alternative modernity. In hindsight, the questions raised in the aesthetic debates during the 1950s and 1960s were, in one way or another, tied to the increasingly intense and frequent ideological and political campaigns in the areas of culture and aesthetics. The relationship between aesthetics and ideology, then, became a compelling issue in the debates.

Reflections on Aesthetics and Ideology

The debates over ideology and aesthetics should be understood both as a criticism of ideology, and as an endeavor to productively examine the tangled relationship between ideology and aesthetics. The interrogation of ideology in the debates challenged and problematized the official concept, and the difficulties encountered by aesthetic Marxists in their attempts to constitute an original ideological critique are themselves quite revealing.

The project of Chinese aesthetic Marxists parallels Althusser's undertaking of roughly the same period. There is, of course, a remarkable irony in Althusser's Chinese connection. Althusser was more than an admirer of Mao and the Chinese Cultural Revolution, like many French radicals of the 1960s. As previously discussed, his theoretical work bears significant imprints of Mao, especially his central concepts of "contradiction and overdetermination" and "structural causality." Althusser's interests in Chinese Marxism might have influenced Michel Foucault, his student, whose notion of the discursive formations and relationship between power and knowledge are traceable in Mao's view of cultural revolution.[60] But Althusser's work has been viewed in China quite unfavorably, by both the orthodox Marxists who categorically relegate Western Marxism to the ranks of bourgeois social democrats, and the liberal intellectuals who condemn Althusser's sympathies for Maoist radicalism. During the humanist Marxist protests against "alienation under socialism" in the 1980s, however, Althusser's antihumanist Marxist position was smuggled in by Hu Qiaomu, a member of and official spokesperson for the CCP's politburo, who reproached the humanist "distortions" of Marxism by referring to the earlier "unscientific" Marx of the *1844 Manuscripts*. These complex conceptual transmigrations reaffirm the sociohistorical determinations of thought, an empirical fact often obscured by voracious impulses for theoretical sophistication and the poststructuralist obsession with language. These kinds of border crossings are especially relevant to the inquiries of ideology in which Althusser and Chinese aesthetic Marxists were engaged under similar historical conditions.

This historical conjuncture, specifically, was the crisis of socialist ideology prompted by the process of de-Stalinization in the Soviet Union. Althusser was devoted to the search for productive answers to the questions raised by the denunciation of Stalinism at the Twentieth Congress of the Soviet Communist Party in 1956. Toward that end, as Valentino Gerratana has written, Althusser felt it "necessary to draw up a Marxist balance sheet of Marxism itself—of its far-from-linear history and its largely unexplored potential for further development. The main stress was on the philosophical aspects of the undertaking."[61] One major contribution was Althusser's celebrated notion of ideology as a representation of the imaginary relationship of individuals to real conditions. Althusser's objective was to differentiate ideology from science, "in order to dare to be the beginning of a scientific (i.e. subject-less) discourse on ideology."[62] Clearly, Althusser wanted to defend Marxism as a true science vis-à-vis ideology and "Ideological State Apparatuses" (ISA). Yet his tenacious distinction of the "ideological" and "scientific" Marx, as a result of the so-called "epistemological break," was not Althusser's most valuable contribution; rather, it was his original analysis of the workings of ideology. The Chinese, such as Zhu, also intended to revive a true Marxist notion of ideology and art, not so much against anti-Marxist, bourgeois humanist distortions as against "mechanical materialism" or "metaphysical thinking," coded terms for Mao's ideological orthodoxy. Nonetheless, it would be misleading to say that the opposition of Chinese aesthetic Marxists to Mao's ideological state apparatuses was an act of political dissent. Instead, Chinese aesthetic Marxists wanted to constitute a constructive cultural space as compared with Mao's destructive idea of class struggle.

Zhu began his discussion of ideology by saying that "the distortions of Marxism have created great obstacles to the aesthetic path."[63] These "distortions," he suggested, are caused by one of the sacrosanct tenets of the orthodoxy: Lenin's reflection theory. Lenin, of course, could not be criticized explicitly, but the misappropriations of his view could and were: "The aesthetic inquiries in China," Zhu wrote, "invariably apply Lenin's reflection theory simplistically and uncritically, based on his 'Materialism and Empiriocriticism' as the sole classic text."[64] To say that our consciousness mirrors objective reality is a correct materialist statement, Zhu observed, yet only to a certain extent: insofar as "red" is a sensation caused by the material property of things as objective existence, it is accurate to say that our senses reflect reality; when we say art is a reflection of reality, however, that is an altogether different matter. Art manifests reality in much more intricate ways than mere sensory and scientific reflection, for art is historically and socially conditioned, whereas sensory and scientific reflections are not. Art is a refraction of reality as ideology. To bolster his argument, Zhu quoted a famous passage from Marx and Engels's *The German Ideology*: "If in all ideology men and their circumstances appear upside down as in *camera obscura*, this phenomenon arises just as much from their life-process as the inversion of objects on the retina does from their physical life-process."[65] Zhu's emphasis is on ideology as a relatively autonomous realm with particular sociohistorical determinations:

Ideology does not simply reflect the [economic] base of the same historical period, for superstructure may lag behind base. That is to say, ideology at a given historical period contains both new and old strata, the new reflecting the contemporary base, and the old, the residual influence of the previous one or more historical periods. This simple fact has much to do with many critical issues in literature and the arts, including traditional form, traditional ideas, the continuity of and opposition to tradition, the limits and immanent contradictions of authors, etc. Finally, as a superstructure of the same base, one ideology can influence another ideology. For example, literature and the arts can reflect legal, political, religious, and philosophic views of the time.[66]

Anticipating Raymond Williams's distinctions of the cultural "dominant," "residual," and "emergent" in complex ideological formations, Zhu unremittingly insisted on the necessary differentiations and correlations between ideology, superstructure, and economic base.[67] In his 1979 preface to *A History of Western Aesthetics*, Zhu revised his earlier position on ideology by underscoring its relative independent and autonomous position in relation to the general superstructure. He contended that such a view can be found in Marx's well-known formulation of base and super-structure: "The sum total of these relations of production constitutes the economic structures of society, the real foundation, on which rises a legal and political superstructure and to which correspond definite forms of social consciousness."[68] The relationship between "legal and political super-structure" and ideology ("social consciousness") is, in Marx's definition, parallel rather than hierarchical. In other words, ideology neither merely belongs to, nor is subjugated to, the superstructure. Zhu asserted that the distinction between ideology and superstructure sustains a Marxist notion of the social division of labor: "The ideology of each different realm has its distinct historical continuity and relative autonomy in the historical process."[69] Moreover, Zhu saw the concepts of superstructure and base as relational and metaphoric: "'Superstructure' is relative to 'economic structure' or the 'real foundation,' and these terms are all metaphors. The gist of it lies not so much in terminology as in three essentially different driving forces of history. These are: 1) economic structure or real foundation; 2) legal and political superstructure; and 3) ideology in a broad sense as a system of ideas and values."[70] Analogous to Althusser, Zhu substituted the doctrine of linear historical causality or determinism with a notion of multilinearity or overdetermination.

The Chinese reinvention of the Marxian notion of ideology clearly evidences what Pierre Bourdieu calls the struggle for "symbolic capital" or battle against "symbolic violence."[71] If ideology is a heavily contested battlefield of symbolic warfare, then the debate about ideology itself strikes at the very heart of the contention. The significance of Zhu's advocacy of the relative autonomy of ideology from "legal and political superstructure" must be seen in this light: when everything is politicized by the absolute authority of the party or monologic ISA, the relative autonomy of culture is no small symbolic capital to gain.

Aesthetic reflection is ideological rather than scientific not only because of its historical and social determinations, but also due to the constitutive role played by subjectivity in the formation of ideology and aesthetic experience. Zhu's notion that subjectivity was ineradicable in aesthetic experience, contrary to Althusser's theory of subjectivity through interpellation, argued that ideology requires the active force of subjectivity in its formation. The workings of ideology are "extremely complicated," Zhu wrote, and the process of ideological formation is "often unconscious. The ideological totality of an individual's lived experience and cultural upbringing, his world view, his view of life, and his class consciousness, etc., is imbued with emotional colors. . . . Ideology and lived experience are inseparable to the extent that ideology works through an individual's lived experience." Because "ideology is an emotional, affective system of thought which determines the individual's attitudes toward things and his ideals about life and art," aesthetic experience is ideology par excellence.[72] Althusser likewise emphasized the emotional, affective, and unconscious aspects of ideology, and as Terry Eagleton points out, if ideological statements by Althusserian definition are both subjective and universally valid, ideology has a certain affinity with the Kantian notion of aesthetics.[73] In this respect, the similarity between Zhu and Althusser's concepts is obvious. Still, they differ markedly on the question of subjectivity. If Althusser's view of subjectivity and ideology smacks of a certain "political pessimism," as Eagleton observes, Zhu's more optimistic stance cannot be simply interpreted as an expression of radical idealist utopianism.[74] (Although, indeed, Zhu clearly espoused a Marxist utopianism, as shown in frequent statements such as "the aim of aesthetic cognition is not the disclosure of objective truth but the discovery of ideals of life.")[75]

Ironically, Zhu and his Chinese colleagues may be more justified than Althusser in asserting the repressiveness of the political mechanism of interpellated subjectivity under Mao's rule. Their recognition of the constructive possibilities inherent in material practice, however, have directed them away from remaining locked into the issues of consciousness and ideas. In fact, Zhu has been repeatedly criticized by Li and others for his lingering idealism, which resulted in his ambiguity about material practice. Li views material practice, first and foremost, as the productive labor of making and using tools in changing the material reality—that is, economic activity as the "real foundation" for change in a historical materialist sense.

Yet Li himself is far from consistent on this issue. His concept of the objectivity of social existence is, as we have seen, para-structuralist. Li's view of ideology also indicates this structuralist propensity. He regards ideology as some Janus-faced thing, subjective insofar as ideology is a social consciousness reflecting the objective economic base; and as a given fact in the social reality partaking of that very process of social formation, it is part of the objective, material social existence. Li underscores the materiality of ideology, but by materiality he does not mean language or the process of signification. It is worth noting that Li maintains a strong aversion to the language-centered modern Western philosophy and aesthetics. Certain Western Marxists or post-Marxists identify language as the material form and substance of ideology, drawing on structuralist and poststructuralist notions. Yet in Li's theory, it is unclear what constitutes the mediating link between the material practice of productive labor and cultural formations, because he leaves no room for language and sign making in his notion of practice.

A difficulty arises, then, concerning the problem of representation. Zhu had already broached the issue of mediation and signification in the 1960s, proposing a distinction between "thing" (thing A) and the "image of thing" (thing B) in aesthetic experience. Thing A is a natural object unrelated to human beings, whereas thing B is a socially and ideologically determined and mediated human perception. Zhu drew on Henri Lefebvre's differentiation of *l'object presenté* and *l'object present*, maintaining that former refers to thing A and the latter to thing B.[76] Between the late 1970s and early 1980s, the heated debate about "imaginary thinking" or "imagination" became a major event within literary and art criticism circles. The debate was essentially concerned with the issue of representation: the Chinese phrase *xingxiang siwei*, literally meaning imaginary thinking or "thinking in images," concisely summarized the search for new forms of representation that would free literature and the arts from the straitjacket of nonimaginative, formulaic "socialist realism." Zhu, then already more than eighty years old, was most energetic in the debate, promoting imaginary thinking.[77]

Representation was also a major issue in the humanist Marxist protests against "alienation under socialism." It was brought to bear on the phenomenon of ideological alienation, referring to the Maoist hegemony that had turned a revolutionary theory into a quasi-religious dogma. Wang Ruoshui, an outspoken critic of socialist alienation, accused the Maoist ISA of manipulating representation to encourage Mao's personality cult:

> Marx in his work *The Eighteenth Brumaire* analyzed the small farmers. . . . inability to form a "national bond." As a result, "they cannot represent themselves, they must be represented. Their representative must . . . appear as their master, as an authority over them, as an unlimited governmental power that protects them against the other class and sends them rain and sunshine from above." This kind of socio-economic condition nurtures monarchical thinking and produces the personality cult.[78]

The humanist Marxist upheavals of the early 1980s, reproved and crushed by the CCP as "bourgeois spiritual pollution," brought the crisis of Maoist ideological representation into sharp relief. From the debate over imaginary thinking in literature and the arts to the protests against alienation under socialism, the issue of representation became crucial in China's cultural politics. Bill Brugger and David Kelly have observed the complicity of the discursive formation of "socialist alienation" with the radicalist discourse of the Red Guards during the Cultural Revolution.[79] The problem of representation reemerged as a central issue in the Cultural Reflection of the late 1980s, only to be registered in the other side of the problematic: representation was then less about installing new voices than finding an audience not only responsive to, but also constitutive of, its new forms. Ironically, the focus of Mao's 1942 *Talks*—the question of audience—resurfaced in the postrevolutionary China of the 1980s. For Mao, the primary audience of cultural and aesthetic production was the peasant population, as noted earlier. Toward the agents or subjects of cultural production—that is, urban intellectuals—Mao's strategy was a thought-reform that subjected them to ceaseless self-condemnation and moral cleansing. But the undeniable fact was that, however ruthlessly and constantly Mao's purgatory campaigns of thought-reform or intellectual bashing were waged, the tensions and contradictions between the CCP cadres and urban intellectuals remained unresolved during Mao's reign, and were exacerbated during the Cultural Revolution.

The question of ideological legitimacy in the post-Mao era had much to do with Mao's failure to garner the crucial support of urban intellectuals as one of the essential forces of the Chinese Revolution. After Mao's death, urban intellectuals felt deeply disillusioned with his ideology. Consequently, China plunged into a profound "spiritual and intellectual crisis" that threatened to wreak havoc on the very hegemonic foundation of the nation. Such a claim of the significance of urban intellectuals is no exaggeration. They played a central role in the Chinese Revolution, and up until the mid-1980s, there were no new social formations that could exert a strong influence on social life. Urban intellectuals, as the only social group with direct access to and involvement with cultural and ideological institutions, had therefore to bear the excessive burden of political, ideological, and social representation. The peculiar status of Chinese intellectuals shifted only in the 1990s, when economic development radically altered the social formations and shattered the old social structure under Mao's reign. Under the current circumstances of a developing free market economy and the suppression of any ideological discussions, urban intellectuals have gradually become marginalized. Their much-weakened position by no means signals a satisfactory solution to political and ideological representation. To the contrary, representation has now become a site of intense contention, potentially explosive. The present-day CCP has virtually no hegemonic discourse and ideology to legitimize its policy of fully embracing the capitalist economic world system, while maintaining its political role under a Maoist system. Although urban intellectuals have by and large been successfully displaced from the political and ideological center, it is now the disenchanted working class, especially the millions and millions of unemployed workers recently laid off from former state-owned enterprises, that have become increasingly impatient with the current ways of political and ideological representation.

Yet in the 1980s, the burning issue was how to win over the deeply resentful and disenfranchised urban intellectuals. In this regard, Chinese aesthetic Marxists, Li's theoretical formulations in particular, proved to be immensely successful. Li's aesthetics of practical subjectivity had captured the imagination of thousands of young Chinese scholars. That his abstract philosophical monograph on Kant sold nearly 100,000 copies, inducing a "Kant Fever" of no small scale among China's intelligentsia in the 1980s, cannot be explained as merely a result of an interest in "theory."[80] It is no coincidence that the Chinese aesthetic Marxists, Li especially, were prominent in this intellectual movement that signaled a watershed in China's cultural scene. Although Chinese aesthetic Marxism no longer has the centrality in China's intellectual milieu that it once enjoyed, the critical space and momentum it created has had lasting impacts, not the least of which is the problematic that it formulated in the Cultural Reflection. In the 1990s, the dilemma of cultural transformation and reconstruction becomes more complicated, as it must now confront capitalism in its current phase of transnational/flexible production, which inevitably involves China in a process of globalization that makes any self-sufficient, enclosed socialism meaningless. Moreover, escalating socioeconomic inequalities and ethical-moral disorientations, compounded by prevalent political corruption, are rapidly reaching a new crisis, in which the issues of ideological and political representation and legitimacy again become a powder keg.

As another turn of the century fast approaches, Chinese aesthetic Marxism seems to have quickly lost its audience in a time of global expansion of capitalism and its ideologies. In an age of the "end of ideology," ideology and hegemony will reassert themselves in more pervasive ways than ever, and therefore counterhegemonic voices, such as Chinese aesthetic Marxism, will hardly lose their relevance. That Li's original work has offered rich symbolic capital to an audience impoverished of spiritual nourishment is obvious enough; the point is that in Chinese aesthetic Marxists's undertakings lies the powerful appeal of their reinvention of Marxism, which not only unsettles the monolithic orthodox of Maoism, but more significantly, breeds a constructive alternative that is at once utopian and practical. In China, at least, Marxism remains a vitally productive and positive discourse. Apart from being a predominantly critical theory of capitalism, Marxism in China can offer a meaningful reconstructive vision against the CCP's instrumentalization of Marxism as ISA. This vocation, however, is socially and historically grounded, just as Marxism in the West today sees the critique of the postmodern condition, or "late capitalism," as both its historical occasion and mission.

CHAPTER 5

Subjectivity and Aesthetic Marxism: Toward a
Cultural Topology of Postrevolutionary Society

Contemporary cultural criticism has an impulse to historicize, yet it paradoxically tends to project some ahistorical, transcendental categories by
which the effort to historicize is ultimately undermined. In the West, a
transnational and global capitalism provides the social conditions for, and
sets the structural limits to, cultural criticism. Hence, the commodification of all social spheres, cultural and aesthetic ones in particular, is a major structural determinant. But in contemporary Western cultural criticism, the decisive power of the economy has always already been
displaced and infinitely deferred by "sign," "language," and "discourse."
Lately, the displacement takes on a host of more substantive guises than
sign itself. One witnesses a proliferation of critical discourses, assuming
nonsystematic, nontotalizing, and decentering forms of micropolitics,
multiculturalism, diversity, and postcoloniality. In a complicated and
subtle manner, ideological traces of cultural production, especially the obvious connections between cultural and symbolic production and economic production, are carefully effaced or obfuscated. Cultural criticism
or theory is not immune to the process of displacement. The popularity of
Gramsci's concepts, such as hegemony and interregnum, is one example
of the neglect of the central problem of global economic inequality today.
The current usage of Gramsci valorizes a fragmented "war of positions" or
micropolitics, with radical political claims predicated on a historical
anachronism that ignores Gramsci's concrete concerns for the Italian
Communist Party's political strategies during the antifascist wars. The
Italian Communist revolution in the 1930s seems to have no bearing on
contemporary cultural criticism in the U.S. academy today, where new
kinds of "identity politics" deploy Gramsci in academic debates couched
in abstract and rarefied theoretical discourse. In an era where revolution
appears to have become decidedly a thing of the past, theoretical displacement of revolutionary and insurgent ideas is the order of the day.

In China, aesthetic and cultural debates have undergone a curious double movement similar to Western cultural criticism. The resurgence of the aesthetic as the leitmotiv of the Chinese cultural scene in the 1980s was, from the outset, a politically engaged endeavor to historicize the recent past. On the other hand, the aesthetic debates addressed issues of transcendence, universality, and generality, capitalizing on the ambiguity and polysemy of the concept of the aesthetic. During the 1980s, China was saturated with imported goods, from Sony televisions to Sartre's existentialism. This was a period of tremendous excitement and anxiety, and a "Culture Fever" in the second half of the decade surged across the nation, embodying the volatile social mood and psychology at a time of fundamental social change. An interesting phenomenon of this cultural ferment was that ideas that were historically and politically specific in the West became transcoded and displaced into something abstract and ahistorical in China. Poststructuralism, for instance, was largely a product of the radical cultural revolution in France in the 1960s, inextricably linked to Maoism and the Chinese Cultural Revolution. When China imported it in the 1980s as a brand-new intellectual product from the West, it ironically served to debunk the Chinese revolutionary legacy that inspired French poststructuralists from the start.

In order to understand the twisted migrations and mutations of ideas, an effort to historicize and periodize the recent past is necessary. Such an effort cannot be narrowly focused or fragmentary; it must account for broader, systemic, and indeed, global transformations in a general sense. Granted, this is a difficult task. The question of what metanarrative is embedded in such a historical account is bound to arise. Yet if there is any metanarrative at all, it should be the dialectic of history itself. To be sure, history is overdetermined by a multitude of structural determinants, and does not seem to follow a unilinear and teleological trajectory. By the same token, however, history does not move randomly or entirely by chance. History has an intrinsic dialectic that unfolds itself in the very historical movement. As Fernand Braudel puts it, "our effort is to interpret history, not to discover its secret laws."[1] The dialectic of history can only be interpreted, because the interpretation itself partakes of the historical dialectic, instead of standing outside it. Engels claimed that Marx discovered history's secret laws. Nevertheless, once Engels made that statement, he undermined the fundamental principle of historical dialecticism that any "secret laws" and "ultimate truth" cannot exhaust the dialectic of history itself. The dialectic of history sometimes foregrounds its fragmenting, decentering side prominently, and conceals its unifying and homogenizing other side. Hence, we are faced with immediate, dramatic, and overwhelming movements of rupture and fragmentation. Still, decentering and fragmentation are only one part of the dialectic, displayed with a high intensity at the time of profound change. At such moments, one arguably needs a stronger sense of the general and totalizing movement in order to come to grips with the true dialectic of history.

To comprehend the more specific and "local" Chinese developments, it is also necessary to examine the ways in which certain "foundational" and "universal" texts are reinvented in enumerating China's cultural history. The reinvention of Kantian aesthetics, central to Li Zehou's ambitious philosophical project of aesthetic subjectivity, then, serves as a focal point in this chapter to interrogate the cultural ferment and debates of the 1980s. The debates spawned conceptual frameworks within which Chinese history and modernity could be analyzed, and a Chinese aesthetic Marxism with the twofold objective of critique and reconstruction. In addition, a cultural topology emerged, allowing radical transformations and elastic deformations of geometric configurations of cultural space to be interrogated.

This cultural topology, which will be explored in detail below, can be seen as the historical dialectic at work: Chinese intellectuals strove to come to grips with history in order to find answers to China's modernity or an alternative modernity. The interpretation, or reinterpretation, of history then became a major task of making history. A universalizing, totalizing mood dominated the debates of the 1980s. One may accuse such a broadly encompassing universality and historical totality of essentialism, but the historical momentum that gave rise to this sensibility cannot be neglected. For all their limits and blind spots, Chinese intellectuals, especially aesthetic Marxists, scored remarkably in their endeavors to grapple with history. They played a significant role in making history, too, even if their expectations for historical development did not necessarily correspond to real events.

From Cultural Revolution to Cultural Reflection: Periodizing the Era from the 1960s to 1980s

In spite of all the confusion and chaos, the central objective of the Cultural Reflection in the 1980s was to problematize both recent history, the Cultural Revolution in particular, and the less tangible historicity of the concepts and categories by which historical events are mapped. It thus bears a strong structural resemblance to what are generally known as the postmodernist debates in the West in roughly the same period. And the connections between the Chinese and Western controversies in the 1980s (extending into the 1990s) are also historically substantial, in that both the Chinese and Western debates derived their epistemological and ideological problematics from the upheavals of the late 1960s, when cultural revolution virtually swept across the entire globe. The late 1960s constituted an extraordinary episode in twentieth-century world history, a major historical conjuncture in modernity. The conjuncture was marked by, for instance, May 1968 in Western Europe; the Vietnam War; the Soviet invasion of Czechoslovakia; and the Chinese Cultural Revolution. Therefore, an account of the Cultural Reflection of the 1980s entails a necessary rethinking of the 1960s and 1970s as its historical precondition within a global context. In the tempestuous decade of the 1960s, in particular, the internal tensions and contradictions of modernity erupted. This, in turn, fundamentally altered the world order, despite the fact that capitalism itself was only profoundly shaken, not destroyed. Indeed, transnational capitalism emerged around roughly the same decade, as new technologies of communication rapidly changed the capitalist mode of production and distribution. Capitalism entered a distinct new phase of postindustrialism or postmodernism. To a large extent, capitalism's transformation was a response to the social and cultural changes that began in the 1960s. That historical conjuncture was first theorized by Mao, Sartre, Althusser, and Marcuse, among others, and retheorized by the poststructuralist and postmodernist critics in the West and the Chinese aesthetic Marxists of the late 1970s and 1980s.

In order to illustrate the dialectical tensions in history, an attempt to recontextualize the period from the 1960s to 1980s is worthwhile. First of all, the contradictions of the voracious self-reflexive, metacritical impulses underlying a variety of critical approaches need to be examined. These approaches or theories question specific, internal schisms of historical events, while extrapolating and perpetuating some new extraneous categories, such as otherness and difference. In the U.S. academy, one witnesses the recent replacement of the older binary oppositions with new fetishized geopolitical divisions and microgroups, like the "Third World," "subalternity," or "ethnicity," vis-à-vis the "First World," "Eurocentrism," the "dead white male," and so forth. In China, the old binary oppositions between "tradition" and "modernity," "Westernization" and "Chineseness," rehashed with some "newer" terminology or conceptual schemes such as hermeneutics, "system theory," and "cybernetics," have tended to externalize the tensions generated from within China's modernity or an alternative modernity. Of course, none of the fragmented micropolitics or identity politics are unimportant. Insofar as these critical forces are committed to systematic and worldwide social transformation, they continue the global social movement that began in the 1960s, aiming to create a just and democratic alternative to capitalism. Still, the curious absence of historical reflection and recontextualization is striking in this regard.

Philosophically, as Fredric Jameson notes, the story of the Althusserianism of the mid-to-late 1960s "is the most revealing and suggestive of the various 'structuralisms,'" which inserted language or the symbolic as the new paradigm of the "politics of otherness."[2] This politics of otherness, in the context of the 1960s, was closely related to the movements of decolonization that marked the "Third World beginnings." Decolonization forced "First World" intellectuals to reexamine fundamental assumptions about Western civilization and modernity, predicated on a whole system of binary oppositions and dichotomies. These "metaphysical assumptions"—such as the sovereign subject, or binary oppositions of self/other, master/slave, center/margin, West/Non-West, and so on—were broken down, as a "Third World" self-consciousness, represented by such revolutionary intellectuals as Frantz Fanon, was on the rise. Capitalism in its new phase, with new information and communication technologies as well as transnational market expansions, also contributed to the degeneration of the older metaphysical assumptions. These historical conditions constituted, as Jameson argues, the "third term," or "referent," in a poststructuralist scheme of the symbolic. Yet it can be construed inversely, too: the symbolic can be seen as merely a cultural third term, which functions not just as a referent, but as an "interpretant," in a Peircian sense.[3] As such, it mediates the internal tensions and contradictions of modernity as a global condition of existence.

The Althusserian politics of otherness, in connection with structuralism and poststructuralism, tried to offer a cultural, symbolic solution to the social conditions of capitalist modernity. It illuminated both possibilities and limitations of cultural and aesthetic solutions, especially when these solutions were translated into real and concrete social practice. This was precisely the mid-to-late 1960s period, when Althusser painstakingly searched for conceptual alternatives by way of critiquing Hegelianism, Stalinism, and bourgeois humanism. It was, as Jameson points out, the moment of Maoism, that made Chinese Marxism a universal Marxism. "What is less often remembered," Jameson continues, "but what should be perfectly obvious from any reading of *For Marx*, is the origin of this new problematic in Maoism itself, and particularly in Mao Zedong's essay 'On Contradiction,' in which the notion of the complex, already-given *overdetermined* conjuncture of various kinds of antagonistic and nonantagonistic contradictions is mapped out."[4]

Mao's notion of contradiction is acknowledged by Jameson as one of the most significant theoretical formulations of the 1960s. But Jameson's characterization of Maoism and Althusser's Maoist connections is not without its own irony and contradiction. While critiquing the "ludicrous features of Western Third-Worldism" that perceived Mao's theory and practice through certain exotic, Orientalist angles, Jameson nevertheless tends to subscribe to the very dichotomy of "First World/Third World" it-self, as he discusses the postmodern expansion and penetration of "First World" capital into the "Third World," the "unconscious," and "Nature."[5] The concept of the "Third World" in Mao's original formulation was pri-marily military and strategic, derived largely from his experience of peas-ant guerrilla warfare. Mao's idea of world revolution had the goal of elim-inating the "three worlds" division through the "Third World" rural guerrillas' encirclement of "First World" urban centers.[6] Ironically, in contemporary cultural criticism in the West, Mao's *military* concept of the "Third World" is turned into a *cultural* category. Mao's political and military strategies of global reintegration through revolution, together with Chinese Marxism and indeed China itself, are externalized and iso-lated once again. Hence, the "Third World," other non-Western nations, and China are perceived as "imagined communities," only to be interro-gated by "First World" critics or "Third World" intelligentsia who reside in the "First World."[7] Of course, Mao's military "Third-Worldism" proved to be a gross miscalculation of the global situation. On the other hand, the displacement of concrete economic, political, and social divisions and conflicts by "imagined," symbolic, or aesthetic representation is no less preposterous than Mao's quixotic extravaganza of world guerrilla revolution.

What becomes hopelessly tangled in theoretical quibbles over the issue of the "Third World" is the paradoxical function of cultural revolution it-self. Cultural revolution in Mao's view was not only a theoretical hypothe-sis, but primarily a political solution to China's problems arising from its own trajectory of an alternative modernity, which nevertheless bore many contradictions of modernity as a global condition of existence. Mao's con-ception of cultural revolution was based on his observation of the "Soviet experience" after the Twentieth Congress of the Communist Party of the Soviet Union (CPSU), as Khrushchev's de-Stalinization and liberalization, in Mao's opinion, betrayed socialism by furthering the bureaucratization and centralization of Stalinist "economism." Mao sensed that the Stalin-ist and post-Stalinist Soviet Union provided no alternative to capitalist modernity, and could therefore serve only as a negative example for China. The Soviet Union's bureaucratization and economic centralization, and its reliance on technocracy and a police state at the expense of social de-mocratization and the participation of the masses, were perceived by Mao as negative consequences that China could avoid only by means of a vigor-ous and continuous revolution at the superstructural level, or through a cultural revolution.[8]

In order to seek new alternatives to capitalist modernity within the ad-vanced capitalist system, Althusser drew inspiration from Mao's notion of contradiction. He then formulated several important concepts to critique Hegelianism and capitalist modernity, including overdetermination, structural causality, and structural totality. Althusser characterized his project as a theoretical critique. Throughout his life, he insisted on "theoretical practice" as distinct from political and material practices. He wrote: "My aim was equally clear: to make a start on the first *left-wing* critique of Stalinism, a critique that would make it possible to reflect not only on Khrushchev and Stalin but also on Prague and Lin Piao; that would above all help put some substance back into the revolutionary project in the West. . . . [F]or me philosophy is something of a battlefield."[9] Ironically, Althusser's primarily cultural and theoretical critique had a political twist that he never expected. In China, where Lin Piao (Lin Biao) served as Mao's most important chieftain of the Cultural Revolution until his death, the Cultural Revolution turned into an episode of bloodshed and violence among radical groups and ordinary citizens. What started out in the cultural sphere, or on "symbolic battlefields," as Althusser perceived it from a distance, became nationwide chaos, only to be suppressed by the People's Liberation Army, Mao's "army of guns" again. At the time, Althusser and his French colleagues could hardly comprehend the serious consequences. Nor could he have imagined earlier that China would be put under virtual martial law for the rest of the Chinese Revolution, from 1969 to 1976, until Mao's death.

At the beginning of the Cultural Revolution, the tendency to politicize culture was evident. It then escalated into a massive "grand cultural inquisition," not unlike medieval Europe's Christian Grand Inquisition in its fervor and paranoia. The politicization of culture severely undermined Mao's efforts to wage the Cultural Revolution as a mass democracy that could challenge and subvert the CCP's bulky, inefficient, and increasingly corrupt bureaucracy. Mao, however, labeled this bureaucracy as the "bourgeoisie within the CCP," thus conflating the notion of the bourgeoisie as a social class that amasses large capital through exploitation in privately owned businesses with the state apparatuses that bred bureaucracy as such.[10] This was a serious conceptual mistake, for Mao simply displaced the fundamental Marxist principle of class analysis based on economic status above anything else. Mao's class identification of the bourgeoisie, or the bourgeoisie within the CCP, was based primarily on ideological grounds—the political, ideological, and even moral affiliations and dispositions of the bureaucrats and other members of society. Mao always suspected that bourgeois ideas and values had infiltrated and corrupted his revolutionary troop of cadres and intellectuals. (The intellectuals were categorized almost already as petty bourgeoisie, even though they had been subjected to endless thought-reform.) Mao's reasoning was that because ideology and culture played a decisive role in eroding the minds of thousands, thus turning them into a "newly bred bourgeoisie" (*xin sheng de zichan jieji*), it was necessary to start from cultural and ideological spheres to launch a revolution.

The Cultural Revolution began as a campaign against dramatists and novelists. In 1961, Wu Han, the vice mayor of Beijing and a well-known Communist historian and playwright, wrote a historical play, *Hai Rui ba guan* (Hai Rui is stripped of the post of governor). The play eulogized Hai Rui, a seventeenth-century governor known for his uprightness as well as his straightforward criticism of the imperial system's bureaucracy and corruption. Wu wrote the play in response to Mao's call at a CCP convention for attacks on the bureaucracy, which Mao viewed at the time as eroding the CCP's support of and connection with the popular masses. Yet, four years later, in 1965, Mao saw an urgent need to save the nation from the "sabotage of the class enemies," referring to a political rivalry he suspected. Mao felt increasingly estranged from the CCP Central Committee, managed by his handpicked successor, Liu Shaoqi, then the president of the People's Republic, and Deng Xiaoping, then the CCP general secretary. Mao chose to attack Wu's play as a prelude to the Great Cultural Revolution. This time, he smelled the smoking gun from Wu's otherwise loyalist and propagandist play, which was dictated by Mao's own, earlier decree.

There was a conceptual slippage involved in notions of class enemies and bourgeoisie, shown in the interpretation of Wu's play. Such an interpretation is normally conducted in cultural and symbolic realms. When translated into real political struggles, however, the consequence of this hermeneutic act can be deadly (indeed, it cost Wu his life in less than two years). To use a structuralist analogy, the "floating signifier"—class enemies or bourgeoisie—would have its definitive "signified" in the political arena, which could blast its material "referent"—Wu the dramatist, and Liu and Deng at the highest levels—into pieces. Grotesquely, the "free float" of bourgeoisie as a political signifier opened up a Pandora's box filled with all sorts, from wills to power, to fears of terror, to sadistic and masochistic instincts, which quickly sent the whole country into a veritable house of madness. In the post-Mao, anti-Cultural Revolution campaigns sanctioned by Deng, numerous horror stories emerged, enumerating the "armed battles" (*wudou*) among the radical mass organizations along with the ruthless persecutions of class enemies during the two year period from 1967 to 1968. Alarmed by the chaos and bloodbath, Mao ordered the People's Liberation Army to intervene, and the long, dreadful period of undeclared martial law began. Order was restored; radicals declared the "glorious victory of the Cultural Revolution." Yet despite the fanfare over and deification of him at the Ninth Congress of the CCP in 1969, Mao was quite disturbed by the outcome of what he conceived as a genuine mass democracy against bureaucracy and bourgeois values. However ambivalent about the so-called "personality cult" that Lin Biao, his newly designated heir apparent, cultivated around him, Mao was dissatisfied with the superficial stability and order. He not only sensed Lin Biao's true intention to seize ultimate power from him, but felt disappointed at what he perceived as the incomplete project of the Cultural Revolution. Subsequently, Mao called on the broad masses to wage new rounds of campaigns to denounce more class enemies.

Enter the 1970s. For China, the decade was punctuated by a series of political and ideological events: the death of Lin Biao (1971); Richard Nixon's visit to China (1972); the gradual rehabilitation of ousted CCP cadres, represented by the first comeback of Deng (1973); Deng's project of revamping the defunct economy, and his confrontation with the Cultural Revolution radicals led by the "Gang of Four," which ended in Deng's second downfall (1974–1976); the death of Mao, and the arrest of the Gang of Four (1976); the second comeback of Deng (1977); and the Third Plenum of the Eleventh Central Committee of the CCP (1978). The last event formally marked the end of the Cultural Revolution, and the beginning of *gaige* (reform) and *kaifang* (opening up), which set China squarely on a new trajectory of economic development and modernization all the way through the 1980s and into the 1990s. Amid all the ups and downs, a gradual and irreversible trend emerged: the revolutionary hegemony lost not only its momentum, but its ideological hold on the minds of nearly one billion Chinese people by the end of the 1970s.

Mao was wrong. Contrary to his expectations, the legitimacy of the revolutionary regime was by no means strengthened by the incessant ideological campaigns and class struggles. The revolution severely damaged the legitimacy and credibility of the CCP. Moreover, the country was devastated by a backward, stagnant economy with one of the lowest gross national products rates and extremely inefficient productive infrastructures. "Revolution does not mean poverty," Deng enjoined after his second comeback, reflecting on the mounting resentment of the populace in the wake of the Cultural Revolution. Meanwhile, the world economy entered a new era: transnational capitalism. During the 1970s, a revolutionary sea change occurred in China's neighborhood, not only in terms of information technologies, but also in relation to the rapid modernization of East Asian countries—the much talked about "East Asian Economic Miracle." This miracle, in hindsight, contained all the internal tensions and contradictions of a capitalist world system, as financial and economic crises have swept many parts of the world, particularly East and Southeast Asian countries, into an unimaginable abyss recently. But at the end of the 1970s, the glamour of a successful capitalist modernization was all that could attract the less developed world, China in particular. Multinational, or transnational, global capitalism was closely linked with these new economic developments and the rise of the East Asian economic powers. Under such circumstances, China's desire to modernize and "catch up with" its neighbors was reflected, in no small measure, by an eagerness to denounce its revolutionary experiments. In the West, global capitalism, and its accompanying waves of a global free market, further displaced and fragmented the radical social and intellectual movements in the West. The cultural revolution of the 1960s that opened up the possibility of an alternative, seemed to be closed by the political events in China, not to mention the economic, technological, and social developments in the capitalist world.

Toward the end of the 1980s, however, new social momentum gathered in the intellectual, academic circles of the West for a renewed effort at challenging capitalist modernity. It is ironic, and symptomatic, too, that after a decade's displacement, starting in the mid-1980s, culture again became the central stage on which intense intellectual, political, and ideological dramas were played out. This resurgence of culture ought to be understood within the context of global economic development and expansion. In an effort to rethink the cultural revisionism of the 1980s, the historical connection between the 1960s' Cultural Revolution and the 1980s' Cultural Reflection should be kept in mind. The "interregnum" of the 1970s created a necessary distance to reflect on the fervor and excitements of the 1960s, and at the same time, prompted self-reflexive inquiries that still carried the passions of the 1960s. This was shown in the interventionist positions of secular criticism, represented, among others, by Edward Said and Fredric Jameson in the United States and the "Birmingham School" of Cultural Studies in Britain. In China, too, Li Zehou and Liu Zaifu took the lead in launching a cultural critique that questioned that country's tradition and modernity or alternative modernity. To understand culture's regained significance in the 1980s, then, we need to go back to both the legacy of the 1960s that spawned the first global "cultural revolution," and the displacement of culture in the 1970s, and indeed, to the collapse of cultural and aesthetic realms into other spheres in those two decades.

In China, a total politicization of culture eliminated the last vestiges of the semiautonomy or autonomy of culture. Ironically, culture held the spotlight in China during Mao's reign, for he always privileged the cultural sphere over and above others. In retrospect, Chinese intellectuals had also always stood out in Mao's time, serving alternately as "frontal assault troops," and the first victims of political campaigns. The death of Lin

Biao proved to be a decisive event, in that it set into motion a process of de-mystification of the revolutionary hegemony by unraveling the instrumentalist and manipulative nature of the Cultural Revolution. It should be added that a majority of the Chinese, especially young students and intellectuals, had committed themselves to the Cultural Revolution with sincerity and enthusiasm, contrary to the perception that they were largely forced to conform to the CCP's dictates. The revolutionary hegemony was persuasive and effective, thanks to Mao's thirty-some years endeavor starting in Yan'an. But revolutionary hegemony could not, nevertheless, solve the fundamental contradiction between revolution and reconstruction. The fate of Chinese intellectuals testifies to this: caught between a self-contradictory double commitment to incessant revolution and building a postrevolutionary culture, intellectuals found no sense of cultural and political identity and subjectivity for themselves, except as tools being used by, and subjected to, endless political manipulation and instrumentalization.

In the West, on the other hand, the 1970s marked the onset of what was later labeled postmodern cultural trends. The customary representation of postmodern culture in the West often identifies the following cluster of features as its major characteristics: the death of the subject; the culture of the simulacrum; the disappearance of any sense of "depth" and historicity; and the conflation of high and mass culture.[11] Most obvious and decisive in shaping postmodern culture was both the technological revolution and the new development of capitalism. Yet any statement of this link between the capitalist economy and postmodern culture is often denied or rejected outright by postmodern critics and ideologues alike, as either overtly "reductionist" or "economic determinist." This is, of course, symptomatic of postmodern culture's dialectic, which, according to Jameson, manifests itself by simultaneously conflating and collapsing the autonomous space of culture in the modernist era, and by culture's prodigious expansion and penetration into all spheres of social life. It then turns every economic production into an eminently "cultural" one. This process is accompanied by the global expansion and penetration of transnational capital into every corner of the world. In other words, postmodern culture is characterized by a double movement of the commodification of culture and "acculturation" of commodity production and consumption on a global scale.

Under these conditions of globalization, cultural changes in China seem to share some common features with the West, most appropriately delineated by the classical concepts of alienation and reification. It can be said that, in China, the politicization of the cultural sphere ultimately alienates and reifies culture or aesthetics as autonomous or semiautonomous, whereas in the West, the commodification of culture and aesthetics poses a serious threat to the cultural sphere as resistance to alienation and reification. Such a characterization, however, is only partial. Commodification and consumerism may also have positive and transformative impacts, when economic development may mean improvement in material well-being for a vast majority of the population, and when the market economy can help resist the politicization and moralization of people's material everyday life. This is a truism that merits reaffirmation, especially when a country like China struggles to leave behind a legacy that deprived the material rights and enjoyments of people by illusory and semireligious promises of the moral good. On the other hand, the erosive impacts of consumerism cannot be overlooked, when the ideological and moral vacuum is being rapidly filled by the most brutal and reckless kinds of egotism and individualism. The global "triumph" of the capitalist market and consumerism actually effaces grave economic and political inequality and injustice in today's world. Thus, resistance to the "false consciousness" of commodified ideology itself is complex and contradictory, overdetermined by a host of divergent factors in different geopolitical areas and nations. In this regard, the explanatory inadequacy of the notions of alienation and reification becomes evident, since one needs to account for intricate economic and political conflicts, fragmented and superimposed by racial, ethnic, and religious contentions.

In studying the 1980s in China, there is also the crucial issue of the mutual interaction between political economy and culture. Post-Mao China's reform and opening up have started an irreversible process of economic decentralization and social transformation. This broad social milieu provided powerful momentum to cultural diversity, which in turn, boosted economic reform. Modernization emerged as the leitmotiv in China's social consciousness. Yet as a discursive formation, modernization was grounded in a textual landscape filled with tensions and contradictions. First of all, the "principal contradiction" in social consciousness was the twofold problematic of revolution and reconstruction that constituted Chinese modernity or an alternative modernity. Second, China was rapidly integrated into the globalizing capitalist world system from an economically peripheral position, when the capitalist "center"—the West—was at a critical historical conjuncture known as postmodernity. Hence, the Cultural Reflection of the 1980s was as much a strong reaction to the revolutionary legacy and hegemony as a renewed endeavor to chart the atlas of China's social reconstruction. The central objective of the Cultural Reflection was both deconstructive and constructive, aimed at the dilemma of revolution and reconstruction. The Chinese problematic localized and internalized the contradictions of global modernity, while

China attempted to reposition itself in relation to postmodernity. Such a vested, entangled textual space unavoidably entailed a Chinese version of "schizophrenic discourse." It had to address the alienation of culture and the aesthetic as a historical consequence of its own revolutionary hegemony. This cultural and ideological alienation under socialism was exacerbated by a postmodern cultural production that infiltrated China as a result of the modernization drive and reform. And finally, the Cultural Reflection had to fulfill its self-imposed burden of seeking ways to reconstruct a modern and national culture, a task raised over and over again in China's modern history.

The themes of "modernity and tradition" and "Westernization and Chineseness" that had held sway in the early twentieth century reemerged in the 1980s under various guises. Although these old ideas had already been deconstructed by Mao's revolutionary hegemony, when that hegemony was undermined by its own movements, the old ideas managed to stage a "homecoming" not without bitter irony and vengeance. Neo-Confucianism gradually made its way back to China's intellectual arena by the end of the 1980s. It was promoted by Hong Kong- and Taiwan-based "cultural neoconservatives" and North American scholars of sinology, which include many overseas Chinese. More appealing was the introduction of garden-variety liberalist and bourgeois humanist ideas, associated with Western intellectual luminaries such as Max Weber, Friedrich A. Hayek, Daniel Bell, and Richard Rorty. These intellectual exchanges and transactions in the 1980s were made possible by Deng's opening-up policy and the intellectual "joint ventures" of many sources. United States academics made numerous lecture trips to Beijing, Shanghai, and other major Chinese cities; massive translation projects allowed Chinese readers to savor the new intellectual achievements from the outside—primarily the United States—unknown to the Chinese for decades; and most important, intense debates dominated China's cultural scene in the late 1980s, debates that thousands of middle-aged scholars and college students either read about or participated in. Behind all this was the powerful support of liberal-minded CCP General Secretary Hu Yaobang and his politically short-lived successor, Zhao Ziyang, as well as institutions and foundations from overseas—from North America and Western Europe.

Apart from the old themes, more interesting ideas surfaced in the 1980s. These were closely associated with contemporary intellectual trends in the West, from phenomenology and hermeneutics, to the Frankfurt School and poststructuralism. The new ideas were largely articulated by two groups. One group tended to subscribe to a scientistic framework, represented by Jin Guantao's rereading of Chinese history as a manifestation of a "hyper-stable system" drawing on system theory, cybernetics, and other scientific paradigms. The other group was inclined to humanistic schemes of hermeneutics, represented by Gan Yang and his young colleagues in their "China and the World" editorials, in which they tried to reconfigure the spatial and geocultural concept of "East-West" into the temporal concept of "past-present" in interpreting China's modernity.[12] Despite their different perspectives, these intellectuals often confronted the problematic of revolutionary hegemony on its own terms, taking it as a central issue in China's modernity. It is not surprising that Jin Guantao, Gan Yang, and other Chinese scholars concentrated on the revolutionary legacy, given the gravity of the topic in China's modern history. It is, however, quite revealing that they showed a keen interest in appropriating contemporary Western cultural criticism and critical theory in their analyses of China.

In the late 1980s, many other ideas also appeared, vying for space. One such view was the radical and wholesale rejection of traditional Chinese culture mounted by Liu Xiaobo, an iconoclastic literary critic. Liu's rhetoric was extremely militant, reminiscent of the Maoist discourse dominating the Cultural Revolution. But Liu vehemently attacked Mao, using Mao's radical strategies and discourse. Liu has been frequently discounted as an unselfconscious critic whose ideas and language remained captive to Maoist hegemony. An extreme contrast appeared in the messianic vision of Liu Xiaofeng (no relative to the other Liu), couched in a Christian and theological idiom. On the surface, Liu Xiaofeng's discourse seemed to offer a counterhegemonic alternative to the radicalist view of Liu Xiaobo, who was still entrenched in Maoist discourse. On closer look, however, Liu Xiaofeng's efforts to bring out a purely spiritual and transcendental *zheng-jiu* (salvation) contradicted his secular and politically motivated campaigns against *xiaoyao* (carefreeness, a euphemism for moral degeneration and a coded term for political apathy).[13]

Among all the critical formations, only Li Zehou's notion of aesthetic subjectivity raised the fundamental contradiction between revolution and reconstruction as a theoretical question. Li was also the first to offer an answer to this question from a Marxist perspective that was nonetheless different from the official orthodoxy. At the beginning of the 1980s, a series of debates about ideology and revolution took place. The most notable of these focused on "humanist Marxism" and "socialist alienation."[14] Still, none of these debates systematically theorized the issues under discussions. In this respect, Li's theoretical efforts to reinvent Kantian aesthetics and Marxist historical materialist concepts are groundbreaking. He brought the question of subjectivity to the forefront of the contemporary Chinese cultural scene. By doing so, he captured probably the most compelling issue of the time, when post-Mao China was experiencing a profound legitimation crisis. A major part of this crisis concerned the identity of Chinese "cultural workers" or intellectuals, a consequence of the separation of cultural activity from the party's political agenda. Having been simultaneously captives as well as guardians of the party ideological state apparatuses for decades, intellectuals now felt immensely liberated from CCP fetters, and as such, were disoriented as to their new social identity in an increasingly open, commodified, and contradictory society, where the dominant power still remained in the hands of the CCP. There was, then, an urgent need to establish a new identity, an independent and autonomous rationality for scholars themselves. This identity had to be sought in a Lebenswelt, or cultural system, resistant to bureaucratic control and autonomous from the power structures of domination and subordination. Subjectivity, thus, became key to a new rationality in post-Mao China. Put in the context of institutional changes occurring over the years, reflections on subjectivity can be seen as a self-conscious effort to redefine the intellectual self as an autonomous, self-determining, self-regulating, and free subject.

Reinventing Kant: Li Zehou and Aesthetic Marxism

From the late 1970s, Li took up the burden of recovering the independent subject through rereading and reinventing Kantian aesthetics and classical Marxist notions of historical materialism. This was a continuation of his earlier views in the aesthetic debates, but he substantially modified his positions under different circumstances. In the 1950s and early 1960s, revolutionary hegemony was still on the rise, and had a firm grip on social consciousness. The issue of subjectivity was then concerned primarily with constructing a revolutionary collective identity in a cultural space, where reconstruction of social life, rather than class struggle, would be the dominant objective. The Cultural Revolution demolished the constructive cultural space, thereby precipitating the process of "self-alienation" in cultural and aesthetic domains. Hegelianism had been transcoded in the discursive system of the Cultural Revolution as a term for Maoism, and from then on, it connoted a cultural and ideological determinism responsible for the massive politicization during Mao's reign.

In this respect, Li's "recovery" of Kant has the symbolic value of critiquing Hegelianism, or Maoism. Concurrently, a critique of Kantian "idealism" has enabled Li to respond to contemporary intellectual trends in the West, Western Marxist critical theory in particular, from a unique perspective that resituates the proper Marxian problematic of the mode of production, or the economic as the "ultimately determining instance," back to the center of cultural and aesthetic domains. Kantian aesthetics also provides Li with a theoretical foundation for reinventing a constructive and utopian vision of culture and society. Significantly, this utopian vision draws on the classical tradition of Confucianism as well. Li conceives of a utopian, aesthetic world through classical Chinese conceptions, reinterpreting Chinese tradition as a "pleasure-oriented culture" and Confucian thought as a "practical rationality." His reinterpretation of Chinese tradition is based on his understanding of Kantian aesthetics. Li's ambitious undertaking amounts to a dialectic "transcoding" of Kantianism, Confucianism, and Marxism. He calls it a project of "transformative creation," an idea borrowed from Lin Yu-sheng, a historian at the University of Wisconsin, whose notion of "creative transformation" had considerable popularity in the Cultural Reflection of the 1980s.[15] Li wants to emphasize creation rather than transformation, for he believes that a new modern culture should be created by synthesizing at least Confucius, Marx, and Kant, rather than by merely transforming traditional Chinese culture.

Since the late 1970s, Li has emerged as a leading philosopher and thinker. His appeal to the younger generation—college students in particular—was enormous in the 1980s. Many considered him a "mentor of spiritual enlightenment."[16] He earned this honor by breaking new ground in the study of Marxism, the foremost subject of learning in China. Li returned to Marx's intellectual origins, German idealist philosophy, to search for a solid theoretical base for a Marxist theory of subjectivity. This he found in Kant, rather than Hegel, for Kant laid the foundation for a modern "self-reflection" of subjectivity, nature, and society. In 1979, Li's *Critique of the Critical Philosophy: A Study of Kant* (hereafter *Critique*) was published. The second revised edition came out in 1984, with his important 1981 lecture, "The Philosophy of Kant and the Theses on the Construction of Subjectivity," included as an appendix. *Critique* is Li's major philosophical work. It is a critique of Kantian philosophy from the historical materialist point of view of "practice." The main goal of *Critique* is to spell out a Marxist practical philosophy in order to lay the philosophical foundation for a Marxist notion of subjectivity, which can then serve as a conceptual framework for examining Chinese culture and history. The book is difficult. Li admits that "probably my book is really affected by the style of *The Critique of Pure Reason*, notorious for its repetitiveness, monotony, and obscurity."[17] Surprisingly, the first edition of 30,000 copies sold out quickly, and the second edition of some 40,000 copies was just as popular. Indeed, the book induced a "Kant Fever" of no small scale in China's intellectual circles.

Li tried to establish connections between historical materialist categories and Kant's reflections on human rationality and consciousness. Li's emphasis on historical materialism, as he later acknowledged, was intended as a critique of Mao's "idealist" valorization of dialectical materialism.[18] Kant, according to Li, was the first to place the issue of subjectivity at the heart of philosophical thought by examining three essential constituents of human nature—knowledge, will, and feeling—in his three critiques of epistemology, ethics, and aesthetics. The a priori representations or concepts of understanding in Kant's first critique, the *Critique of Pure Reason*, functioned as a mediation between the human mind and sensory data. The transcendental synthesis formed the kernel of Kant's "Copernican Revolution," which reconciled the idealist insistence on speculative consciousness as the sole resource of understanding and the empiricist dependence on sense perception for knowing the world. Kant tried to establish a rationality that redefined humanity's troubled relationship with nature, and the relationships between reason and sensuousness, mind and matter. The way Kant solved this problem was, in short, to give humans superior legislative power over nature.

Kant's second critique, in the realm of ethics, concluded by postulating moral law as a pure form of universal legislation. Humankind's supremacy over nature was then guaranteed with the inscription of rationality in ethics. The second critique, therefore, reinforced Kantian rationality in the domains of ethics and will, approximating more closely the relationship between the phenomenal and noumenal worlds, and glancing over once again the unknowable and mysterious Ding an sich.[19] In Li's view, Kant's greatest contribution to the philosophy of subjectivity was his reflections on the complex formation of human rationality. These reflections lead to an "anthropological ontology of subjectivity," as opposed to the various "idealist ontologies based on experience [desire], language, or logic."[20] This Kantian notion serves as a point of departure for a Marxist theory of subjectivity. Drawing on historical materialist assumptions, Li divides subjectivity into a material component and a psychological one. He calls the former, the world of society and technology, and the latter, a "cultural-psychological formation" (*wenhua xinli jiegou*). Subjectivity is conceived as a complex, open-ended, and overdetermined formation, rather than a monadic, metaphysical entity of a sovereign and autonomous subject. It would thus be grossly misleading to identify Li's (and to some extent Liu Zaifu's) theorization of the subject position as a belated "recovery" of the Cartesian cogito under a Kantian guise, which only reflected a post-Mao China's longing for the self-centered individualism that Chinese culture lacks.

The two components of subjectivity—the social-technological and cultural-psychological—are closely connected to two other elements— social collectivity and individuality. The complex ensemble of these four interdependent, interrelated constituents fills out subjectivity as a dynamic structural relationship, rather than a static "essence." The social-technological forms the exterior dimension, while the cultural-psychological makes up the interior.[21] The social collectivity is both exterior and interior: exterior to the individual self and interior to the objective social-technological world of materiality. It should be noted that Li's configuration of the four terms of subjectivity is asymmetrical and involves two different schemes of hierarchy, which are more than conceptual or epistemic. The category of the social-technological, or the material practice of toolmaking as a distinct social and anthropological behavior, has an ontological status that subsumes all other terms, and in Li's view, has preceded in historical reality the formation of the cultural-psychological, the social collective, and individual or personal. The two configurations can be sketched as follows:

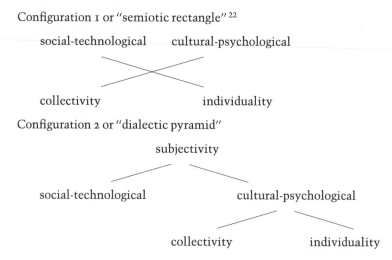

Configuration 1 or "semiotic rectangle"[22]

    social-technological   cultural-psychological

    collectivity   individuality

Configuration 2 or "dialectic pyramid"

               subjectivity

    social-technological   cultural-psychological

           collectivity   individuality

The above two schemes indicate that the relationships between the four terms are not simply dichotomous or logical; they should be seen as a dialectical "antinomy" in the Kantian sense. The second scheme presents the third term, collectivity or the dialectic synthesis, as subjectivity itself. Such a configuration also contains an antinomy: the relationship between the social-technological and subjectivity. Li thinks that the social-technological presides over everything else, including subjectivity. But subjectivity now must synthesize all these terms, including the social-technological. Althusser recognized this antinomy inherent in Marxism as well. His solution was to conceive a structural totality to history, in which all contradictions would be overdetermined by a multitude of contradictions. An ontological status of the totality or history itself is thus implicit in Althusser's theory, despite his efforts to de-ontologize or de-essentialize philosophical categories. Li tries to solve this problem differently. He retains the category of antinomy as the inner logic of his philosophy, asserting that "the antinomy of historicism and ethicism" is the very logic underlying both history itself and its conceptualization.[23] For Li, an insistence on the priority of the social-technological is necessary, as he remains faithful to the historical materialist distinction of base and superstructure. Subjectivity is the third missing term or synthesis of the dialectic of the objective (social-technological) and subjective (cultural-psychological).

To resolve the antinomy of such a configuration, Li's original and creative move was to place great emphasis on the constitutive character of "practice." The notion of practice is often synonymous with subjectivity, and Li emphatically calls his philosophy a "practical philosophy of subjectivity." Li defines practice as the material production and practice of tool-making, rather than "praxis," which is used most frequently in Western Marxist writings to include theoretical and cultural production. Engels characterized toolmaking as the defining feature of humanity, separating human beings from nature, and constituting humankind's subjectivity and self-consciousness. But how exactly subjectivity is formed through toolmaking and material practice is not explained by Engels. It was Kant who theorized the complex process of the constitution of subjectivity. Kantian philosophy, however, is known for its eclecticism, compromising materialism with idealism. In order to overcome Kant's idealist impasse and restore Kantian rationality to its "true" material basis, the reinvention of a historical materialist concept of practice was necessary.[24]

Significantly, Li's reinterpretation of historical materialism appears in a negative characterization and critique of Western Marxism. Li mounts his severe criticism of the Frankfurt School and Western Marxism in his chapter on "Kantianism in Social Theories":

> [In] Western Marxism . . . some stress the priority of thought, and some consider cultural revolution and cultural critique more important preconditions for economic reform and political revolt. Some, like Marcuse, escaped to aesthetics, or, like Habermas, to communication, as their shelter of "revolutionary" or reformist theories. Therefore they like to use the term "praxis" to include one's every activity, as opposed to historical materialism.[25]

In defense of historical materialism, Li contends that "practice must be defined in terms of the use and making of tools, in order to unify the philosophy of practice and historical materialism."[26] Western Marxism, as Li puts it, "severs [the Marxist] philosophy of practice from historical materialism," with serious practical consequences in political reality. Drawing on Chinese lessons, Li admonishes: "the Chinese Great Leap Forward of 1958 was indeed a grand practice. But it violated the historical law and had only negative consequences. Thus [although] a philosophical presupposition may look far removed from reality, it in fact always has significant bearings on social reality. The Cultural Revolution was another grave instance. The momentous student movement of the 1960s in the West did not yield any accomplishments either."[27] It is no coincidence that Sartre, Althusser, and other Western Marxists touted the Chinese Cultural Revolution as a great praxis because of the fundamental affinity of "impetuous, petit bourgeois ethical utopianism" inherent in Maoist radical leftism as well as Western Marxism.[28] Clearly, Li's critique of Western Marxism is based primarily on the historical experience of Chinese Marxism, Maoist "idealism" and "voluntarism" in particular. His emphasis on toolmaking and material practice is also overshadowed by post-Mao China's overriding concern with modernization projects.

Contrary to the Western Marxists's fascination with the young Marx's Hegelian conception of the overcoming of alienation as the ultimate end, Li sees a genuine historical materialist solution to the future of humankind in Marx's formulation of a humanized nature in the *Economic and Philosophical Manuscripts*.[29] The notion of a humanized nature, as mentioned earlier, was developed by Zhu Guangqian and the then-young Li in the early aesthetic debates in China. In his study of Kant, however, Li further elaborates on how practice finally humanizes nature. Here, he draws not only on Kant, but also the cognitive psychology of Piaget and Ludwig Wittgenstein's theory of language-game as social practice. Li is mainly interested in Wittgenstein's later thoughts on the interrelation of language and social practice, yet is quick to point out the basic difference between Wittgenstein and Marx: the former errs precisely in prioritizing language over social practice.[30] (Ironically, it is the same later Wittgenstein who reversed his early notion of the determination of prelinguistic reality over the structure of language, and placed greater stress on language as a constituting force rather than a constituted entity. For Wittgenstein, language and social practice were inseparable, whereas Li insists on the absolute determination of material practice over language.)[31]

Key elements of Li's theory of subjectivity are the concepts of *nehua* (internalization) and *jidian* (sedimentation). The notion of nehua is derived primarily from Piaget. Although the term jidian has far more influential currency, it is largely a variation of the concept of internalization based on the Piagetian theory of cognitive and affective development.[32] Li gives Piaget a prominence unparalleled by any other twentieth-century Western thinker in his system of thought:

> I value Piaget highly, because he almost repeats in the microfield of child psychology what Marx and Engels discovered in the macro-

world of history in the nineteenth century: it is not a priori internal rationality, nor logic and linguistic grammar, but practical and operational activity [sic] that forms the basis and origin of a human being's intellect, reason, and thought. . . .

Piaget . . . notices the key determination of [physical] action and operation in the formation of logical thinking as well as the whole open structure of cognition. He thus provides the important materialist basis for a scientific description of cognitive origin and development."[33]

Interestingly, Jürgen Habermas, whose "reformist" position is rejected by Li, also leans heavily on Piaget in his rationalist social analysis, which is eminently Kantian. Habermas rules out the radical contingency of the world in his communicative reason, favoring a vision of political order based on a somewhat idealized classic model of bourgeois stability. The appeal to Piaget is indeed curious and symptomatic. It may represent a tendency within contemporary Marxism to resuscitate certain materialist positions from rationalist and scientist models, without confronting the unnerving issue of identity and nonidentity in materialism that the Frankfurt School philosophers brought up in their rethinking of Freud's psychoanalysis.[34]

As regards Li's concept of sedimentation, an effort to integrate rationalist discourse with historical materialism is also evident. According to Li, the material practice of humans gives birth to the ability of symbolic production—that is, language—and at the same time, this material practice has internalized people's sensuous experience into a psychologically deep structure at the level of unconscious. In other words, the material practice has made possible an extremely long, complex process by which people's sensuous experience, their intuitive faculty of conceptualizing, knowing, and understanding—the categories of time and space in Kant's parlance —has sedimented, or congealed, into a rational, cultural-psychological formation.

Li's cultural-psychological formation roughly corresponds to the Freudian notion of unconscious.[35] Still, there is a basic difference: Li's psychic formation is a thoroughly rational and cultural product, while in Freud and Jacques Lacan, the unconscious signals an irreconcilable hiatus between cultural constraints and natural instincts and drives. In Lacan's view specifically, only the mediation of the symbolic—as in language— can establish rational order to the chaotic and undifferentiated unconscious, but at a high price: the formation of subjectivity through the mediation of language involves essentially repressive processes of condensation and displacement, whereby the real is absent and can never be fully grasped. Li, in contrast, relying on Piagetian, biologically oriented cognitive and developmental psychology, denies the decisive role of linguistic mediation. For his sedimentation process, rationality always has its plenitude, or full presence of totality. The mediation of the symbolic does not appear critical in the constitution of subjectivity.[36]

If Li's formulation of the Marxian concept of practice has a negative and critical edge concerning the Maoist and Western Marxist valorization of cultural praxis, then the idea of a cultural-psychological formation contains his critical response to another principal intellectual trend in the West: the language-centered philosophy and aesthetics dominating much of the twentieth century. Li contends that the linguistic or discursive revolutions and class struggles of some Western Marxists are profoundly influenced by modern language-centered philosophies and thinking in the West. In the philosophy of Kant, the general categories of time and space, logic, and causality appear a priori transcendental, divorced from the concrete material practices of making and using tools.[37] Subsequently, language is also abstracted and ontologized in modern philosophy. The ontological status accorded to language in a modern Western philosophy intent on subverting traditional metaphysics and ontology, paradoxically, only reinscribes a self-contradictory, self-effacing "metaphysics of language" devoid of any concrete substance and meaning except vacuous signifying chains of "difference of differences." It perpetuates rather than resolves the Kantian antinomies.

In order to reconceive a constructive notion of culture based on a new concept of subjectivity, Li stresses that the fetishism of language in modern Western thinking must be demystified.[38] Language is, as Claude Lévi-Strauss acknowledged, the foundation of culture and humanity that distinguishes humankind from animals. Yet Wittgenstein (in his later years especially) sought to locate the origin of semantics and the actual use of language in everyday life or praxis. These thinkers conceded that there was something prior to, and more fundamental than, language per se. The ineradicable and ultimate real (the "referent," in structuralist idiom) that precedes language is, in Li's view, the material practices of making and using tools. It was through material practice as a social, collective enterprise that human beings were constituted as Homo sapiens. In other words, collective material practice engendered a unique rationality distinguishing humanity from the animal world. The rationality of humankind was the product of collective, communal activities of primitive sacrificial rituals and shamanism that stored, transmitted, and regulated the sensuous experience of individual human beings derived from material practice. Sacrificial rituals, shamanism, totems, and taboos were the pristine forms of culture that came into being simultaneously with the real symbolic system of humankind or language. Once culture and language established the social formations, orders, and regulations of both external social behavior and internal psychology, material practice was endowed with a purposiveness that governed its natural causality and empowered human beings with a subjectivity vis-à-vis nature.

Rather than taking language or the symbolic as the predominant formation of culture, Li proposes a historical dialectic by which language and material practice are interrelated and interdependent. In the long historical process, language originated from the material practices of making and using tools, and transcended them in the process of cultural formations. The suprabiological, social existence of humanity has been formed by the symbolic production of culture and rationality grounded in a material practice. As to the complex and extremely important question of how language or symbolic production is imbricated with material production in the modern world, Li concedes that Habermas's theory of communication points to a fruitful direction of inquiry.[39] Yet Habermas's formulation of communicative rationality commits the very same error as many schools of modern Western philosophy by exclusively prioritizing the function of language. Jacques Derrida's view of "écriture" vis-à-vis "speech," on the other hand, can be seen as an effort to break the epistemological foreclosure and impasse of modern language-centered philosophy, since écriture can be understood as a more general symbolic structuration or cultural formation than the narrowly defined speech as pure language.[40]

Li grants relative autonomy to linguistic and cultural productions, and urges that this autonomy be understood within the overall totality of social existence, in which economic production is ultimately determinant. He maintains that "after all, it is not language but material practice that constitutes and sustains the life and existence of humankind. This point can never be overemphasized and is one of the essential propositions of the constructive philosophy drawing from historical materialism."[41] Language, or the symbolic, is only a constitutive component in Li's system of cultural-psychological formation through sedimentation. Although his system is derived primarily from classical German thought, Kantian aesthetics in particular, Chinese cultural tradition is the other intellectual resource for Li's thinking. He reinterprets and modifies this tradition through Kantian and Marxist perspectives. It is Marxist historical materialism that brings logical coherence to the whole system, by which the convergence of subjectivity, nature, and history can be mapped out.[42]

Aside from his reliance on Piaget, Kant, and Marx, Li labors to relate the psychologically oriented Confucian notion of *ren* (benevolence, as it is inadequately rendered in English), to the process of sedimentation and the constitution of a cultural-psychological formation. Briefly, Li interprets ren as a psychological internalization of *li* (propriety, rite), the external rules governing human behavior, derived from the rules and regulations of the rituals of ancestor worship. Fundamental to these two concepts—li and ren—is the emphasis on kinship rather than sexuality. The corporeal pleasure of sexuality, along with its attendant tension and guilty conscience, is epitomized by the fall of Adam and Eve as well as the Oedipus complex. Li regards such cultural conceptions as the foundation of Western culture. But Confucian tradition stresses kinship as well as parental love and care, related essentially to the procreative, anthropological, and biological aspects of sexuality. As the Confucian system of li—rites and rituals—indicates, sexuality from very early on was rationalized and anthropomorphized in Chinese society.[43] Apparently, this has certain significant bearings on Li's almost complete disregard of Freud in his discussion of sedimentation and cultural-psychological formation, since Freudianism always looks suspect in view of Confucian rationalist psychology (reinterpreted, of course, through Li's appropriation of certain Western models).

Li's central goal of philosophical and aesthetic thinking is, above all, constructive and ontological: a construction of an "ontology of instrument"—that is, economic, material well-being—and an "ontology of psychology"—culture and unconsciousness. Not surprisingly, his "ontological thinking" is not so much concerned with the metaphysical question of the relationship between being and God as with the existence of human beings as such. It is, therefore, anthropological rather than onto-theological.[44] Furthermore, it is primarily aesthetic, in that the aesthetic, in Li's judgment, is the ultimate state for humankind as suprabiological, social, and anthropological beings. The seeds for the final convergence, or completion, of a thoroughly anthropomorphized and psychologized subjectivity, however, were sown by Kant in his third critique on aesthetic judgment. Li regards *Critique of Judgment* as the keystone of Kant's philosophical arch: "As a middle point between Rousseau and Hegel, the social man is the true center, the true point of departure and basis for Kant's thinking."[45] *Critique of Judgment* embodies Kant's wholesale resolution of the contradictions, antitheses, and antinomies between the particular and general, sensuousness and rationality, nature and society, freedom of will and law of morality. In the two preceding critiques, Kant had wrestled with those antinomies strenuously without a successful resolution. Since Kant's goal was to prove that humans are the final purpose of nature in its complete freedom, only aesthetic judgment could fulfill this objective.

Aesthetic judgment is the moment whereby people's meditation of their own purposiveness without utilitarian purpose is fully realized. This realization amounts to nothing less than the eventual fulfillment of humanity's self-regulating, self-referential, autonomous, and free subjectivity, which coincides perfectly with the final purpose of nature. The aesthetic, of course, also constitutes the core of Li's constructive philosophy. He contends that the central task for a constructive philosophy at present is to sketch out some preliminary contours and directions for humanity in terms of the ontology of psychology in which subjectivity holds a crucial position. The reconstruction of the ontology of psychology entails the establishment of a "new sensibility," out of both the mechanization or dehumanization caused by the unconstrained expansion of the ontology of instrument, and the various irrational impulses of nihilism, cynicism, religious fundamentalism, and so on, prevalent in the twentieth century, that reduce humankind's mode of being to animalistic instincts and desires. The new sensibility cannot stem from an exterior, transcendental, and hypostatized notion of God. Instead, it will arise from a cultural sedimentation (or cultural-psychological formation, or cultural unconscious) of practical, sensuous, and aesthetic modes of being, in which the classical Chinese wisdom of the harmonious relationship between nature and humanity holds sway, forming subjectivity in a socially objective world. This is precisely what Marx envisioned as the state of a humanized nature in his *Economic and Philosophical Manuscripts*.

Kant recognized that logic alone cannot exhaust the problem of subjectivity in epistemology, and that subjectivity as such was an ethical and moral "categorical imperative" that transcended the particular and individual interests of a given time or social formation. In the end, subjectivity is best embodied by what Kant referred to as the "aesthetic judgment" of the free form of beauty that unifies the social characteristics of humankind, namely regularity and teleology. As a cultural-psychological formation that corresponds to the free form of beauty, aesthetic experience is the highest integration and unity of rationality and sensibility. This, indeed, is the final achievement of humanity's subjectivity, its clearest and most distinct manifestation, for aesthetic experience as such congeals, or sediments, the totality of humankind (its subjectivity) in the individual, the rational in the sensuous, the social in the natural.[46] It should be clear that subjectivity in a Kantian-Marxian sense (through Li's reinterpretation) is not the unique, particular, individual self, but humankind as a collective totality, as the aggregate of every single individual human being in the long historical process of sociocultural formation. Individual subject position is undeniable and ineradicable, insofar as the social totality or collectivity, or the "Big I," can never exist without the unique, individual human being through his/her material practice as well as his/her sensuous experience.

In short, the Kantian aesthetic not only guarantees the universality of human being's freedom, but also establishes the condition for the complete humanization of nature or the naturalization of humankind. This condition, obviously, lies at the heart of Marx's *Economic and Philosophical Manuscripts*. Marx's fundamental propositions were that humanness comes into being through humanizing nature, and that the exercise of human senses, powers, and capacities was an absolute end in itself. In his seminal lecture of 1982, "The Philosophy of Kant and Theses on the Construction of Subjectivity," Li not only used aesthetic subjectivity as the master trope to define his whole theoretical enterprise, but also to constitute the paramount "topological paradigm" for reinterpreting, and ultimately transforming, Chinese culture.[47]

Discourse of the Aesthetic-Historical: Toward a Cultural Topology

In assessing the Cultural Reflection of the 1980s, it is essential to comprehend the self-reflexive efforts to rethink history, which problematize both historical events and the concepts of existing historiography. These efforts to develop conceptual frameworks and analytical codes can be grasped as attempts to construct a cultural topology, or a metacritical "cognitive mapping." Topology here is used figuratively, suggesting the topographical study of a particular cultural space in terms of both its diachronic and synchronic mutations and transformations. The notion can also learn from certain conceptual implications in the modern mathematical branch, concerned with those properties of geometric configurations (such as point sets) that are unaltered by elastic deformation (such as stretching or twisting) within a topological space. There are interesting conceptual and methodological affinities between the Althusserian notion of "structural totality" and "topological space," as the latter refers primarily to the *structural* relationship between sets, subsets, and the collection or constellation of sets and subsets. Topological space defines a set with a collection of subsets that must satisfy the following conditions: that both the empty set and the set itself belong to the collection; that the union of any number of subsets is also an element of the collection; and that the intersection of a finite number of subsets is an element of the collection.[48] In Althusserian parlance, the sets and subsets can be seen as semiautonomous, yet interdependent and overdetermined contradictions and formations within a structural totality. This totality or history is an "empty set" or "absent cause," which in turn, is determined and overdetermined by all the integral components of social formations, or sets and subsets, in a topological space.

The methodological and analytical code of this cultural topology is mainly represented by Li's thinking. And perhaps the single most influential debate of the 1980s in this regard was the one that focused on history and culture, labeled here as "the discourse on the aesthetic-historical."

Li's interrogation of classical Chinese culture allows him to develop a dialectic view of the relationship between Chinese tradition and an alternative modernity. His analyses of Chinese classical philosophy, ethics, and the arts demonstrate that Chinese traditional thinking exhibits a practical or pragmatic rationality. In Li's view, this pragmatic rationality represents a sober, optimistic, pleasure-oriented, and aesthetic view of life. In contrast to the Judeo-Christian assumptions of desires, sinfulness, and redemption as human nature, the pleasure-oriented Chinese classical philosophy takes delight in *rational* life itself. This worldview interfuses sensuous experience with a naturalist rationality, embodied by the principle of the "unity of man [sic] and heaven (*tian ren heyi*)." In this respect, classic Chinese thinking is also essentially aesthetic: it takes the unity of sensuous experience with the rational order of the universe as its ultimate goal, to be fulfilled in a profoundly psychological and internalized mode of life. But Li holds that this emphasis on harmony and equilibrium has its negative implications, too. It severely hinders the development of humankind's capacity to conquer nature and fully realize one's own humanity. Furthermore, as history evolved toward the modern period, traditional rationality ossified into an intractable and oppressive dogma, detrimental to the healthy unfolding of social consciousness. This was the time when traditional Chinese society gradually disintegrated in the face of the Western powers. The West, with its advanced sciences and technology, outshone China's ancient civilization.[49] Clearly, Li's account of Chinese cultural history is based on a rationalist and evolutionary concept of history, and in turn, such a concept is undoubtedly derived from the enlightenment rationality that modern Chinese intellectuals since the May Fourth movement have espoused. Indeed, interpretations of history and tradition have been major vehicles to convey intellectuals' concerns about China's modernity from the May Fourth era onward.

Likewise, problems of modern history and culture are central to Li and other critics of the Cultural Reflection. Li explains China's painful struggle toward modernity as the "dual variation of enlightenment and national salvation."[50] This view captures the antinomy of revolution and reconstruction. Briefly, Li claims that the turning point in modern China was the May Fourth movement of 1919, which offered a cultural critique and, at the same time, aimed to transform traditional ways of life into modern ones. This cultural enlightenment, however, ended up in a political struggle for national salvation when the country was besieged by imperialist invasions and domestic corruption. The enlightenment themes of individuality, subjectivity, freedom, and democracy were then superseded by the militant imperatives of collective class struggle. The success of the communist revolution in China reinforced the military and political battles of the national salvation movement at the expense, according to Li, of the individual, who was subordinated to the state with the reinstitution of the autocratic and "feudalist" tradition that the May Fourth iconoclasts had challenged.[51]

The theme of a "dual variation" has its own paradoxes and contradictions. Not surprisingly, it has been subjected to heated disputes. A main criticism is that Li made a logical and factual error by confounding cultural movements and political struggles, and by separating the interrelated and inextricable needs of modernization (enlightenment) and revolution (national salvation). Another common criticism is to stress the fact that all the May Fourth themes of enlightenment showed the unmistakable intentions of national salvation and revolution. Valid as these criticisms are, they miss a crucial theoretical point in Li's thesis. Li may have misconstrued the intentions and objectives of the May Fourth enlightenment, but his thesis opens up the antinomy of revolution and reconstruction as a central question in China's modernity. The controversies that his position aroused problematized the concepts and categories by which Chinese modernity had been represented and interpreted. The dual variation offers a critical perspective through which to examine a whole range of tensions and incongruities in modern Chinese history. In other words, Li conceives of a core problematic by which revolution, national salvation, modernization, and enlightenment can be understood. The dual variation moves beyond the dichotomies of tradition/modernity and Westernization/Chineseness. The single leitmotiv—modernity—entails a dialectic approach to the intrinsic contradictions of modernity, thereby breaking the externalizing and dichotomous paradigms of modernization theories. Although Li's concept was formulated without much exchange with scholarship outside China, the parallels between his views and the revisionist trends in the social sciences in the West that critique modernization theories are obvious.

Li also proposes a constructive and creative solution to the antinomy of the dual variation. The incomplete project of the Chinese enlightenment ought to be fulfilled, as he suggests, by reinscribing the May Fourth thesis of "Westernization" from a Marxist perspective. This reinscription radically alters the ideological content of the idea in its original form. Ostensibly, the proposition of *xiti zhongyong* (Western substance/Chinese function) is formulated against the last century's reformist stance of *zhongti xiyong* (Chinese substance/Western function), which externalized the internal contradictions of China's modernity. The fundamental difference between the two theses, Li argues, lies in their definitions of "substance"

—*ti*. Li's ti has a distinct Marxist connotation of *benti*, or the ontology of social existence, which includes material, scientific-technological, and cultural-psychological formations. By contrast, the Chinese ti that the old reformists insisted on was merely Confucian ideologies and their cultural legacy. As Li himself admits, however, the definitions of and arguments over ti (essence) and *yong* (function), which include his own thesis, are imprecise and can sometimes be misleading. Short of an intention to engage in a pedantic discussion of the definitions, Li claims that what constitutes ti in modern times is nothing less than a subjectivity that is well conceived and articulated, if not completely realized, by modern Western enlightenment. Li's plea is to create a modern Chinese subjectivity by revitalizing the Chinese classic rationality of the "unity of man [*sic*] and heaven" based on the Marxian notion of a humanized nature.[52]

A clue to Li's usage of ti or benti as "Western" or Marxist lies in his critique of Mao's Marxism and the roots of the Cultural Revolution. Li contends that Chinese Marxism was deeply influenced by the traditions of practical or pragmatic rationality and utopianism inherent in Confucianism, Taoism, and Chinese Buddhism. Without a powerful tradition of religion as a spiritual mode of life, the Chinese have fostered from antiquity a strong reliance on rationality to guide social and material practices. Marxism happens to be precisely a rationality that corresponds to Chinese rationalism. Self-consciously atheist, Marxism is at once practical and utopian, and is firmly anchored in Enlightenment rationality. Thus, Marxism appeared congenial to the practical-minded Chinese, who had been nurtured in a tradition that had always favored a rationalized, sensuous experience derived from everyday material practice. By Li's account, Marxism appealed to Chinese intellectuals as an ideology, a system of values and beliefs, rather than a science or systematic explanation of social history. The idea of class struggle, then, became the cardinal principle of Chinese Marxism, not because it offered an objective and scientific analysis of society, but because it implied a strong value judgment and promised a way to right wrongs.

Li's analysis of the origin of Chinese Marxism is a major part of his undertakings. He holds that Marxism offered an alternative way of thinking about and affecting modernity. Hence, it was embraced by the Chinese as a guiding ideology for the revolution, and it was social revolution, rather than anything else, that brought China to its own history of modernity. In the very historical process of China's modernity, a Chinese Marxism was generated. This was the moment when Mao's thought was formulated, in the throes of revolutionary struggle. In Li's view, Mao's thought, as the first stage of Chinese Marxism, was not simply a local application of Eurocentric, classical Marxist ideas. Deeply rooted in concrete Chinese historical circumstances, Mao's thought articulated a non-Western Marxism in the sense that it broke with the classical Marxist notion of history embodied in historical materialism. Nevertheless, it was a genuine Marxism, for it interpreted creatively, and most crucially, put into practice, classical Marxist notions of class struggle and dialectical materialism, thus rendering Marxism a truly universal and practical theory of human emancipation. Mao rewrote China's modern history with Marxism, and in so doing, he also revised the Marxist view of history, following in the footsteps of Lenin, by creating a socialist, alternative, and Chinese modernity. Marx hardly ever envisaged an alternative modernity for China, limited as he was by his teleological notion of the inevitable law of history and his lack of understanding of the non-Western world's struggles with capitalism, his sincere sympathy with exploited nations and peoples notwithstanding.[53]

Chinese Marxists achieved the goal of revolution by seizing state power, which laid the foundations for economic reconstruction and social transformation. But Li argues that in the nearly three decades after the founding of the People's Republic, Mao's utopian project of social engineering failed to deliver on its promise of an economically developed, socialist alternative modernity. The "permanent" or "uninterrupted revolution" and "class struggle" that culminated in the Cultural Revolution only brought China to a disastrous "dialectical negation" of Mao's revolutionary goals and ideals in the spheres of culture and ideology. During the revolutionary war period, revolutionary idealism was proven to be most effective in mobilizing millions of Chinese to support the revolution. Yet when the war ended and social reconstruction began, revolutionary ideology performed poorly. As Li observes, it hardly transpired into effective guiding principles or psychological incentives to raise economic productivity, and enhance the quality and quantity of the productive forces under the socialist mode of production.

Mao's other central objective, as discussed earlier, was to combat the new bureaucratic, privileged, and corrupt class within the revolutionary party itself. Mao thought that this new class would undermine the revolution, and create social injustice and inequality. As early as the 1950s, Mao admonished that the bureaucracy of the CCP had become estranged from the people and would inevitably signal the death knell for socialism. In Li's mind, this great insight was proven by the collapse of the former Soviet Union, which was caused, in no small measure, by the widening schism between stagnant, self-serving bureaucratic apparatuses and ordinary citizens. But in China, the problem took a different turn. The Cultural Revolution brought excessive damage and disorder to society, and the unjust mob terror and massive persecution that occurred overshadowed the noble objectives of encouraging democratic participation and preventing bureaucratic abuses of power. (To understand the fact that in China, unlike the former Soviet Union, socialism, primarily linked with the legacy of Mao, has never been rejected in toto by millions of Chinese people, it is necessary to reevaluate Mao's singular insistence on and practice of ceaselessly dismantling the formation of a privileged class within the revolutionary party against the interests of the people.)

Mao's contributions, Li argues, can be seen by analyzing his flaws from both historical and theoretical perspectives. The thrust of Mao's Marxism was class struggle. Yet, as Li puts it, "such a narrowly defined notion of historical materialism reflects more the conflict-ridden historical circumstances and the practical, revolutionary imperatives of Mao's Marxism than Marx's complex views of the totality of history, in which the economic, material practice is the single most important driving force."[54] Li also holds that Mao's Marxism was closer to dialectical materialism than historical materialism in that it clung to a dialectic notion of class struggle and social revolution as opposed to the historical process of material progress. In the end, the materialist dimension was gradually attenuated and nearly vanished, as Mao increasingly shifted his attention to class struggles in cultural and ideological spheres.

"It is worth noting," writes Li, "that Mao's dialectics has little to do with the Hegelian or Western dialectics; rather, it is intimately related to the classical Chinese concepts of dialectics, derived largely from military strategies and the arts of war."[55] Mao's theory of practice emphasized "dialectical materialist epistemology," and his notion of "contradictions" consisted primarily of actual, practical, and essentially military strategies, originating from Mao's practical experience in peasant revolutionary warfare. Mao translated Marxist dialectics into the practices of a revolutionary war, rather than merely theorizing it. In sum, Li believes that Marxism became "sinified" through a complex process—Mao integrated Marxist dialectical materialism with both social reality and tradition. The peasant revolutionary war was waged with a strategy based on Chinese classical military dialectics. This, in Li's view, was the nature of the sinification of Marxism.

On a theoretical level, both the strength and weakness of the historically conditioned Chinese Marxism reside in its creative incorporation and transformation of dialectical materialist notions of revolution, class struggle, and the subjective will and consciousness in "making revolution." Furthermore, as Confucian ethical pragmatic rationality never differentiated the separate domains of politics, culture, and consciousness, the public and personal, Chinese Marxism hardly develops a notion of the relative autonomy of these domains. Instead, it tends to conflate polity with morality, private ethics with social responsibilities. During the Cultural Revolution, Li observes, the conflation of these domains had dire consequences. Political and social issues were registered in primarily moral and ethical imperatives, thus inducing quasi-religious, moral, and ethical fervor in social movements. Moreover, the conflation of different social domains radically altered the *rational* objective of the Cultural Revolution, turning it into near insanity and irrationality.[56] Contrary to the prevailing opinion that the Cultural Revolution was a purely irrational nightmare, Li's analysis probes into the complex causes of history. And, indeed, the Cultural Revolution itself in Li's view, testifies to the very "antinomy of historicism and ethicism": the historical necessity of revolution is turned against itself, so to speak, by the ethical imperatives conditioned by historical needs. By the same token, the dual variation of the enlightenment and national salvation rests on the same antinomy: enlightenment entails not only cognitive self-education, but moral and ethical regeneration, whereas national salvation is a clear response to China's historical crisis. In the final analysis, modernity itself can be understood by this antinomy. Alienation, Li contends, is historically necessary and inevitable for achieving a humanized nature, but it runs counter to human being's ethical values, thus generating a fundamental contradiction of modernity.[57]

Li's own thinking also resides on a series of antinomies. First, Li's optimistic, constructive, and forward-looking vision is decidedly constrained by mixed feelings over the past, and an ethos of recovery and return: a return to May Fourth humanism and enlightenment, to Chinese cultural traditions, and to classic Marxism. Second, despite his appropriations of certain modern conceptions—say of Wittgenstein, Piaget, and Clifford Geertz—Li's reflections remain locked in the categories of classical German thought. The term *fansi* (reflection), which had preeminent currency in the 1980s, contains a major paradox: it is, on the one hand, self-reflexive of the Chinese tradition, especially the revolutionary legacy; on the other hand, it is oblivious to its metaphysical underpinnings of classical German philosophy. Third, reactions to Mao's legacy and the Cultural Revolution may have compelled him to put more stress on the ultimate determination of the economic than on ideology and culture. Ironically, the historical materialist distinction of base and superstructure seems to be dissolved in his culturalist resolutions. Instead of relying on economic developmentalism and modernization models, Li tries to reintegrate the Kantian aesthetic subject, Marxian notion of a humanized nature, Piagetian developmental psychology, and Confucian ren (benevolence) and tian ren heyi (unity of humans [sic] and heaven) into a final, grandiose resolution of the dilemma of China and the world.

Last but not least, there is the antinomy of the aesthetic itself. Li's historical materialist and dialectical method seems to be suspended when he comes to define subjectivity and the humanization of nature in exclusively aesthetic terms. Aesthetic subjectivity from Kant to Marx has had strong political bearings. Kantian universal subjectivity, however versatile and ambiguous, was a projection of the late-eighteenth-century German middle class, "in image if not in reality, as a truly universal subject." This bourgeois subject has posed "an ideological challenge to the ruling order" and served as a "counterstrategy to political dominance."[58] Li is not unaware of the political and ideological specificity of the Kantian notion of aesthetic subjectivity, but when he applies it to the Chinese condition, he seems to bracket the historical particularity of the concept by valorizing the aesthetic over the political. Despite Li's strong reservations about the Frankfurt School, he actually practices an analogous supradisciplinary critique. His is a mixture of philosophy, intellectual history, aesthetic theory, art criticism, and anthropological analyses. In addition, the culturalist and aestheticist tendencies in his political and historical criticism also bear some resemblance to Western Marxism.

The inherent contradiction or antinomy between political engagement and a depoliticizing, aestheticizing tendency is evident in many critical formations of the Cultural Reflection; Liu Zaifu's theory of literary subjectivity is a prominent example. Liu's formulation of literary subjectivity was, as he acknowledged, largely inspired by Li's aesthetic theory of subjectivity. It was also occasioned by China's literary scene of the mid-1980s. Since 1985, the contemporary Chinese literary scene has undergone a series of changes in terms of form and language. In the words of critic Li Tuo, these changes amount to nothing less than a "cultural avalanche," a "revolution of language" that threatens to subvert the hegemony of "Maoist discourse."[59] A new oppositional political consciousness and an aesthetic vision have emerged.

Concurrently, new avant-garde critics have displayed a strong political self-consciousness in their deconstructive undertakings. The rediscovery of modernism and the introduction of postmodernist writings have fueled an innovative and oppositional avant-garde in Post-Mao China. The self-referential, self-reflexive, experimental fiction of Yu Hua, Ma Yuan, Can Xue, Ge Fei, Su Tong, and others, invariably creates the effects of estrangement and defamiliarization through the cultivation of a new linguistic medium that expresses feelings of alienation, disillusionment, and existential *Angst* in Mao's China. Translating poststructuralist assaults on cultural hegemony in the Western tradition into critiques of cultural institutions in Maoist China, the Chinese avant-garde critics celebrate the demystifying power of the discourse of experimental literature. The younger generation of critics in the PRC is fascinated by this avant-garde literature, and at the same time, feels deeply frustrated that its theoretical mode and vocabulary remain enmeshed in Stalinist-Maoist criticism. The old-fashioned theoretical tools, bereft of the procedures of formal analysis, are far too inadequate to grasp the formal inventiveness of this new literature.

Liu, in his early career in the late 1970s, took the lead in challenging the conceptual basis of the dominant Marxist theoretical model. His critical study of Lu Xun, published in 1979, was a self-conscious attempt to do away with sociological platitudes. Liu's landmark essay, "On the Subjectivity of Literature" (1985), and other writings triggered a major controversy over the principal issues in literary theory and criticism. This debate in the field of literary studies then became a major component of the general cultural debate in China that began in the mid-1980s.

When Liu's "On the Subjectivity of Literature" appeared, literary criticism in China stood at an intersection, bewildered by the busy traffic of new styles and trends, yet unable to locate its own path in the cultural co-ordinates of the post-Mao era. The terrorist "literary criticism" of the Cultural Revolution, much despised and maligned, was no longer dominant. But Chinese criticism under the straitjacket of Soviet socialist realism suffered a fatal deficiency: its embarrassing inability to engage literary texts as literature, rather than as political and ideological documents. Under the leadership of liberal-minded CCP General Secretary Hu Yaobang and Premier Zhao Ziyang who were then backed by China's paramount leader Deng Xiaoping, in 1984 Liu had been appointed director of the Institute of Literature Research at the Chinese Academy of Social Sciences, and the editor-in-chief of *Wenxue pinlun* (*Literature Review*), the leading scholarly journal in the field. With such powerful positions, Liu was expected to be a spokesperson for the party's literary policy. But his 1985 subjectivity essay contained an unmistakable criticism of the party's interference in the realms of literature and the arts, while advocating a humanist, independent literature of subjectivity as an alternative. Party loyalists smelled the smoke of dissent and deviation in Liu's work. His critics, representing the official and orthodox view, characterized him as being politically radical and subversive.[60] But such charges only reflected the kind of political paranoia that locked up the minds of the orthodox critics themselves (Chen Yong, for instance, who during the debate most vehemently attacked Liu's "political heresy," was himself a victim of the earlier Anti-Rightist Campaign and Cultural Revolution). The majority of Chinese writers and critics hailed the article for its bold challenge to the party's literary orthodoxy.

The thrust of Liu's formulation is a dialectical recovery of creative subjectivity as well as literature itself ("return to the subject and return to the text," so to speak.)[61] The effacing of the individual subject in official literary criticism is politically and ideologically determined in ways that cannot be explained in purely literary and cultural terms. Liu's aesthetic reconstruction of subjectivity is therefore counterhegemonic, continuing Hu Feng's efforts of subject formation within a revolutionary hegemony. On the other hand, Liu's strategy differs from Hu's, in that Liu tends to ontologize aesthetic subjectivity. By equating the aesthetic with the essence of a human being and then defining literature as that which embodies the level at which the human being understands itself, Liu's formulation endows the aesthetic with the power to transgress the border of the imaginary and real, thereby challenging the notion of aesthetic representation. As for Liu's theory, the sociopolitical reality of China that denies the very existence of subjectivity is not real; the real is the aesthetic being, or the subject in Liu's terms, that has been totally alienated, and hence, must be reconstructed by literature and the arts. Liu writes: "The significance of the thesis that 'literature is the study of human beings' [wenxue shi renxue] is self-evident, for it restores the practical subjectivity of humankind and spiritual subjectivity in the realm of literature. The enrichment and development of subjectivity marks the progress of history. As a study of human beings, literature develops itself at a pace paralleling the level at which human beings understand themselves."[62]

In Liu's frame of reference, "the progress of history" as a Marxist teleology maintains the romanticist utopianism that distinguished the young Marx in the *Economic and Philosophical Manuscripts*. Liu transfigures this Marxian utopian vision into the contemporary world, asserting that

> humankind nowadays has already left the immediate daily process of labor behind them. Labor and aesthetic activity come to unite into one, and human nature has continued to enrich, develop and perfect itself. . . . Never has the self-consciousness of human subjectivity as a whole become so manifest. Human beings are longing to modernize themselves as they demand the modernization of society.[63]

Liu emphasizes the emancipatory function of the aesthetic experience of reading. From a Schillerian-Marxian perspective of aesthetic education, he describes this as a process whereby one realizes his or her free, complete, and self-conscious being. Reading is equated with the unfolding of humanity, and the human essence of freedom and self-consciousness.[64] For many years in China, aesthetic judgment was subordinate to the cognitive function of literature and the arts in revolutionary hegemony. Liu's aesthetic experience of reading as a return to humanity challenges the politicization and instrumentalization of aesthetic experience. The aesthetic serves an eminently counterhegemonic and political purpose by invoking humanity, universality, and freedom as the proper goals of revolution itself. In this respect, Liu's notion of aesthetic experience should be grasped as a dialectical solution to the antinomy of revolution and revolutionary hegemony, rather than a reaffirmation of bourgeois humanism through romanticizing subjectivity and aesthetic experience, as both his orthodox critics in China then and the ideologues of bourgeois humanism and liberalism now would depict it for different reasons.

After "On the Subjectivity of Literature," Liu published several books and numerous articles, further developing his view of literary subjectivity. In a book coauthored with the young critic Lin Gang, *Tradition and the Chinese Person* (1988), the emergence of individualist values and subjectivity are identified as hallmarks of Chinese modernity. His historically accurate description of modern Chinese intellectual development, however, gives way to an aestheticized account of universal subjectivity, following Li's theory, as the ultimate goal of China's project of enlightenment and modernity.[65] Also, Liu portrays modern and contemporary Chinese literature as essentially a process of discovering humanity and human subjectivity at different historical conjunctures. He views literature as part of a profound cultural reflection on Chinese tradition. The centrality of this cultural reflection is the question of subjectivity.[66] Liu's theory of subjectivity constitutes a cultural theory from which to study modern Chinese literature. In a 1986 interview, Liu proposed cultural studies as a new approach to modern Chinese literature, as opposed to the dominant political and sociological avenues. Here, he contended that the most important feature of modern Chinese culture was the transformation of cultural conceptions, characterized by the recognition of the primacy of individuality and subjectivity.[67]

Liu's theory of subjectivity rests on the humanist view embodied in Hegelian metaphysics. He criticizes mechanical theories of reflection by valorizing creative subjectivity and literature as representations of the human essence of freedom. But Liu is keenly aware of the immense incompatibility between historically different social conditions and abstract systems of thought. At the heart of his theoretical reflection is the distinction between politics and culture. Much of Li and Liu's works were intended to stake out or relocate an autonomous site or a cultural space for the displaced intellectuals themselves. In this respect, their philosophical and literary notions can be seen as strategies of reterritorialization, as well as efforts to construct a cultural topology of postrevolutionary society. A staggering amount of difficulties and contradictions appeared in their endeavors, and like Li, who posits a fundamental antinomy in philosophy (which must logically include his own), Liu copes with the tensions in his own thought by turning to critical reflexivity.

In recently thinking over his critical enterprises of "literary subjectivity" and "cultural studies," Liu admits that one of his main objectives is to counter the dominant philosophical discourse in China, namely "the dualism of mind and matter."[68] This dualism refers specifically to the deterministic and teleological traits inherent in historical materialism. Liu is also aware that his own thinking habits are deeply entrenched in a "dualistic mode," something with which he has wrestled throughout his career. His book of prose poems, *Tragic Songs of Quest*, is replete with contradictory romantic yearnings for love, harmony, and universality, along with trepidations about a strident reality.[69] In Liu's theoretical musings, antagonistic dichotomies seem to permeate every corner of life: at the level of social life, there are binary oppositions such as politics/culture, tradition/modernity, Westernization/sinification; at the theoretical level, those of mind/matter, feeling/reason, conscious/unconscious cut across his work. One of his famous formulations is the "dual composition of literary character." He insists that the literary character is not a homogeneous monad, but possesses complex, dual features. In another celebrated essay, "On Desire," Liu deals with conflicts between human instincts and desires, and social orders and norms.[70]

A careful reading of Liu's major statements on subjectivity indicates the hybrid resources of his theoretical arguments. Liu has borrowed freely from existentialism and phenomenology to reinforce his ontological depictions of aesthetic subjectivity. He is receptive to archetypal criticism, structuralism, reception theory, and psychoanalysis, engaging Heidegger, Freud, Lacan, and Derrida. In a recent article, Liu writes: "Subjectivity is not simply consciousness. . . . it is being itself. . . . Subjectivity is first and foremost a question of ontology rather than epistemology. . . . The highest value is man's ontological value of being. . . . no matter whether it exists in the temporal form of 'present' or in the 'past,' the highest value of his being is always already embodied in the meaning of being here and now." By treating literature as "the symbolic world of one's spiritual freedom," Liu actually repeats Heideggerian aesthetic existentialist propositions on literature and the arts. Liu also suggests that human subjectivity has a dimension of opposition and transcendence over cultural and symbolic constructs, which will enable Liu to ultimately overcome the aporia of the language prison and cultural constraints he himself has built. It will, therefore, remedy the Lacanian "extreme pessimism."[71] His main frame of reference, however, remains that of traditional Marxist categories, and his classic literary examples come primarily from the nineteenth-century European romanticist and realist works and the classical Chinese tradition.[72]

The prime impulse of Liu's aestheticizing enterprise is a desire to counter the dominance of political theories of reflection and representation with an aesthetic theory of subjectivity. Liu's generation of Chinese intellectuals has become disillusioned with politics, and tries to distance itself from politics as much as possible. Yet politics inevitably intervenes at the very moment of depoliticization. Liu attempts to transcend politics by proposing aesthetic universals, but his aesthetic enterprise betrays the political intent he is unwilling to acknowledge.

More influential than Li and Liu's elite, academic discourse is a hybrid kind, mingling intellectual exchange with popular tales and myths, articulated through the powerful medium of television. The television documentary series *He Shang (River Elegy)* of 1988 proved to be the climactic event of the Cultural Reflection, arousing considerable fervor among young intellectuals and college students. When they became the prime forces of the Tian'anmen upheaval in 1989, the documentary immediately drew harsh criticism from the revolutionary old guard and praise from students. Sanctioned by liberal-minded CCP General Secretary Zhao Ziyang, the six-part series was broadcast by CCTV, China's only national channel and the CCP's most important mouthpiece. After its successful debut, the show was rebroadcast two months later during prime time. Millions watched the documentary, and thousands of letters and phone calls flooded CCTV's editorial offices (there were no call-in programs on China's television channels at the time).

Relentlessly iconoclastic, *He Shang* appears to be an indictment against traditional Chinese culture. Yet its manifest intention was to present an unequivocal message about the present political situation. As Xiaomei Chen puts it, the documentary virtually "offers a paradigm for a number of more general and pressing theoretical and political issues, and it thus has a cross-cultural significance that reaches beyond contemporary China and the authorized and unauthorized discourses associated with it."[73] Chen identifies the paradigm as "an anti-official discourse that employs the Occidental Other as a cultural and ideological absence that critiques the oppressive presence of official ideology."[74] The Occidental other refers to the documentary's excessive images of the modern West as a contrast to China, an ingenious or disingenuous manipulation of signification that pits an "unofficial" Occidentalist counterdiscourse against the "official" Orientalism and Occidentalism. To be sure, the documentary's content is superbly skillful, playing off one set of binary oppositions against another, such as East/West, self/other, and tradition/modernity. Its presentation is effective, too. The narrative and audiovisual effects are both emotionally appealing and intellectually persuasive. It shows a carefully choreographed parade of leading Chinese scholars and writers, who offer their authorial and expert commentaries on historical events. The most significant comments are pronounced by the provocative and mesmerizing voice of an offscreen commentator, while sharply contrasted images, colors, and music are synchronized by the producers to maximize the series' effect on a television audience.

The aesthetic plays a crucial role in *He Shang*. Its critical paradigm closely resembles Li's aesthetic-historical framework; indeed, Li's influence is pervasive in the documentary. The series' narrative discourse and visual presentations are primarily registered in dialectical antinomies and paradoxes. Throughout, Li's concepts of sedimentation and cultural-psychological formation are used as "master tropes" in both the narratives and commentaries. *He Shang* contains unmistakable political messages that trespass and challenge the "official" ideological lines. Its defiance is extravagant rather than subtle, not only because the medium itself requires sensationalism and simple, straightforward messages, but because of the general mood at the time—a period of high Culture Fever. The two CCP general secretaries, Hu Yaobang and Zhao Ziyang, backed criticism that bordered on outright condemnation of the revolution and its hegemony, while China experienced a new "honeymoon" with Western culture, American culture in particular. In brief, it was a time of political high drama and emotional excess, and *He Shang*'s much dramatized admiration of Western culture and equally exaggerated reproach of Chinese tradition captured the general ambience. The two top leaders fell respectively, and the highly dramatic mode of presentation in *He Shang* ominously anticipated the events at Tian'anmen in June 1989, which turned out to be, among other things, a sensational global media spectacle filled with violence, PLA's tanks, and a bloodbath.

A more revealing aspect of the documentary is formal, rather than its political content. The extravaganza of parading striking colors and images, of chanting sensational slogans and tunes, is by no means unfamiliar to the Chinese. In fact, it reminds one of the Cultural Revolution's aestheticization of politics. Yet its self-reflexive, self-critical, and intellectual and rational posture clearly presents the new dominant mode of the Cultural Reflection. Furthermore, its "antigovernment" political message also rests on a critical ambiguity. It was antigovernment only to the extent that it criticized the "conservative factions"; meanwhile, it was also "pro-government," insofar as it supported the "liberal factions" within the CCP leadership.

Indeed, the aesthetic-historical form of *He Shang* itself transgresses all neat binary oppositions, be they pro-government/antigovernment, Occidentalist/Orientalist, or ultimately, aesthetic/political. It is this paradoxical and transgressive power of the form that gives rise to the documentary's political and ideological effectivity, and at the same time, determines its limits as a political interventionist strategy. One is, for instance, reminded of the political incidents that occurred the following spring. Unquestionably, *He Shang* was linked quite directly with the student movement; the series' emotionally charged discourse reverberated exuberantly among the demonstrators at Tian'anmen Square. After the government's crackdown, the producers were all charged with instigating political unrest, and many were forced into exile outside China. Most of them fled to the United States as political dissidents. While the *He Shang* crew themselves were either at the center of the demonstrations prior to June 4, or were silenced afterward, the ambiguity and ambivalence of the form was used and abused at Tian'anmen in 1989—not by the Chinese themselves, but by the postmodern, multinational media team headed by CNN. Thanks to CNN's extensive coverage, one got the feeling that "China" had for the first time become "real," entering millions of households through global and transnational electronic media coverage. This is not to suggest a resemblance between *He Shang* and CNN's coverage of Tian'anmen, but rather, to indicate some profound revelation in terms of the role of the aesthetic in the electronic media that reaches beyond political, ideological differences. There is a glaring difference between CNN's flatly consumer-oriented, yet "professionally" and "objectively" produced coverage of current events, and *He Shang*'s highly politicized, much dramatized version of history. But ultimately, one must question the aesthetic-historical, and indeed political-ideological, "content" of the form itself in order to uncover the ideologies in each cultural production.

The fate of *He Shang* epitomizes the possibilities and limits of the Cultural Reflection that intervened in contemporary political life by commenting on recent history through an aesthetic lense. The aestheticizing impulses of the Li Zehous, Liu Zaifus, and other cultural critics, including the *He Shang* crew, seem to parallel a tendency in Western contemporary cultural theories: to engage, paradoxically, in social and historical analyses from cultural and aesthetic perspectives, while distancing both cultural and literary criticism from social engagement.[75] In the West, it is a question related to the escalating interpenetration and fragmentation of social life, which has bewildered Western intellectuals and made radical social engagement increasingly difficult. The recent debates about modernism and postmodernism address fundamental issues in contemporary late capitalist society; but the debates themselves remain confined within academic circles, with little impact on social and political life. Such is also the fate of Marxist cultural theory in the West. Recently, the political and ideological consequences and effects of academic cultural criticism have been intensely debated among the intellectual Left in the West. While hardly any positive alternatives emerge, assertions of critical intervention and participation renew hopes of social effectiveness.

In China, the events of 1989 serve as a powerful reminder of how politics—political struggles in social institutions and daily life—has been entangled with every cultural formation. Compared to the realpolitik in China's cultural spheres, one wonders if the debates in Western academic circles about rhetorical or pragmatic discourses will have any influence relative to the political struggles in society and everyday life. Granted, recent theoretical debates in the West have affected education and scholarly research in the social sciences and humanities. Yet an obsession with language and discourse obscures more grievous issues in society. In this respect, a comparison of the Cultural Reflection in China and the postmodernist debates in the West is illuminating.

The overwhelming preoccupation with "culture" in the 1980s points to a new relationship between culture and politics. The autonomy of culture and its relatively marginal importance in modern Western societies have now been replaced by the close integration (and conflation) of social spheres and the centrality of culture. By the same token, culture has become inseparable from politics in the West, although politics in the United States may take different forms and processes from China or elsewhere. In an advanced capitalist country like the United States, where anticommunism and free market liberalism have long been dominant ideologies, the relationship between culture and politics embodies all the intrinsic contradictions of American capitalism. Needless to say, American society is fundamentally different from China's, and so are the politics and ideologies. But to insist on these differences, as well as the incomparability of political and cultural formations, would only lead to an impasse. In the end, either a cultural relativism that cancels out any meaningful universality or a universalism that privileges one kind of ideological system—often the Western kind—would prevail. To avoid this, one needs to see the underlying political and ideological motivations of cultural and conceptual claims.

Moving beyond the facile arguments of relativism and universalism, cultural practices can be viewed as political practices and interventions that function differently in different societies. Contemporary Western critical theories have concentrated on critiquing and deconstructing the ideologies and myths underpinning the concepts of modernity, democracy, freedom, and development that are basic to capitalist societies. These concepts are also embedded in the thought of Chinese intellectuals, such as Li Zehou and Liu Zaifu, in their attempt to establish a new cultural myth for the future of China. Interestingly, they have engaged in critique and deconstruction, too, but their target is not capitalist modernity and its ideologies. Instead, it is the Maoist legacy of politicization and instrumentalization. The humanist, aesthetic "essence" of Marxism that the Chinese aesthetic Marxists tried to recover is, ironically, an ideological myth now subjected to rigorous demystification by their Western contemporaries. Such a conceptual incommensurability cannot be simply explained as a result of fundamental differences. Instead, it is better grasped as a manifestation of the profound tensions and contradictions of modernity at a crossroads or critical conjuncture. From such a historical perspective, one may proceed to examine the very role of the aesthetic, which mediates, reconciles, and negotiates widely different and heterogeneous tensions and contradictions.

At the end of the twentieth century, there is little indication that the role of the aesthetic is fading away. Still, it is changing quite significantly. Globalization has accelerated the process of the commodification of cultural and aesthetic spheres on a global scale. Meanwhile, efforts to aestheticize, and hence neutralize, real political and economic inequalities and conflicts tend to perpetuate the myth of capitalist modernity. Aesthetic sensibilities and tastes, moreover, have been increasingly identified with ethnic and national peculiarities in the claims of localized, ethnic, nativist, and nationalist interests. The dominant depoliticizing mode in China's cultural scene nevertheless surreptitiously reinforces neoconservative political upsurges under the discrete guises of nationalism, "neoliberalism," and various "post-isms"—from postmodernism to postcolonialism. These new intellectual fashions in China have one thing in common: one way or another, they submit to the ideas of the "final triumph of capitalist modernity" and "death of socialist alternatives."[76] For instance, it has became trendy to debunk the 1980s' Cultural Reflection, invariably subscribing to the categories of transcendence and autonomy vis-à-vis political engagement and intervention. Consequently, the efforts of the Li Zehous and Liu Zaifus are now accused of being either too obsessed with the secular and ideological issues of the present, or too deeply engrossed in the Enlightenment grand récit or Western "master narratives." As the new waves of consumerism are quickly pushing the intellectual elite to the periphery of social life, aesthetic transcendence or autonomy transpires into a new binary warfare between a cultural elitism and commercialized popular culture. Paradoxically, the newly manufactured cultural heterogeneity or hybridity tends to homogenize and conceal intense economic and political confrontations and polarizations. Both pessimists and optimists alike (depending, of course, on which ideological camp one belongs to) concede that the CCP itself has substantially transformed from a revolutionary, idealist party into a powerholder and corporate manager in a capitalist economy and autocratic political system. A consensus seems to prevail, though implicitly, in China today: revolution is dead and socialism only retains its name, insofar as the CCP still rules.

But can revolution die? Jacques Derrida's latest book, *Specters of Marx*, suggests that revolution as a specter will never disappear, even though "in the name of the revolution," as the title of one chapter indicates, revolution remains an "impure impure impure history of ghosts."[77] And there are not only ghosts. In China, the tradition of revolution itself lives, and "must learn to live finally," with both the living and dead.

My narrative of the genealogy of the aesthetic in modern China, particularly in its Marxist incarnations, must come to an end now. Narratives, of course, try to construct a coherent and meaningful story with a beginning and an end. While it certainly appears naive to suggest that the end of narratives correspond to, or at least corroborate, the end of real events, the meaning of aesthetic beginning and ending must be sought elsewhere. William Shakespeare wrote eloquently: "So long as men can breathe, or eyes can see / So long lives this, and this gives life to thee." These lines testify to the aesthetic meaning of narratives, as well as to the paradox or antinomy that the genealogy of the aesthetic embodies. The aesthetic aspires to capture the transient, the ephemeral, the historical, with something eternal, immutable, and transcendental. During this process, it has been charged with enormous moral, ethical, and libidinous passions, desires, and energies, which nevertheless can never transcend the historical necessity, nor reach "beyond good and evil." Nor can it ultimately efface the irreducible heterogeneity and difference of the world, be it economic, ideological, racial, sexual, or ethical, by its "imaginary," "symbolic," and "discursive" mystification or demystification. The aesthetic, however, can illuminate, self-reflexively, its own role (and the role of culture by extension) in the makings of revolution, modernity, and an alternative modernity that traverse historical and geographical boundaries. Its genealogy in Chinese modernity or an alternative modernity epitomizes all the antinomies and paradoxes inherent in modernity itself, as it has trespassed temporal and spatial borders that have marked the fragmented, fragmenting, yet globalizing and unifying contemporary world. Most important, perhaps, the aesthetic seems to point toward infinite possibilities of seeking alternatives. This is testified to not only by the modern intellectual tradition of Western Marxism. It is also shown in the efforts of Chinese aesthetic Marxists, which can neither be neglected nor forgotten.

NOTES

Chapter 1. Aesthetics, Modernity, and Alternative Modernity: The Case of China

1 Max Horkheimer and Theodor Adorno, *Dialectic of Enlightenment*, trans. John Cumming (New York: Continuum, 1994), 3.

2 Terry Eagleton, *The Ideology of the Aesthetic* (Oxford: Basil Blackwell, 1990).

3 Ibid.

4 For a study of the ti-yong dualism and its major proponent, see Daniel Bays, *China Enters the Twentieth Century: Chang Chih-tung and the Issues of a New Age, 1895–1909* (Ann Arbor: University of Michigan Press, 1978).

5 For an analysis of the ideological nature of the aesthetic concept from a Western Marxist perspective, see Eagleton, *Ideology of the Aesthetic*. See also Josef Chytry, *The Aesthetic State: A Quest in Modern German Thought* (Berkeley: University of California Press, 1989); and J. M. Bernstein, *The Fate of Art: Aesthetic Alienation from Kant to Derrida and Adorno* (University Park: Pennsylvania State University Press, 1992).

6 Liang Qichao, *Yinbingshi heji* (Collected essays from the ice-drinker's studio), vol. 4 (Shanghai: Zhonghuan shuju, 1936), 176.

7 Cai Yuanpei, *Cai Yuanpei xuanji* (Selected works of Cai Yuanpei) (Beijing: Zhonghua shuju, 1963), 328.

8 Lin Yu-sheng, *The Crisis of Chinese Consciousness: Radical Antitraditionalism in the May Fourth Era* (Madison: University of Wisconsin Press, 1979), 28.

9 See Arif Dirlik, *The Origins of Chinese Communism* (Oxford: Oxford University Press, 1989); and Arif Dirlik, *After the Revolution: Waking to Global Capitalism* (Hanover, N.H.: Wesleyan University Press, 1994).

10 "Westerners have gone through great turmoils, and shed [a] great deal of blood, in order to embrace Mr. Science and Mr. Democracy. . . . We now must have firm confidence in them as the cures of China from the political, moral, scholarly, and intellectual abyss" (Chen Duxiu, "Ben zhi zui'an zhi dabian shu" [A self-defense of our journal's "criminal case"], *Xin qingnian* [New youth] 6, no. 1 [1915]: 1).

11 See Hu Shi, "Du Liang Shuming xiansheng de *Dongxi wenhua ji qi zhexue*" (Comment on Liang Shuming's *East/West cultures and philosophies*) (1923) and "Women duiyu xiyang jindai wenming de taidu" (Our attitude toward modern Western cul-

ture) (1926), in *Cong "xihua" dao xiandaihua* (From "Westernization" to modernization), ed. Luo Rongqu (Beijing: Beijing daxue chubanshe, 1990), 108–22, 158–69.

12 For a survey of Jin Guantao's "scientistic Marxism," see Bill Brugger and David Kelly, *Chinese Marxism in the Post-Mao Era* (Stanford, Calif.: Stanford University Press, 1990).

13 Michel Foucault, "What Is Enlightenment?" in *Foucault Reader*, ed. Paul Rabinow (New York: Pantheon Books, 1984), 39. For a discussion of the May Fourth intellectuals' conceptualization of both democracy and science, see Vera Schwarz, *The Chinese Enlightenment* (Berkeley: University of California Press, 1986), 107.

14 See, for instance, Andrew Nathan, *Chinese Democracy* (Berkeley: University of California Press, 1985); and Merle Goldman, *Sowing the Seeds of Democracy in China* (Cambridge, Mass.: Harvard University Press, 1994).

15 Eagleton, *Ideology of the Aesthetic*, 16.

16 Fredric Jameson, *Postmodernism, or, The Cultural Logic of Late Capitalism* (Durham, N.C.: Duke University Press, 1991), 48.

17 For critical rethinking of Japanese modernity and the Western discourse of Japan, see, for instance, the two collections edited by Masao Miyoshi and H. D. Harootunian, *Postmodernism and Japan* (Durham, N.C.: Duke University Press, 1989) and *Japan in the World* (Durham, N.C.: Duke University Press, 1993); and Masao Miyoshi, *Off Center: Power and Culture Relations between Japan and the United States* (Cambridge, Mass.: Harvard University Press, 1991).

18 China specialists in the West are interested primarily in cultural events with political consequences. Hence, Western studies of intellectual currents in the PRC mainly focus on "voices of dissent." See, for instance, Merle Goldman et al., eds, *China's Intellectuals and the State: In Search of a New Relationship* (Cambridge, Mass.: Council on East Asian Studies at Harvard University, 1987). On the other hand, studies of Chinese Marxism have yet to tackle the issue of alternative Marxist thinking in China in cultural and aesthetic domains. See Brugger and Kelly, *Chinese Marxism*; and Arif Dirlik and Maurice Meisner, eds., *Marxism and the Chinese Experience* (New York: M. E. Sharpe, 1989).

19 One of the aims of this book is to critique certain basic assumptions of China studies, including postcolonial (and postmodernist) perspectives on modern Chinese cultural history. For a preliminary critique of the ideological assumptions underlying studies of modern Chinese literature and culture, see Kang Liu, "Politics, Critical Paradigms: Reflections on Modern Chinese Literature Studies," *Modern China* 19, no. 1 (1993): 13–40.

20 Marshall Berman, *All That Is Solid Melts into Air: The Experience of Modernity* (New York: Penguin Books, 1988), 15.

21 Miyoshi, *Off Center*, 13–14.

22 Recent research credits this to an essay by Xu Dachun, "Shu meixue" (Introduction of aesthetics), *Dongfang zhazhi* (The Orient) 1, no. 1 (1915) (see Chen Wei, *Zhongguo xiandai meixue sixiang shigang* [A brief history of modern Chinese aesthetic thought] [Shanghai: Shanghai renmin chubanshe, 1993], 8–10).

23 Joseph Levenson, *Liang Ch'i-ch'ao and the Mind of Modern China*, 3d ed. (New York: Harper and Row, 1966), 9.

24 Ibid., 219.

25 Philip C. Huang, *Liang Ch'i-ch'ao and Modern Chinese Liberalism* (Seattle: University of Washington Press, 1972).

26 Hao Chang, *Liang Ch'i-ch'ao and Intellectual Transition in China, 1890–1907* (Cambridge, Mass.: Harvard University Press, 1971), 149–54.

27 Ibid., 298.

28 Ibid., 307.

29 Liang Qichao, "Xiaoshuo yu qunzhi zhi guanxi" (On the relationship between fiction and the government of the people), in *Zhongguo jindai wenlun xuan* (Selected modern Chinese literary essays), vol. 1 (Beijing: Renmin wenxue chubanshe, 1981), 157–61.

30 Liang Qichao, quoted in Lin Yu-sheng, *Crisis of Chinese Consciousness*.

31 Liang Qichao, "Meishu yu kexue" (Art and science), in *Zhongguo meixue ziliao xuanbian* (Selected essays on Chinese aesthetics), vol. 2 (Beijing: Zhonghua shuju, 1981), 410.

32 Liang Qichao, "Ziyou shu: wei xin" (Treatise on liberty: On mind), in *Yinbingshi heji*, vol. 3, 235.

33 Chang, *Intellectual Transition in China*, 224–25.

34 Liang Qichao, "Ou you xinying lu" (Impressions of the journey to Europe), in *Yinbingshi heji*, vol. 5, 79.

35 Ibid., 81.

36 Henri Bergson, quoted in Monroe C. Beardsley, *Aesthetics from Classical Greece to the Present* (New York: Macmillan, 1966), 325–27.

37 Liang, "Ou you xinying lu," 77.

38 Raymond Williams, "The Bloomsbury Fraction," in *Problems in Materialism and Culture* (London: Verso, 1980), 168.

39 See Joey Bonner, *Wang Kuo-wei: An Intellectual Biography* (Cambridge, Mass.: Harvard University Press, 1986).

40 See Liu Mengxi, " 'Wenhua tuo ming' yu Zhongguo xiandai xueshu chuantong" ("Cultural will-passing" and the modern Chinese tradition of scholarship), *Zhongguo wenhua* (Chinese culture), no. 6 (spring 1992): 107.

41 Ibid., 106.

42 The hermeneutic paradigm of tradition/modernity was promoted by a group of young scholars associated with the journal *Wenhuan: Zhongguo yu shijie* (Culture: China and the world) and the translation project Twentieth-Century Western Scholarly Classics. Without counting the influence of the same paradigm dominating modern China studies in the West, the purpose of the Chinese hermeneuticists of the 1980s was to replace the older paradigm of Chinese culture/Western culture with tradition/modernity in their reinterpretation of modern Chinese cultural and intellectual history. While they did not purposefully elide and suppress the revolutionary hegemony and legacy as a central problematic, these hermeneuticists took the problematic of modernity (of the Western origin, at least as an epistemological issue) as their guiding episteme without questioning its historical specificity. See Gan Yang, ed., *Zhongguo dangdai wenhua yishi* (Contemporary Chinese cultural consciousness) (Hong Kong: Sanlian shudian, 1989).

43 For a critique of national learning, see Kang Liu, "Is There an Alternative to (Capitalist) Globalization? The Debate about Modernity in China," in *The Cultures of Globalization*, ed. Fredric Jameson and Masao Miyoshi (Durham, N.C.: Duke University Press, 1998).

44 Charles Baudelaire, *The Painter of Modern Life and Other Essays* (London: Phaidon, 1964), 13.

45 Malcom Bradbury and James MacFarlane, eds., *Modernism, 1890–1930* (New York: Penguin, 1976), 446.

46 For a discussion of Wang's attitudes toward Kant and Schopenhauer, see Bonner, *An Intellectual Biography*, esp. chaps. 5 and 6, 56–80.

47 Wang Guowei, "*Honglou meng* pinglun" (Comments on *Dream of Red Chamber*), in *Zhongguo meixue ziliao xuanbian*, (Collection on Chinese aesthetics), vol. 2 (Beijing: Zhonghua shuju, 1982), 432.

48 Wang Guowei, quoted in Bonner, *An Intellectual Biography*, 45.

49 Wang Guowei, "*Guoxue congkan xu*" (Foreword to *National learning journal*), in *Wang Guowei yishu* (Collected works of Wang Guowei), vol. 4 (Shanghai: Shangwu yinshuguan, 1940), 7.

50 Wang Guowei, quoted in Bonner, *An Intellectual Biography*, 47.

51 For an illuminating discussion of modern Chinese literary trends, see Marston Anderson, *The Limits of Realism: Chinese Fiction in the Revolutionary Period* (Berkeley: University of California Press, 1990).

52 Pierre Bourdieu, *Algeria 1960* (Cambridge: Cambridge University Press, 1979), vii.

53 Wang Guowei (Wang Kuo-wei), *Poetic Remarks in the Human World: Jen Chien Ts'u Hua*, trans. and ed. Tu Ching-i (Taipei: Chung-hua shu-chü, 1970).

54 Raymond Williams, "A Hundred Years of Culture and Anarchy," in *Materialism and Culture*, 8.

55 For a study of Cai Yuanpei, see William Duiker, *Ts'ai Yüan-p'ei: Educator of Modern China* (University Park: Pennsylvania State University Press, 1977).

56 For a study of Hu Shi, see Jerome Grieder, *Hu Shih and the Chinese Renaissance* (Cambridge, Mass.: Harvard University Press, 1971).

57 Cai Yuanpei, "Zhexue yu kexue" (Philosophy and science), in *Cai Yuanpei xiansheng quanji* (Complete works of Cai Yuanpei) (Taipei: Shangwu yinshuguan, 1968), 492–93.

58 Cai Yuanpei, "Yi meiyu dai zongjiao shuo" (On replacing religion with aesthetic education), in *Cai Yuanpei xiansheng quanji*, 730.

59 Ibid., 731.

60 Cai's interest in Kant is abundantly demonstrated in his own work. He has written about and translated several German neo-Kantian philosophers, including Friedrich Paulsen and William Wunde (see, for instance, "Zhexue dagang" [An outline of philosophy] and "Zhexue yaoling" [Introduction to philosophy], in *Cai Yuanpei xiansheng quanji*, 103–44, 252–99). While a young library assistant at the Peking University Library, Mao was introduced to Paulsen's neo-Kantian philosophy by Cai. For Cai's concern with Kantian aesthetics and philosophy, see William Duiker, "The Aesthetic Philosophy of Ts'ai Yuan-p'ei," *Philosophy East and West* 22, no. 4 (1972): 385–401. For young Mao's interest in neo-Kantianism, see Li Zehou, "Young Mao Zedong," in *On Marxism in China* (Hong Kong: Joint Publishers, 1993).

61 Cai Yuanpei, "Zhongguo de wenyi zhongxin" (China's renaissance), in *Cai Yuanpei xiansheng quanji*, 814.

62 Cai Yuanpei, "Duiyu jiaoyu fangzhen zhi yijian" (My opinion on educational policy), *Cai Yuanpei xiansheng quanji*, 456.

63 Cai Yuanpei, "Meiyu yu rensheng" (Aesthetic education and life), in *Cai Yuanpei xiansheng quanji*, 639–40.

64 Drawn from Chen Wei, *Zhongguo xiandai meixue sixiang shigang*, 113.

65 Ibid., 127.

66 Hu Shi coined the English phrase "alternative modernization" in "Conflicts of Cultures," in *The China Christian Yearbook, 1929* (Shanghai: Christian Literature Society, 1930), 113.

67 For discussions of "Westernization" and "modernization" in the 1920s and 1930s, see Luo Rongqu, ed., *Cong "xihua" dao xiandaihua* (From "Westernization" to modernization) (Beijing: Beijing daxue chubanshe, 1990).

Chapter 2. The Formation of Marxist Aesthetics: From Shanghai to Yan'an

1   For a discussion of the relationship between revolution and modernity, see Perry Anderson, "Modernity and Revolution," *New Left Review* 114 (March–April 1984): 96–113.

2   Marie-Claire Berges, a French scholar, argues that Chinese civil society and its public sphere in the early twentieth century never fully developed, largely due to the weak yet stable structure and power of the state. But she also concedes that the relationship between state and society is dynamic, and even development has great impact on such relationships (see Marie-Claire Berges, *The Golden Age of the Chinese Bourgeoisie*, trans. Janet Lloyd [Cambridge, U.K.: Cambridge University Press, 1989]).

3   For a recent discussion by China specialists in the United States on the issue of civil society/public sphere in modern China, see the symposium "'Public Sphere'/'Civil Society' in China?" *Modern China* 19, no. 2 (April 1993). See also Timothy Brook and B. Michael Frolic, eds., *Civil Society in China* (Armonk, N.Y.: M. E. Sharpe, 1997); and Baogang He, *The Democratic Implications of Civil Society in China* (New York: St. Martin's Press, 1997). The main problem is that these scholars all seem to take Western epistemic assumptions for granted in their discussions of whether or not China has had a civil society.

4   Li Zehou, "Qimeng yu jiuwang de shuangchong bianzou" (The dual variation of enlightenment and salvation), in *Zhongguo xiandai sixiang shi lun* (Essays on modern Chinese intellectual history) (Beijing: Dongfang chubanshe, 1987), 7–49.

5   For studies on the Chinese Revolution and Marxist cultural theories and ideology, see Arif Dirlik, *The Origins of Chinese Communism* (Oxford: Oxford University Press, 1989); Maurice Meisner, *Li Ta-chao and the Origins of Chinese Marxism* (Cambridge, Mass.: Harvard University Press, 1967); and Benjamin Shwartz, *Chinese Communism and the Rise of Mao* (Cambridge, Mass.: Harvard University Press, 1951). Surprisingly, while political and documentary works as well as personal testimonials and memoirs about the Cultural Revolution abound, there are few studies, both in and outside China, that deal with the role of cultural revolution in the Chinese Revolution as a whole in any historical or systematic fashion, let alone with theoretical analysis. For studies of the Cultural Revolution in English, see, for instance, Lynn White, *Policies of Chaos: The Organizational Causes of Violence in China's Cultural Revolution* (Princeton, N.J.: Princeton University Press, 1989); Bill Brugger, ed., *China: The Impact of Cultural Revolution* (London: Croom Helm, 1978); and Merle Goldman et al., eds., *China's Intellectuals and the State: In Search of a New Relationship* (Cambridge, Mass.: Council on East Asian Studies at Harvard University, 1987).

6   Mao Zedong, *Selected Works of Mao Tse-tung*, vol. 2 (Peking: Foreign Language Press, 1967), 372.

7   Paul Pickowicz, *Marxist Literary Thought in China: The Influence of Ch'ü Chiü-pai* (Berkeley: University of California Press, 1981).

8   For Chinese studies, see, for instance, Wang Yao, *Lu Xun zuopin lunji* (Essays on Lu Xun's works) (Beijing: Renmin wenxue chubanshe, 1984); Liu Zaifu, *Lu Xun meixue sixiang lungao* (Essays on Lu Xun's aesthetic thought) (Beijing: Zhongguo shehui kexue chubanshe, 1981); and Lin Fei and Liu Zaifu, *Lu Xun zhuan* (Biography of Lu Xun) (Beijing: Zhongguo shehui kexue chubanshe, 1981).

9   For studies of Lu in English, see Leo Ou-fan Lee, *Voices from the Iron House: A Study of Lu Xun* (Bloomington: Indiana University Press, 1987); Leo Ou-fan Lee, ed., *Lu Xun and His Legacy* (Berkeley: University of California Press, 1985); William Lyell, *Lu*

Hsün's Vision of Reality (Berkeley: University of California Press, 1976); and V. I. Semanov, *Lu Hsün and His Predecessors* (White Plains, N.Y.: M. E. Sharpe, 1980). On the self/society conflict, see Lee, *Voices*. On Lu's moral ethos, see Lin Yü-sheng, "The Morality of Mind and Immorality of Politics: Reflections on Lu Xun the Intellectual," in Lee, *Lu Xun*.

10   See Pierre Bourdieu, *Outline of a Philosophy of Practice* (Cambridge: Cambridge University Press, 1977); and Pierre Bourdieu, *Distinction: A Social Critique of the Judgment of Taste* (Cambridge, Mass.: Harvard University Press, 1984).

11   See Fredric Jameson, *The Political Unconscious* (Ithaca, N.Y.: Cornell University Press, 1981), 74–102.

12   Ibid., 95.

13   For a discussion of the artistic features of Lu's zawen essays, see "The *Zawen*: Sundry Visions of Life and Reality," in Lee, *Voices*, 110–13.

14   Lu's translations of literary theory and criticism include *Literature and Criticism* and *On Art* by Lunacharsky, *On Art* by Plekhanov, and *Symbols of Mental Anguish* by Hakuson (all collected in Lu Xun, *Lu Xun quanji* [Completed works of Lu Xun], 16 vols. [Beijing: Renmin wenxue chubanshe, 1973]).

15   See Fredric Jameson, "Third World Literature in the Era of Multinational Capital," *Social Text* 15 (fall 1986): 65–88.

16   Ibid., 73.

17   Ibid., 77.

18   Lu Xun, *Lu Xun quanji*, vol. 4, 175.

19   Zhang Longxi, "Out of the Cultural Ghetto: Theory, Politics, and the Study of Chinese Literature," *Modern China* 19, no. 1 (January 1993): 77.

20   Aijaz Ahmad, "Jameson's Rhetoric of Otherness and the 'National Allegory,'" *Social Text* 19 (fall 1987): 3–25.

21   Martin Jay, *The Dialectical Imagination* (Boston: Little, Brown and Co., 1973), 15.

22   Walter Benjamin, *The Origin of German Tragic Drama* (London: Routledge, 1977), 34.

23   For studies of Benjamin, see Eugene Lunn, *Marxism and Modernism: An Historical Study of Lukács, Brecht, Benjamin, and Adorno* (Berkeley: University of California Press, 1982); Richard Wolin, *Walter Benjamin: An Aesthetic of Redemption* (New York: Columbia University Press, 1982); and Terry Eagleton, *Walter Benjamin, or Towards a Revolutionary Criticism* (London: Verso, 1981).

24   Walter Benjamin, *Charles Baudelaire: A Lyric Poet in the Era of High Capitalism* (London: New Left Books, 1973).

25   Theodor Adorno, quoted in Hannah Arendt, "Walter Benjamin, 1892–1940," introduction to *Illuminations*, by Walter Benjamin (New York: Schocken Books, 1969), 12.

26   Hannah Arendt, "Walter Benjamin, 1892–1940," introduction to *Illuminations*, by Walter Benjamin (New York: Schocken Books, 1969), 14.

27   Lu Xun, *Lu Xun quanji*, vol. 11, 79.

28   Lu Xun, *Selected Stories of Lu Hsün* (Peking: Foreign Language Press, 1972), 6.

29   Walter Benjamin, *Illuminations*, trans. Hannah Arendt (New York: Schocken Books, 1969), 258.

30   See Fredric Jameson, *Marxism and Form* (Princeton, N.J.: Princeton University Press, 1971), 60–63.

31   Shanghai, as arguably the most modern of Asian cities at the time, was by no means a purely "exotic" and irrelevant background for André Malraux's drama of the "human

destiny." The Western concessions within the city, and the international conspirators and events involved in Malraux's novel, were as real and literal as they were integral components of the cosmopolitan life of Shanghai. See André Malraux, *Man's Fate (La Condition humaine)* (New York: Vantage Books, 1968).

32   See T. A. Hsia, "Lu Hsün and the Dissolution of the League of Leftist Writers," in *The Gate of Darkness: Studies on the Leftist Literary Movement in China* (Seattle: University of Washington Press, 1968); Maruyama Noboru, *Rojin to kakumei bungaku* (Lu Xun and revolutionary literature) (Tokyo: Kinokuniya shoten, 1972); and League of Left-Wing Writers, *Zuolian huyi lu* (Memoirs of the league of left-wing writers), 2 vols. (Beijing: Zhongguo shehui kexue chubanshe, 1982).

33   Terry Eagleton, *The Ideology of the Aesthetic* (Oxford: Basil Blackwell, 1990), 349.

34   Theodor Adorno, *Asthetische Theorie: Gesammelte Schriften*, vol. 7 (Frankfurt: Suhrkamp, 1970), 339.

35   Ibid., 347.

36   For criticism of Adorno's defeatism, see, for instance, A. Benjamin, ed., *The Problem of Modernity: Adorno and Benjamin* (London: Verso, 1988); and Stephen Bronner, *Of Critical Theory and Its Theorists* (Oxford: Blackwell, 1994).

37   Lu Xun, *Lu Xun quanji*, vol. 4, 123.

38   Ibid., 166.

39   Lu Xun, *Lu Xun xuanji* (Selected works of Lu Xun), vol. 4 (Beijing: Renmin wenxue chubanshe, 1983), 223–28.

40   Ibid., 226.

41   See Hu Qiuyuan, *Wenxue yishu lunji* (Collected essays on literature and art), 2 vols. (Taipei: Xueshu chubanshe, 1979); and *Geming wenxue lunzheng ziliao xuanbian* (Selected materials from the revolutionary literature debate), 2 vols. (Beijing: Renmin wenxue chubanshe, 1981).

42   Marston Anderson, *The Limits of Realism: Chinese Fiction in the Revolutionary Period* (Berkeley: University of California Press, 1990), 58.

43   Lu Xun wrote a series of essays attacking the third category, collected in *Erixin ji*, vol. 4 of *Lu Xun quanji*. "Lun 'disan zhong ren'" (On "third category"), in particular, was one of Lu's most important statements of his Marxist position on the class character of literature and art.

44   The polemical essays Lu Xun wrote during the Two Slogans dispute, like the essays critiquing the third category, are among the most significant works of his criticism (collected in *Lu Xun quanji*, vol. 6).

45   See Hsia, *The Gate of Darkness*, 101–45.

46   Lu Xun, "Da Xu Maoyong bin guanyu kang-Ri tongyi zhanxian wenti" (An open reply to Xu Maoyong on the question of the anti-Japanese united front), in *Lu Xun quanji*, vol. 6, 536.

47   Lu Xun, "Geming shidai de wenxue" (Literature in the revolutionary era), in *Lu Xun xuanji*, vol. 2, 334–36.

48   For an English translation and analysis of the central passages of Lu's essay "Literature in the Revolutionary Era," see Wendy Larson, *Literary Authority and the Modern Chinese Writer* (Durham, N.C.: Duke University Press, 1991), 89–93.

49   Lu Xun, *Lu Xun xuanji*, vol. 2, 338–39.

50   Lu Xun, "Wenyi yu zhengzhi de qitu" (The Divergent roads of art and politics), in *Lu Xun sanshi nian ji* (Collected works of Lu Xun over thirty years) (Hong Kong: Xinyi chubanshe, 1971), 111.

51   Ibid., 116.

52 Lu Xun, *Lu Xun xuanji*, vol. 2, 15.

53 Lu Xun, "Wenyi yu zhengzhi de qitu," 117.

54 Ibid., 118.

55 Pickowicz, *Marxist Literary Thought in China*. For studies that discuss Marxist literary thought in China, see Jaroslev Prusek, *The Lyrical and the Epic: Studies of Modern Chinese Literature*, ed. Leo Ou-fan Lee (Bloomington: Indiana University Press, 1980); Jaroslev Prusek, ed., *Studies in Modern Chinese Literature* (Berlin: Akademie-Verlag, 1964); Bonnie McDougall, *The Introduction of Western Literary Theories into Modern China, 1919–1925* (Tokyo: Center for East Asian Cultural Studies, 1971); Leo Ou-fan Lee, *The Romantic Generation of Modern Chinese Writers* (Cambridge, Mass.: Harvard University Press, 1973); Marián Gálik, *Mao Tun and Modern Chinese Literary Criticism* (Wiesbaden: Franz Steiner Verlag, 1969); and Merle Goldman, ed., *Modern Chinese Literature in the May Fourth Era* (Cambridge, Mass.: Harvard University Press, 1977).

56 Edward Said, *Orientalism* (London: Routledge, 1978), 7.

57 Ibid., 12.

58 Edward Said, *The World, the Text, the Critic* (Cambridge, Mass.: Harvard University Press, 1983), 243.

59 Gayatri Spivak, "Can the Subaltern Speak?" in *Marxism and the Interpretation of Culture*, ed. Cary Nelson and Lawrence Grossberg (Urbana: University of Illinois Press, 1988), 271–316.

60 Qu Qiubai, "Zhu Bajie: Dong-Xi wenhua yu Liang Shuming, Wu Zhihui" (Zhu Bajie: East/West cultures, and Liang Shuming and Wu Zhihui), in *Qu Qiubai wenji* (Collected essays of Qu Qiubai), vol. 1 (Beijing: Renmin wenxue chubanshe, 1953), 226.

61 Qu Qiubai, "Cong mingzhi zhuyi zhi shehui zhuyi" (From democracy to socialism), in *Qu Qiubai wenji*, 77.

62 The main points elucidated here concerning Qu Qiubai's critique of Europeanization can be found in the following important essays, all collected in *Qu Qiubai wenji*: "Ouhua wenyi" (Europeanized literature and art); "Dazhong wenyi de wenti" (Questions of popular literature and art); "Women shi shei?" (Who are we?); "Xuefa wansui!" (Long live the literary warlords!); and "Lu Xun zagan xuanji xuyan" (Preface to Lu Xun's collected essays).

63 Qu Qiubai, *Qu Qiubai wenji*, vol. 2, 855.

64 Ibid., 856.

65 Ibid., 880–88.

66 Ibid., 596.

67 Ibid., 880.

68 Ibid., 885.

69 May Thirtieth refers to the "Shanghai Massacre" in that city's British concession on May 30, 1925, as a result of workers' strikes and demonstrations, which triggered a major CCP-led urban insurgency across the whole country.

70 *Modenghua*, translated here as "modern trends," literally means "modernized" with the derogatory connotation of being driven by vogue. *Trans.*

71 Qu Qiubai, *Qu Qiubai wenji*, vol. 2, 996.

72 See Pickowicz, *Marxist Literary Thought*, esp. "'Europeanization' and the Literary Left," 99–111.

73 See Li Zehou, *On Marxism in China* (Hong Kong: Joint Publishers, 1993), 79.

74 See Antonio Gramsci, *Selections from the Prison Notebooks*, ed. and trans. Quintin Hoare and Geoffrey Nowell-Smith (New York: International Publishers, 1971); An-

tonio Gramsci, *Selections from Cultural Writings,* ed. David Forgacs and Geoffrey Nowell-Smith (London: Lawrence and Wishart, 1985); and the significant translation of Antonio Gramsci's *Quaderni del carcere* in English, *Antonio Gramsci Prison Notebooks,* ed. Joseph Buttigieg, vol. 1 (New York: Columbia University Press, 1992). Studies of Gramsci now abound. See, for example, Walter Adamson, *Hegemony and Revolution: A Study of Antonio Gramsci's Political and Cultural Theory* (Berkeley: University of California Press, 1980); Alistair Davidson, *Antonio Gramsci: Towards an Intellectual Biography* (London: Merlin Press, 1977); Chantal Mouffe, ed., *Gramsci and Marxist Theory* (London: Routledge, 1979); and the two special issues of *boundary 2* dedicated to Gramsci, vol. 14, no. 4 (spring 1986) and vol. 21, no. 2 (summer 1994).

75 Qu Qiubai, *Qu Qiubai wenji,* vol. 2, 880.

76 Ibid., 889.

77 Gramsci, *Selections from the Prison Notebooks,* 132.

78 Ibid., 132.

79 Ibid., 9.

80 For a study of the cultural popularization movement in modern China, see Chang-tai Hung, *Going to the People: Chinese Intellectuals and Folk Literature, 1918–1937* (Cambridge, Mass.: Council on East Asian Studies at Harvard University, 1985).

81 Qu Qiubai, *Qu Qiubai wenji,* vol. 2, 856–930.

82 Gramsci, *Selections from the Prison Notebooks,* 350.

83 Ibid., 350.

84 Ibid., 23.

85 Qu Qiubai, *Qu Qiubai wenji,* vol. 2, 1008–9.

86 Ibid., 1010.

87 See Pickowicz, *Marxist Literary Thought,* 177.

88 Qu Qiubai, quoted in Sima Lu, *Qu Qiubai zhuan* (A biography of Qu Qiubai) (Hong Kong: Zilian chubanshe, 1962), 132–36.

89 See Ernesto Laclau and Chantal Mouffe, *Hegemony and Socialist Strategy: Towards a Radical Democratic Politics* (London: Verso, 1985).

90 David Forgacs, "National-Popular: Genealogy of a Concept," in *The Cultural Studies Reader,* ed. Simon During (London: Routledge, 1993), 188.

91 Pickowicz, *Marxist Literary Thought,* 225.

Chapter 3. Hegemony and Counterhegemony: National Form and "Subjective Fighting Spirit"

1 Mao Zedong, *Selected Works of Mao Tse-tung,* vol. 1 (Peking: Foreign Language Press, 1967), 308.

2 For studies of different aspects of Mao's thought in English, see, for instance, Stuart S. Schram, *The Political Thought of Mao Tse-tung* (New York: Praeger Publishers, 1971); Frederic Wakeman Jr., *History and Will: Philosophical Perspectives of Mao Tse-tung's Thought* (Berkeley: University of California Press, 1975); Raymond Wylie, *The Emergence of Maoism: Mao Tse-tung, Ch'en Po-ta, and the Search for Chinese Theory, 1935–1945* (Stanford, Calif.: Stanford University Press, 1980); Maurice Meisner, *Marxism, Maoism, and Utopianism* (Madison: University of Wisconsin Press, 1982); Li Zehou, *On Marxism in China* (Hong Kong: Joint Publishers, 1993); and Arif Dirlik, "Mao Zedong and 'Chinese Marxism,'" in *The Encyclopedia of Asian Philosophy* (London: Routledge, 1995).

3 Raymond Williams, *Keywords* (Oxford: Oxford University Press, 1983), 145.

4 Mao Zedong, *Selected Works*, vol. 4, 413.

5 Vladimir Ilyich Lenin, "Left-wing Communism: An Infantile Disorder," in *Selected Works of Lenin*, vol. 3 (New York: International Publishers, 1943), 379.

6 Louis Althusser, "Contradiction and Overdetermination," in *For Marx* (London: New Left Books, 1977).

7 Mao Zedong, *Selected Works*, vol. 4, 413.

8 Ibid., vol. 1, 305.

9 Ibid., vol. 1, 336.

10 Arif Dirlik, *The Origins of Chinese Communism* (Oxford: Oxford University Press, 1989), 10.

11 Karl Marx, "Theses on Feuerbach," in *The Marx-Engels Reader*, ed. Robert Tucker (New York: W. W. Norton, 1972), 108.

12 Arif Dirlik, "The Predicament of Marxist Revolutionary Consciousness: Mao Zedong, Antonio Gramsci, and the Reformulation of Marxist Revolutionary Theory," *Modern China* 9, no. 2 (April 1983): 182–211. See also Nigel Todd, "Ideological Superstructure in Gramsci and Mao Tse-tung," *Journal of History of Ideas* 35 (January/March 1974).

13 It is instructive to note Western academicians' appropriation of Gramsci's views centering on the notion of an interregnum, while totally neglecting questions of strategy in a postrevolutionary society. For a recent statement concerning Gramsci and an interregnum, see Paul Bové, *In the Wake of Theory* (Hanover, N.H.: Wesleyan University Press, 1992).

14 Dirlik, "Mao Zedong and 'Chinese Marxism.'"

15 Mao Zedong, *Selected Works*, vol. 2, 382.

16 See Althusser, "Contradiction and Overdetermination," 87–128. On the relationship between Mao and Althusser in detail, see Kang Liu, "The Legacy of Mao and Althusser: Problematics of Dialectics, Alternative Modernity, and Cultural Revolution," in *Critical Perspectives on Mao Zedong Thought*, ed. Arif Dirlik and Nick Knight (forthcoming).

17 See Mao Zedong, *Selected Works*, vol. 1, 316, 329, 330.

18 Arif Dirlik considers "On Contradiction" a "revolutionary hermeneutics" (see "Mao Zedong and 'Chinese Marxism'").

19 See *Mao Zedong, Selected Works*, vol. 1, 332.

20 Ibid., 333.

21 Ibid., 336.

22 Ibid., 336.

23 Ibid., 337.

24 See ibid., 342.

25 Mao Zedong, "Lun xin jieduan," in *Mao Zedong ji* (Collected works of Mao Zedong), ed. Takeuchi Minoru, vol. 6 (Hong Kong: Po Wen Book Co., 1976), 260–61. This ten-volume collection contains Mao's texts in their original versions. All of Mao's writings underwent extensive revision and editing in the definitive *Mao Zedong xuanji*, appearing in English translation as the *Selected Works of Mao Tse-tung*. For the corresponding text of the quotation in the *Selected Works*, see vol. 2, 209–10.

26 The notions of constative and performative statements are taken from J. L. Austin's "speech act" theory (see *How to Do Things with Words* (Cambridge, Mass.: Harvard University Press, 1962).

27 Mao Zedong, *On New Democracy*, in *Selected Works*, vol. 2, 339–84. Out of this ex-

tended treatise of some fifty pages, just over one page is devoted to the issue of economics.

28 Mao Zedong, *Mao Zedong ji*, vol. 7, 155 (again, this refers to the edition that reproduces Mao's unaltered original text).

29 Compare Mao Zedong, *Mao Zedong ji*, vol. 7, 154–55; and Mao Zedong, *Selected Works*, vol. 2, 344. Another major revision in the *Selected Works* of the text *On New Democracy* is the deletion of the crucial point concerning capitalism as an inevitable historical stage that appeared in the original version. For a discussion of the strategic ramification of this revision, see Wang Zhanyang, *Mao Zedong de jianguo fanglüe yu dangdai Zhongguo de gaige kaifang* (Mao Zedong's strategies of state building, and contemporary China's reform and openness), (Changchun: Jilin renmin chubanshe, 1993), 143.

30 See Mao Zedong, *Mao Zedong ji*, vol. 7, 188.

31 Ibid., 191.

32 Ibid., 191, 202.

33 The nickname stinking No. 9 (*chou laojiu*) was derived from the revolutionary model Peking Opera, *Zhiqu Weihushan* (Strategic seizure of Tiger Mountain), in which hero Yang Zirong, a People's Liberation Army (PLA) agent, is disguised as the No. 9 Guomindang bandit chief. It was said that Mao half-jokingly quoted the line from the opera, "No. 9 can't go," in reference to the indispensable role of intellectuals as scientific and technological instruments. Thus, the nickname No. 9 for intellectuals, with the added qualification "stinking" to indicate their nonproletarian, "reactionary" ideological standpoints.

34 *Mao Zedong ji*, vol. 8, 123 and 6.

35 For a discussion of Mao's contradictory assessment of the May Fourth legacy, see Vera Schwarz, *The Chinese Enlightenment* (Berkeley: University of California Press, 1986), 247–49.

36 Mao Zedong, *Mao Zedong ji*, vol. 8, 147; see also Bonnie McDougall, *Mao Zedong's "Talks at the Yan'an Conference on Literature and Art": A Translation of the 1943 Text with Commentary* (Ann Arbor: University of Michigan Center for Chinese Studies, 1980), 84. This translation is basically an accurate rendition of the unedited original with edited passages appended for comparison.

37 McDougall, *Mao Zedong's "Talks,"* 57.

38 Karl Marx, *The Eighteenth Brumaire of Louis Bonaparte*, in *The Marx-Engels Reader*, 516.

39 Ibid., 516.

40 Louis Althusser, "Marxism Today," in *Philosophy and the Spontaneous Philosophy of the Scientist*, ed. Gregory Elliot (London: Verso, 1990), 278–79. First published in 1978.

41 Terry Eagleton arrogantly declares that "history proper," in the Marxian sense of socialism, has not yet appeared: "So far, nothing particularly special has occurred: history to date has simply been the same old story, a set of variations on persisting structures of oppression and exploitation" (*The Ideology of the Aesthetic* [Oxford: Basil Blackwell, 1990], 215). Such a preposterous denial of historically concrete socialist experiments and alternatives outside the West (yet not outside "history proper") not only betrays Eagleton's Eurocentric parochialism, but also unveils a deep-seated defeatist mode of thinking.

42 Raymond Williams, *Marxism and Literature* (Oxford: Oxford University Press, 1977), 203.

43 McDougall, *Mao Zedong's "Talks,"* 15.

44 For the German Rezeptionästhetik, see Hans Robert Jauss, *Toward an Aesthetic of Reception* (Minneapolis: University of Minnesota Press, 1982); and Robert Holub, *Reception Theory: A Critical Introduction* (London: Routledge, 1984).

45 See McDougall, *Mao Zedong's "Talks,"* 66.

46 Ibid., 115; and 61.

47 See McDougall, *Mao Zedong's "Talks,"* 61.

48 Jauss, *Aesthetic Experience*, 46–110.

49 Ibid., 93–94.

50 This translation is based on Mao Zedong, *Mao Zedong ji*, vol. 8, 126. For different translations and editions, see Mao Zedong, *Selected Works*, vol. 3, 81; and McDougall, *Mao Zedong's "Talks,"* 89. Where McDougall's translation is accurate, it is used; otherwise, passages are translated from the Chinese in *Mao Zedong ji*, and McDougall's are listed as a reference. For crucial passages like this one, all three references are noted.

51 Fredric Jameson, *The Political Unconscious* (Ithaca, N.Y.: Cornell University Press, 1981), 82.

52 Mao Zedong, *Mao Zedong ji*, vol. 8, 128; and McDougall, *Mao Zedong's "Talks,"* 70.

53 Mao Zedong, *Selected Works*, vol. 3, 82.

54 Theodore Huters, "Hu Feng and the Critical Legacy of Lu Xun," in *Lu Xun and His Legacy*, ed. Leo Ou-fan Lee (Berkeley: University of California Press, 1985), 142.

55 See, for instance, C. T. Hsia, *A History of Modern Chinese Fiction*, 2d ed. (New Haven, Conn.: Yale University Press, 1971); and Merle Goldman, *Literary Dissent in Communist China* (Cambridge, Mass.: Harvard University Press, 1967).

56 See Luo Lo, "Sangdai chongxin pingshuo de zhengui yichan: Hu Feng wenyi sixiang pinglun" (Valuable heritage to be reassessed: Hu Feng's literary thought), in *Hu Feng lunji* (Critical essays on Hu Feng), ed. Wen Zhenting and Fan Jiyan (Beijing: Zhongguo shehui kexue chubanshe, 1991), 15–20; and Fan Jun, "Hu Feng: Shang wei jieshu de huati" (Hu Feng: An incomplete issue of inquiry), *Wenxue pinlun* (Literature review) 5 (October 1988): 17–33. To date, no single monograph on Hu's thought has been published in China, despite the numerous journal articles that have appeared because of the last decade's culture debates.

57 Mao Zedong, *Mao Zedong xuanji* (Selected works of Mao Zedong), vol. 5 (Beijing: Renmin chubanshe, 1977), 163.

58 My biographical account of Hu Feng draws on the following sources: Hu's own autobiographical essays, "Lixiang zhuyi zhe shidai de huiyi" (Reminiscence of an idealist) (1936), "Wei yi ge waiguo kanwu xi de zizhuan" (An autobiographical note for a foreign journal) (1941), and "Pinlun ji houji" (Postscript) (1984), all collected in *Hu Feng pinglun ji* (Critical essays of Hu Feng) (Beijing: Renmin wenxue chubanshe, 1984), respectively, vol. 1, 248–57, vol. 2, 157–216, and vol. 3, 371–421; Li Hui, *Hu Feng yuan'an shimo* (Hu Feng's case of injustice) (Beijing: Renmin ribao chubanshe, 1989); and Yang Li et al., eds., *Zhongguo xiandai zuojia da cidian* (An encyclopedic dictionary of modern Chinese writers) (Beijing: Xin shijie chubanshe, 1992), 172–78.

59 See Li Zehou, "Ji Zhongguo xiandai san ci xueshu lunzhan" (Notes on three scholarly debates in modern China), in *Zhongguo xiandai sixiang shi lun* (Essays on modern Chinese intellectual history) (Beijing: Dongfang chubanshe, 1987), 76–87; and Liu Zaifu, "Wusi wenxue qimeng jingshen de shiluo yu huigui" (The loss and recovery of the enlightenment spirit of May Fourth literature), in *Wusi: Duoyuan de fansi* (May Fourth: Pluralist reflections), ed. Ling Yu-sheng et al. (Taipei: Lianjing chubanshe, 1989), 92–122.

60 Hu Feng, *Hu Feng pinglun ji*, vol. 3, 322.

61 See ibid., 322.

62 For discussions of Hu's relationship to Lukács, see Zhang Guo'an, "Hu Feng he Lu-kaqi de xianshizuyi lilun cuowei" (Incongruities between Hu Feng and Lukács's theories of realism), in *Hu Feng lunji* (Critical essays on Hu Feng), ed. Wen Zhenting and Fan Jiyan (Beijing: Zhongguo shehui kexue chubanshe, 1991), 245–76; Ai Xiaoming, "Hu Feng yu Lukaqi" (Hu Feng and Lukács), *Wenxue pinglun* 5 (October 1988): 40–52; and Yue Daiyun, "Guanyu xianshizhuyi de liang chang lunzhan: Lukaqi dui Bu-laixite yu Hu Feng dui Zhou Yang" (Two debates about realism: Lukács versus Brecht, and Hu Feng versus Zhou Yang), *Wenyi bao* (Literature and art gazette), 13 August 1988.

63 Hu Feng, *Hu Feng pinglun ji*, vol. 3, 341–42.

64 See Hu Qiuyuan, "Langfei de lunzheng: Duiyu pipingzhe de ruogan dabian" (Superfluous argument: Some responses to criticism), *Xiandai* (The modern) 2, no. 2 (December 1932): 2–38; and Hu Qiuyuan, "Qianji" (Preface), in *Wenxue yishu lunji* (Collected essays on literature and art), vol. 1 (Taipei: Xueshu chubanshe, 1979), 1–13.

65 See Hu Qiuyuan, *Wenxue yishu lunji*, vol. 2, 682–96, 714–18.

66 See ibid., 42–45.

67 Ibid., 43.

68 Antonio Gramsci, *Antonio Gramsci Prison Notebooks*, vol. 1 (New York: Columbia University Press, 1992), 229–30. See also Marcia Landy, *Film, Politics, and Gramsci* (Minneapolis: University of Minnesota Press, 1994), 75–77, 217–20.

69 Antonio Gramsci, *Selections from the Prison Notebooks* (New York: International Publishers, 1971), 15–16.

70 Hu Feng, *Hu Feng pinglun ji*, vol. 2, 137.

71 Ibid., 137.

72 Ibid., 234, 220–23.

73 Georg Lukács, *Marxism and Human Literature*, ed. E. San Juan Jr. (New York: Delta Books, 1973), 115–16.

74 Hu Feng, *Hu Feng pinglun ji*, vol. 2, 219–20 (italics in original).

75 Ibid., 245–46.

76 Gramsci, *Selections from the Prison Notebooks*, 244.

77 Hu Feng, *Hu Feng pinglun ji*, vol. 2, 254.

78 Ibid., 258.

79 Mao Dun, quoted in Wang Yao, *Zhongguo xin wenxue shi gao* (A history of Chinese new literature) (Shanghai: Xin wenyi chubanshe, 1982), 596–97.

80 Hu Feng, *Hu Feng pinglun ji*, vol. 3, 7.

81 Hu Feng, "Realism Today," in *Literature of the People's Republic of China*, ed. Kai-yu, Hsu, trans. Paul Pickowicz (Bloomington: Indiana University Press, 1980), 64. See also Hu Feng, "Xianshi zhuyi zai jintian" (Realism today), in *Zai hunluan limian* (In the chaos) (Chongqing: Xiwang she, 1943).

82 For an explication of the connection between narration and class consciousness in Lukács's theory, see Fredric Jameson, *Marxism and Form* (Princeton, N.J.: Princeton University Press, 1971), 160–205.

83 Hu Feng, *Hu Feng pinglun ji*, vol. 3, 20.

84 Ibid., 22–23.

85 Ibid., 21.

86 Ibid., 22.

87 Ibid., 18–19.

88 Ibid., 41.

89   Ibid., 77 (italics in original).

90   Ibid., 87.

91   Ibid., vol. 2, 241.

92   For an analysis of Bakhtin's dialogism as a theory of cultural revolution and trans-
     formation in light of the socialist experiences and practices in both Soviet Russia
     and China, see Liu Kang, "Yi zhong zhuanxing qi de wenhua lilun: Lun Bahejin dui-
     hua zhuyi zai dangdai wenlun zhong de mingyun" (A theory of cultural change:
     Bakhtin's dialogism in contemporary critical theory), *Zhongguo shehui kexue* (So-
     cial sciences in China) 86 (spring 1994): 161–77. See also Liu Kang, *Duihua de xuan-
     sheng: Bahejin wenhuan lilun* (Dialogism: Bakhtin and cultural theory) (Beijing:
     Zhongguo renmin daxue chubanshe, 1995).

93   Mikhail Bakhtin, quoted in Michael Holquist, *Dialogism: Bakhtin and His World*
     (London: Routledge, 1990), 24–25.

94   See ibid., 2.

95   Mikhail Bakhtin, *Problems of Dostoevsky's Poetics*, trans. C. Emerson (Minneapo-
     lis: University of Minnesota Press, 1984), 20.

96   Mikhail Bakhtin, *Rabelais and His World* (Bloomington: Indiana University Press,
     1984), 19.

97   Ken Hirschkop, introduction to *Bakhtin and Cultural Theory*, by Ken Hirschkop
     and David Shepherd, eds. (Manchester: Manchester University Press, 1989), 35.

98   Hu Feng, *Hu Feng pinglun ji*, vol. 3, 318–19.

99   Ibid., 149.

100 See Fan Jiyan, "Hu Feng yu 'xianfeng wenhuan'" (Hu Feng and the "avant-garde"),
     in *Hu Feng lunji* (Critical essays on Hu Feng), ed. Wen Zhenting and Fan Jiyan (Bei-
     jing: Zhongguo shehui kexue chubanshe, 1991), 108–23.

101 See Li Zehou, *Zhongguo xiandai sixiang shi lun*, 76.

102 Ibid., 85.

Chapter 4. Aesthetics, Ideology, and
Cultural Reconstruction

1   Mao Zedong, *Selected Works of Mao Tse-tung*, vol. 4 (Peking: Foreign Language
     Press, 1967), 363.

2   Ibid., 364.

3   Rey Chow recently complained that Western Marxist intellectuals often condemn
     consumerism while fully enjoying the benefits of an "affluent society," thus ne-
     glecting the "Third World" needs of modernization or the "eager[ness] to get a share
     of the goodies" ("Response," special issue, "Marxism beyond Marxism?" *Polygraph*
     6/7 [1993]: 211). Although her point on this homogenizing tendency is well taken,
     Rey Chow nevertheless conflates Marxist utopianism with a religious "faith in sac-
     rifice" in her critique of the former. One can certainly argue that West-
     ern Marxists—say Fredric Jameson, who believes in the necessity of utopian
     thoughts—are not merely advocating an idealistic vision of a "sacred future" (in
     fact, Jameson insists, more than any other Western Marxist, on the primacy of ma-
     terial and economic determinants in social life, and the change of material condi-
     tions or "mode of production"); and even more, that Marxist utopianism in China,
     which Rey Chow mentions emphatically, does not simply mean "a corrupt, vic-
     timizing utopianism, bloodshed, violence, and often poverty" ("Response," 209).
     As the discussion herein tries to show, there is at least one humanist utopianism

in Chinese aesthetic Marxism, different from Maoist utopianism. For far more nuanced and certainly sympathetic views on Chinese Marxism, see Arif Dirlik, "Post-Socialism/Flexible Production: Marxism in Contemporary Radicalism," *Polygraph* 6/7 (1993): 133–69; and Fredric Jameson, "Actually Existing Marxism," *Polygraph* 6/7 (1993): 170–96.

4   China specialists in the West are interested primarily in cultural events with political consequences. Hence, Western studies of intellectual currents in the PRC mainly focus on "voices of dissent." See, for instance, Merle Goldman et al., eds., *China's Intellectuals and the State: In Search of a New Relationship* (Cambridge, Mass.: Council on East Asian Studies at Harvard University, 1987). On the other hand, studies of Chinese Marxism have yet to tackle the issue of alternative Marxist thinking in China in cultural and aesthetic domains. See Bill Brugger and David Kelly, *Chinese Marxism in the Post-Mao Era* (Stanford, Calif.: Stanford University Press, 1990); and Arif Dirlik and Maurice Meisner, eds., *Marxism and the Chinese Experience* (New York: M. E. Sharpe, 1989).

5   Fredric Jameson, foreword to *Politics, Ideology, and Literary Discourse in Modern China: Theoretical Interventions and Cultural Critique*, ed. Liu Kang and Xiaobing Tang (Durham, N.C.: Duke University Press, 1993), 6.

6   A recent case in point is the attack on Western critical theory's Marxist orientation mounted by Zhang Longxi in "Western Theory and Chinese Reality," *Critical Inquiry* 19 (1992): 105–30. By setting Western critical theory against "Chinese reality," Zhang Longxi substitutes the real history of an alternative Marxist cultural politics in China with a narrative of political dissidents crying for "human rights" against a totalitarian regime. Using Chinese events as a showcase, he assails Western "leftist intellectuals." Zhang, in effect, argues that the Western Left is complicitous with a totalitarianism that brutally suppresses basic human rights. He then castigates the "absurdity and stupidity of such a mentality." His trenchant attack of the Western Left is based on absolutized and fetishized notions of difference and otherness between things Chinese and Western, which tend to perpetuate the ideological and cultural fragmentation that Arif Dirlik has noted in his critique of postcolonialism. While the postcolonial critics, as Dirlik observes, may use the language of poststructuralism to rephrase the older problem of colonialism, which nonetheless still bears a strong affinity with the cultural politics of the Western Left, an essentially right-wing assault of Marxist tendencies in contemporary criticism can be smuggled in, as in Zhang Longxi's case, by recasting cold war platitudes in poststructuralist concepts. See Arif Dirlik, "The Postcolonial Aura: Third World Criticism in The Age of Global Capitalism," *Critical Inquiry* 20 (1994): 328–56.

7   Edward Said, "Traveling Theory," in *The World, the Text, the Critic* (Cambridge, Mass.: Harvard University Press, 1983), 233–34.

8   Raymond Williams, "Beyond Actually Existing Socialism," in *Problems of Materialism and Culture* (London: Verso, 1980), 255.

9   For a detailed analysis of Mao's determinism and antideterminism, see Liu Kang, "The Problematics of Mao and Althusser: Alternative Modernity and Cultural Revolution," *Rethinking Marxism* 8, no. 3 (fall 1995): 1–26.

10 In *On New Democracy*, economic development was discussed in extremely broad and general terms, while the politics of a "new democracy" was stressed as the concentrated expression of the economy of New Democracy. For CCP documents on modernization, see *Zhongguo gongchandang di ba ci quanguo daibiao dahui wenjian* (Documents of the eighth CCP congress) (Beijing: Renmin chubanshe, 1956).

11 Perry Anderson, "Modernity and Revolution," in *Marxism and the Interpretation of Culture*, ed. Cary Nelson and Lawrence Grossberg (Urbana: University of Illinois Press, 1988), 332.

12 Mao Zedong, "On Correctly Handling Contradictions among the People," in *The Writings of Mao Zedong, 1949–1976*, vol. 2, ed. John Leung and Michael Kau (Armonk, N.Y.: M. E. Sharpe, 1992), 331.

13 Mao Zedong, "Sulian *Zhengzhi jingjixue* dushu biji" (Notes on the Soviet textbook of *political economy*), in *Mao Zedong sixiang wansui* (Long live Mao Zedong thought) (photo reproductions of the Red Guard publications of 1969), 334.

14 Ibid., 347.

15 Hu Feng, *Guanyu jiefang yilai de wenyi shijian qingkuang de baogao* (A report on literary and artistic practices since the liberation), *Xin wenxue shiliao* (Historical documents of new literary history) 3 (1989): 104.

16 For an account by a China specialist in the United States of the Anti–Hu Feng Campaign, see Merle Goldman, *Literary Dissent in Communist China* (Cambridge, Mass.: Harvard University Press, 1967), 129–57.

17 Zhu Guangqian, "Wode wenyi sixiang de fandong xing" (The reactionary aspects of my literary thoughts), *Wenyi bao* (Literary gazette), no. 6 (1956). The essay later appeared in *Meixue wenti taolun ji* (Essays of the debate about aesthetic problems), vol. 1 (Beijing: Zuojia chubanshe, 1957), 1–32.

18 Zhu Guangqian, "Wode wenyi sixiang de fandong xing," in *Meixue wenti taolun ji*, vol. 1, 1.

19 Ibid., 7.

20 Zhu Guangqian, "Zuozhe shuoming" (Author's note), in *Zhu Guangqian meixue wenji* (Collected aesthetic essays of Zhu Guangqian), vol. 1 (Shanghai: Shanghai wenyi chubanshe, 1982), 17.

21 Zhu Guangqian, "Keluoqi pai meixue de piping" (Critique of Crocian school of aesthetics), in *Zhu Guangqian meixue wenji* (Collected aesthetic essays of Zhu Guangqian), vol. 1 (Shanghai: Shanghai wenyi chubanshe, 1982), 165. See also Zhu Guangqian, *Keluoqi zhexue shuping* (A critical introduction to Croce's philosophy), in *Zhu Guangqian meixue wenji* (Collected aesthetic essays of Zhu Guangqian), vol. 2 (Shanghai: Shanghai wenyi chubanshe, 1982), 371–465.

22 Zhu Guangqian, "Keluoqi pai meixue de piping," 153.

23 Zhu Guangqian, "Wode wenyi sixiang de fandong xing," in *Meixue wenti taolun ji*, vol. 1, 22.

24 For Li Dazhao's Marxism, see Maurice Meisner, *Li Ta-chao and the Origins of Chinese Marxism* (Cambridge, Mass.: Harvard University Press, 1967).

25 For discussions of Maoism, see Frederic Wakeman Jr., *History and Will: Philosophical Perspectives of Mao Tse-tung's Thought* (Berkeley: University of California Press, 1975); and Maurice Meisner, *Marxism, Maoism, and Utopianism* (Madison: University of Wisconsin Press, 1982).

26 See Brugger and Kelly, *Chinese Marxism*, chapters 4 and 5. Certain Western Marxists (or "post-Marxists"), such as Ernesto Laclau and Chantal Mouffe, erroneously interpret Mao's contradiction as a concept encouraging a "proliferation of contradictions" in social struggles, and view Mao's metasubjectivity of the "masses" as an alternative to the dogmatic "class identity" of classic Marxism. See Ernesto Laclau and Chantal Mouffe, *Hegemony and Socialist Strategy: Towards a Radical Democratic Politics* (London: Verso, 1985), 62–64. Their position is symptomatic of the Western Marxist appropriation of Maoist radicalism, ignoring the Maoist centralizing tendency evinced by the stress on "objective and universal laws."

27 See Cai Yi, *Meixue lunzhu chubian* (Primary essays on aesthetics) (Shanghai: Shanghai wenyi chubanshe, 1982).

28 Li Zehou, "Mei de keguan xing he shehui xing: Ping Zhu Guangqian, Cai Yi de meixue guan" (Objectivity and sociality of beauty: Comments on the aesthetic views of Zhu Guangqian and Cai Yi), in *Meixue wenti taolun ji* (Essays of the debate about aesthetic problems), vol. 2 (Beijing: Zuojia chubanshe, 1957), 31–45.

29 Zhu Guangqian, "Lun mei shi keguan yu zhuguan de tongyi" (On beauty as the unity of the subjective and objective), in *Meixue wenti taolun ji* (Essays of the debate about aesthetic problems), vol. 3 (Beijing: Zuojia chubanshe, 1957), 26 (italics in original).

30 For a discussion of Chinese philosophical categories, see, for instance, Feng Yu-lan, *A History of Chinese Philosophy* (Princeton, N.J.: Princeton University Press, 1953).

31 Theodor Adorno, "Subject-Object," in *The Essential Frankfurt School Reader*, ed. Andrew Arato and Eike Gebhardt (New York: Urizen Books, 1978), 498–99.

32 Theodor Adorno, *Negative Dialectics*, trans. E. B. Ashton (London: Routledge, 1973), 181.

33 Adorno, "Subject-Object," 504.

34 Zhu Guangqian, "Lun mei shi keguan yu zhuguan de tongyi," 28–29 (italics in original).

35 Herbert Marcuse, *The Aesthetic Dimension: Towards a Critique of Marxist Aesthetics* (Boston: Beacon Press, 1978), 6, 3.

36 Ibid., 5.

37 For a brief discussion in English of the identity debate, see Brugger and Kelly, *Chinese Marxism*, 89–93. For a recent Chinese assessment of the debate, see Wu Jianguo et al., eds., *Dangdai Zhongguo yishixingtai fengyun lu* (Ideological currents in contemporary China) (Beijing: Jingguan jiaoyu chubanshe, 1993), 246–55. Also useful is Yang Xianzhen's own recollection of the debate in *Wo de zhexue "zui'an"* (My philosophical "criminal records") (Beijing: Renmin chubanshe, 1981).

38 See Fredric Jameson, *Late Marxism: Adorno, or, The Persistence of the Dialectic* (London: Verso, 1990), 15–24.

39 Zhu Guangqian, "Meixue de xin guandian bu neng shi 'zhuguan yu keguan xiang fenlie' de guandian" (The new aesthetic view cannot be the one of the 'split of the subject and object'), in *Zhu Guangqian meixue wenji* (Collected aesthetic essays of Zhu Guangqian), vol. 3 (Shanghai: Shanghai wenyi chubanshe, 1982), 312.

40 Antonio Gramsci, quoted in Terry Eagleton, *Ideology: An Introduction* (London: Verso, 1991), 121.

41 See Zhao Shilin, "*Shougao* yanjiu" (Studies of *Manuscripts*), in *Dangdai Zhongguo meixue yanjiu gaishu* (An introduction to contemporary Chinese aesthetics) (Tianjin: Tianjin jiaoyu chubanshe, 1988), 251–85.

42 Zhou Yang, "The Fighting Task Confronting Workers in Philosophy and the Social Sciences." *Peking Review* 1 (1964): 19–20.

43 Adorno, "Subject-Object," 506.

44 Martin Jay, *Adorno* (Cambridge, Mass.: Harvard University Press, 1984), 78.

45 Adorno, "Subject-Object," 499–500.

46 See Brugger and Kelly, *Chinese Marxism*, 119–38.

47 Karl Marx, "Theses on Feuerbach," in *The Marx-Engels Reader*, ed. Robert Tucker (New York: W. W. Norton, 1972), 107.

48 Karl Marx, "Excerpts from the *1844 Economic and Philosophic Manuscripts*," in *The Marx-Engels Reader*, ed. Robert Tucker (New York: W. W. Norton, 1972), 62.

49 Ibid., 75.

50 Zhu Guangqian, "Shengchan laodong yu ren dui shijie de yishu zhangwo: Makesi zhuyi meixue de shijian guandian" (Productive labor and man's artistic grasp of the world: The view of practice in Marxist aesthetics), in *Zhu Guangqian meixue wenji* (Collected aesthetic essays of Zhu Guangqian), vol. 3 (Shanghai: Shanghai wenyi chubanshe, 1982), 290 (italics in original).

51 Ibid., 300.

52 See Terry Eagleton, *The Ideology of the Aesthetic* (Oxford: Basil Blackwell, 1990), 196–234.

53 See Li Zehou, *Meixue lunji* (Essays on aesthetics) (Shanghai: Shanghai wenyi chubanshe, 1980), 153–59.

54 Li Zehou, *Li Zehou zhexue meixue wenxuan* (Collected essays of philosophy and aesthetics by Li Zehou) (Changsha: Hunan renmin chubanshe, 1985), 464–65 (italics in original).

55 Karl Marx, *Grundrisse* (Harmondsworth: Penguin, 1973), 541.

56 Eagleton, *Ideology of the Aesthetic*, 229–30.

57 Ibid., 208–9.

58 Li Zehou, *Pipan zhexue de pipan: Kande shuping* (Critique of the critical philosophy: A study of Kant) (Beijing: Renmin chubanshe, 1979), 402–3.

59 Li Zehou, "Zhexue dawen lu" (Philosophical dialogues), in *Wode zhexue tigang* (An outline of my philosophy) (Taipei: Fengyun shidai chuban gongsi, 1990), 4–6.

60 See, for instance, Michel Foucault, "On Popular Justice: A Discussion with Maoists," in *Power/Knowledge: Selected Interviews and Other Writings, 1972–1977* (New York: Pantheon Books, 1980), 134. But Gayatri Spivak's assertion that "Maoism . . . simply creates an aura of narrative specificity, which would be a harmless rhetorical banality . . . for the eccentric phenomenon of French intellectual 'Maoism,'" is certainly superficial and simplistic ("Can the Subaltern Speak?" in *Marxism and the Interpretation of Culture*, ed. Cary Nelson and Lawrence Grossberg [Urbana: University of Illinois Press, 1988], 272).

61 Valentino Gerratana, "Althusser and Stalinism," *New Left Review* 101/102 (spring/summer 1977): 112.

62 Louis Althusser, "Ideology and Ideological State Apparatuses," in *Lenin and Philosophy and Other Essays*, trans. Ben Brewster (London: New Left Books, 1971), 182.

63 Zhu Guangqian, "Lun mei shi keguan yu zhuguan de tongyi," 14.

64 Ibid.

65 Karl Marx and Friedrich Engels, *The German Ideology*, ed. C. J. Arthur (New York: International Publishers, 1974), 47.

66 Zhu Guangqian, "Lun mei shi keguan yu zhuguan de tongyi," 17.

67 For Williams's concepts, see Raymond Williams, *Marxism and Literature* (Oxford: Oxford University Press, 1977), esp. 121–28.

68 Karl Marx, "Preface to *A Contribution to the Critique of Political Economy*," in *The Marx-Engels Reader*, ed. Robert Tucker (New York: W. W. Norton, 1972), 4.

69 Zhu Guangqian, *Xifang meixue shi* (A history of Western aesthetics), vol. 1 (Beijing: Renmin wenxue chubanshe, 1979), 18.

70 Ibid., 16–17.

71 See Pierre Bourdieu, *Outline of a Theory of Practice* (Cambridge: Cambridge University Press, 1977).

72 Zhu Guangqian, "Lun mei shi keguan yu zhuguan de tongyi," 34.

73 Terry Eagleton, *Ideology: An Introduction* (London: Verso, 1991), 18–20.

74 Ibid., 146.

75 Zhu Guangqian, "Mei shi yishi xingtai" (The aesthetic is ideological), in *Meixue wenti taolun ji* (Essays of the debate about aesthetic problems), vol. 2 (Beijing: Zuojia chubanshe, 1957), 127.

76 Zhu Guangqian, "Lun mei shi keguan yu zhuguan de tongyi," 36–37.

77 See, for instance, Zhu Guangqian's conclusion of *A History of Western Aesthetics*, in which he considers imaginary thinking as key to unlocking the problems of aesthetics. In his later years, Zhu devoted much time to the study of Giambattista Vico's *Scienza Nuova* (*The New Sciences*), concentrating on Vico's concepts of "human science," "poetic wisdom," and "imagination" that anticipate German romantic aesthetics, especially Johann Herder's theory of metaphor and myth as the original language of humankind. Zhu saw strong connections between Vico and Marxism, particularly in the notion of history as a product of human creativity. He also noted approvingly that Terence Hawkes had acknowledged in his *Structuralism and Semiotics* (London: Routledge, 1977) Vico's impact on modern structuralism and semiotics. Zhu's comments on Vico, in effect, served as an observation of his own undertakings in transmitting and transforming Western aesthetic thinking, especially Marxist aesthetics, in relation to modern China.

78 Wang Ruoshui, quoted in Brugger and Kelly, *Chinese Marxism*, 143.

79 See Brugger and Kelly, *Chinese Marxism*, 144–45.

80 Compared to the enormous popularity enjoyed by academic books about cultural subject matters in the late 1980s, the rapidly shrinking academic publishing market of the 1990s appears perhaps more normal than extraordinary, but also depressing to Li's generation: it is now a matter of fact that academic books published even by the most prestigious presses, say Chinese Social Sciences Press, can at best sell no more than 2,000 copies of one edition.

Chapter 5. Subjectivity and Aesthetic Marxism: Toward a Cultural Topology of Postrevolutionary Society

1 Fernand Braudel, *La dynamique du capitalisme* (Paris: Flammarion, 1985), 56.

2 Fredric Jameson, "Periodizing the '60s," in *The Ideologies of Theory*, vol. 2 (Minneapolis: University of Minnesota Press, 1988), 191.

3 For C. S. Peirce's notion of the interpretant in his semiotic theory, see, for example, "Logic as Semiotic: The Theory of Signs," in *Philosophical Writings of Peirce* (New York: Dover Publications, 1955), 98–119.

4 Jameson, "Periodizing the '60s," 191.

5 Ibid., 207.

6 For a statement of Mao's "Third-Worldism," see Lin Piao (Lin Biao), *Long Live the Victory of the People's War!* (Peking: Foreign Language Press, 1967).

7 See, for example, Benedict Anderson, *Imagined Communities* (London: Verso, 1983). Anderson is mistaken when he claims nationalism is a discourse of nationhood simply as an "imagined community" invented by Western capitalist modernity, thus implicitly excluding other alternative modernities in which nationalism and nationhood serve revolutionary purposes in opposition to Eurocentric modernity.

8 For Mao's injunctions on the necessity of a cultural revolution in a postrevolutionary society, see, for instance, Mao Zedong, *Chairman Mao Talks to the People*, ed. S. Schram (New York: Pantheon Books, 1984); and Mao Zedong, *The Secret Speeches of Chairman Mao*, ed. R. MacFarquhar et al. (Cambridge, Mass.: Council on East Asian Studies at Harvard University, 1989).

9 Louis Althusser, quoted in *Radical Philosophy* 12 (winter 1975): 44. For Althusser's

critique of Stalinism, see also Valentino Gerratana, "Althusser and Stalinism," *New Left Review* 101/102 (spring/summer 1977): 111–21.

10 Richard Kraus notes the ambiguous and polysemic conception of bourgeoisie in Chinese Marxist discourse. It may refer to either the remnant bourgeoisie formed in the preliberation years; certain political and ideological attitudes and "class positions"; or the bureaucracy within the CCP (*Class Conflict in Chinese Socialism* [New York: Columbia University Press, 1981], 89–143). Mao clearly had the last group as the referent and target of the Cultural Revolution. Fredric Jameson also points out that Mao's reference to the bourgeoisie involves "an inevitable terminological slippage and displacement" that has "the curious effect of evacuating the class content of these slogans" ("Periodizing the '60s," 189).

11 For accounts of postmodern culture and its relationship to late capitalism, see Fredric Jameson, *Postmodernism, or, The Cultural Logic of Late Capitalism* (Durham, N.C.: Duke University Press, 1991); Steve Connor, *Postmodern Culture: An Introduction to Theories of the Contemporary* (Oxford: Basil Blackwell, 1989); David Harvey, *The Condition of Postmodernity* (Oxford: Basil Blackwell, 1989); and Linda Hutcheon, *Politics of Postmodernism* (London: Routledge, 1989).

12 For a discussion of Jin Guantao's scientist model of China's modern history and his revisionism of Marxism's historical materialism, see Bill Brugger and David Kelly, *Chinese Marxism in the Post-Mao Era* (Stanford, Calif.: Stanford University Press, 1990). For Gan Yang's "new hermeneutics" group, see Gan Yang, ed., *Zhongguo dangdai wenhua yishi* (Contemporary Chinese cultural consciousness) (Hong Kong: Shanlian shudian, 1989); see also Zhang Xudong, "On Some Motifs in the Chinese 'Cultural Fever' of the Late 1980s," *Social Text* 39 (summer 1994): 120–56.

13 Liu Xiaobo made himself known during the late 1980s by attacking most intellectual positions in the debates, especially Li Zehou's, accused by Liu as being "too culturally conservative" (*Xuanzhe the pipan: Yu Li Zehou duihua* [Alternative critique: Dialogues with Li Zehou] [Shanghai: Shanghai renmin chubanshe, 1988]). Liu Xiaofeng criticized Li Zehou's generation from the opposite perspective, charging them as being much too preoccupied with secular and social issues without the transcendental and theological concern of ultimate "salvation" (*Zhengjiu yu xiaoyao* [Salvation and carefreeness] [Shanghai: Shanghai renmin chubanshe, 1988]).

14 See Brugger and Kelly, *Chinese Marxism*, 139–71.

15 See Lin Yu-sheng, *The Crisis of Chinese Consciousness: Radical Antitraditionalism in the May Fourth Era* (Madison: University of Wisconsin Press, 1979); and its Chinese translation, *Zhongguo yishi de weiji* (Guiyang: Guizhou renmin chubanshe, 1988).

16 See Liu Kang, "Subjectivity, Marxism, and Cultural Theory in China," *Social Text* 31/32 (summer/fall 1992): 114–41; some analyses in this chapter draw from this essay. See also Lin Min, "The Search for Modernity: Chinese Intellectual Discourse and Society, 1978–1988; The Case of Li Zehou," *China Quarterly* 122 (fall 1992): 969–98.

17 Li Zehou, *Pipan zhexue de pipan: Kangde shuping* (Critique of the critical philosophy: A study of Kant) (Beijing: Renmin chubanshe, 1979), 438.

18 Ibid., 439.

19 Gilles Deleuze's *Kant's Critical Philosophy* ([Minneapolis: University of Minnesota Press, 1984], 49–50, 68–75) offers a critique of Kant's anthropomorphic tendency, and thus, serves as a good reference to Li's characterizations of Kant. See also P. van De Pitte, *Kant as Philosophical Anthropologist* (The Hague: Hague Press, 1971).

20 Li Zehou, *Pipan zhexue de pipan*, 258.

21 See ibid., 190.

22 For the use and meaning of A. J. Greimas's semiotic rectangle, see Fredric Jameson, *The Political Unconscious* (Ithaca, N.Y.: Cornell University Press, 1981), 46–49, 82–83, 121–27, 166–68.

23 Li Zehou, *Wode zhexue tigang* (An outline of my philosophy) (Taipei: Fengyun shidai chuban gongsi, 1990), 20.

24 See Li Zehou, *Pipan zhexue de pipan*, 310–66.

25 Ibid., 362.

26 Ibid., 363.

27 Ibid., 363.

28 Ibid., 360.

29 See Karl Marx, *Economic and Philosophical Manuscripts*, ed. Karl Coletti (London: Routledge, 1975), 351–54.

30 For Li's discussion of Wittgenstein, see *Pipan zhexue de pipan*, 57–68; and Li Zehou, *Zou wo ziji de lu* (Take my own path) (Beijing: Sanlian shudian, 1986), 284–90.

31 See Susan Easton, *Humanist Marxism and Wittgensteinian Social Philosophy* (Manchester: Manchester University Press, 1983), 83–96; and David Rubinstein, *Marx and Wittgenstein* (Boston: Beacon Press, 1981).

32 See Li Zehou, *Pipan zhexue de pipan*, 53–55, 76–79, 119, 425–26.

33 See Li Zehou, *Zou wo ziji de lu*, 286; and Li Zehou, *Pipan zhexue de pipan*, 55. For an introduction to Piaget's developmental psychology, see Jean Piaget, *Genetic Epistemology* (New York: Pantheon Books, 1970); see also Jean Piaget, *The Principles of Genetic Epistemology* (New York: Columbia University Press, 1972), esp. chapter 3.

34 I owe the point on Habermas's connection to Piaget to Fredric Jameson. For a deconstructive critique of Habermas's Kantian rationalism and appropriations of Piaget, see Michael Ryan, *Politics and Culture: Working Hypotheses for a Post-Revolutionary Society* (Baltimore, Md.: Johns Hopkins University Press, 1989), 27–45. Terry Eagleton also maintains that "it is possible to see in Habermas's ideal speech community an updated version of Kant's community of aesthetic judgment" (*The Ideology of the Aesthetic* [Oxford: Basil Blackwell, 1990], 405).

35 See Li Zehou, *Pipan zhexue de pipan*, 56–68, 160; and Li Zehou, *Zou wo ziji de lu*, 281–96, 274–80.

36 See Li Zehou, *Zou wo ziji de lu*, 284–90. For the Lacanian notion of the unconscious, see Jacques Lacan, *Ecrits* (New York: W. W. Norton, 1977), 2–7, 192–99.

37 For a critique of Kantian transcendental categories, see Li Zehou, *Pipan zhexue de pipan*, esp. chapters 3 and 4.

38 See Li Zehou, *Wode zhexue tigang*, 10–15.

39 See Li Zehou, *Wode zhexue tigang*, 13.

40 See ibid., 15.

41 Ibid., 13.

42 See Li Zehou, *Pipan zhexue de pipan*, 114–18, 325–51, 413–21. See also Immanuel Kant, *Critique of Judgment* (Oxford: Basil Blackwell, 1973).

43 See Li Zehou, *Zhongguo gudai sixiang shi lun* (Essays on classical Chinese thoughts) (Beijing: Renmin chubanshe, 1985), esp. 7–51, 395–423.

44 Li's ontological thinking is inspired largely by Lukács's later works on "social ontology." He suggests that Lukács's *Zur Ontologie des Gesellschaftlichen Seins* (Toward the Ontology of Social Being)—as prolegomena to his more ambitious, but never written treatise on ethics—points to a crucial way of rethinking ontology by developing a theory of subjectivity based on Marxist historical materialist conceptions

vis-à-vis the Heideggerian problematic of "the subjectivity of the subject." See Li Zehou and Liu Kang, "Toward a Constructive Philosophy."

45 Li Zehou, *Pipan zhexue de pipan*, 367.

46 For a brief outline of reinterpretations of the Kantian notion of subjectivity from historical materialist perspectives appearing in English, see Li Zehou, "The Philosophy of Kant and a Theory of Subjectivity," in *Analecta Husserliana*, vol. 21, ed. A.-T. Tymieniecka (Dordrecht: D. Reidel Publishing, 1986), 135–49.

47 See Li Zehou, *Pipan zhexue de pipan*, 422–37.

48 See, for example, the entries on "topology" and "topological space" in the *Encyclopaedia Britannica* (Chicago: Encyclopaedia Britannica, Inc., 1990).

49 Li Zehou's interpretations of classical culture are mainly contained in his *Mei de licheng* (The journey of the beautiful) (Beijing: Renmin chubanshe, 1981), and its English translation, *The Path of Beauty*, 2d ed. (Hong Kong: Oxford University Press, 1994); *Zhongguo gudai sixiang shi lun*; and *Huaxia meixue* (Chinese aesthetics) (Hong Kong: Sanlian shudian, 1988).

50 See Li Zehou, "Qimeng yu jiuwang de shuangchong bianzou" (Dual variation of enlightenment and national salvation), in *Zhongguo xiandai sixiang shi lun* (Essays on history of modern Chinese thoughts) (Beijing: Dongfang chubanshe, 1987), 7–50.

51 See ibid., 46–50. For an English explication of some of Li's concepts of modern Chinese intellectual history, see Li Zehou and Vera Schwarz, "Six Generations of Modern Chinese Intellectuals," *Chinese Studies in History* (winter 1983–1984): 102–26; see also Vera Schwarz, *The Chinese Enlightenment* (Berkeley: University of California Press, 1986), which bases it arguments on China's modern intellectual enlightenment largely on Li's views.

52 See Li Zehou, *Zhongguo xiandai sixiang shi lun*, 311–41.

53 For a fuller account of Mao's thought as the first stage in Chinese Marxism, see Li Zehou, *On Marxism in China* (Hong Kong: Joint Publishers, 1993).

54 Li Zehou, *Zhongguo xiandai sixiang shi lun*, 189.

55 Ibid., 170–76. Classical Chinese dialectics mostly consists in the military philosophies of Taoism and the "arts of war" of Sun Zi (Sun Tsu). See also Li Zehou, "Sun-Lao-Han he shuo" (A synthetic view of Sun Zi, Lao Zi [Lao Tsu] and Han Feizi [Han Fei-tsu]), in *Zhongguo gudai sixiang shi lun*, 77–106.

56 See Li Zehou, "Guanyu 'shiyong lixing'" (Notes on "pragmatic rationality"), *Ershi yi shiji* (Twenty-first century) 21 (spring 1994): 98–103.

57 For a recent reflection on the question of alienation as a historical necessity, see Li Zehou, "Zhexue tanxun lu" (Notes on philosophical inquiries), *Minbao yuekan*, nos. 7–10 (1994).

58 Eagleton, *Ideology of the Aesthetic*, 27.

59 Li Tuo, "Resisting Writing," in *Politics, Ideology, and Literary Discourse in Modern China: Theoretical Interventions and Cultural Critique*, ed. Liu Kang and Xiaobing Tang (Durham, N.C.: Duke University Press, 1993), 273–77.

60 For the debate about literary subjectivity, see *Wenxue zhutixing lunzheng ji* (Essays of the debate about literary subjectivity) (Beijing: Hongqi chubanshe, 1986).

61 Liu Zaifu, "The Subjectivity of Literature Revisited," in *Politics, Ideology, and Literary Discourse in Modern China*, ed. Liu Kang and Xiaobing Tang (Durham, N.C.: Duke University Press, 1993), 57. See also Liu Zaifu, "Fangzhu zhushen: Zhongguo dangdai wenxue pinglun shiji mo de zhengzha" (Exile of gods: The fin de siècle struggles of contemporary Chinese literary criticism), in *Fangzhu zhushen* (Exile of gods) (Hong Kong: Tiandi tushu, 1994), 293–308.

62 Liu Zaifu, "Lun wenxue de zhuti xing" (On the subjectivity of literature), *Wenxue pinglun* (Literary review) 5-6 (May/June 1985): 13-14.

63 Ibid., 15.

64 See ibid., 17.

65 See Liu Zaifu and Lin Gang, *Chuantong yu Zhongguo ren* (Tradition and the Chinese person) (Hong Kong: Sanlian shudian, 1988), 309-20.

66 See Liu Zaifu, "Zhongguo xiandai wenxue shi shang dui ren de san ci faxian" (Three discoveries of humanity in modern Chinese literature), in *Liu Zaifu ji* (Selected essays of Liu Zaifu) (Harbin: Helongjiang renmin chubanshe, 1988), 225-37.

67 See ibid., 181-95.

68 Liu Zaifu, "The Subjectivity of Literature Revisited," 59.

69 See Liu Zaifu, *Xunzhao de bei ge* (Tragic songs of quest) (Hong Kong: Tiandi tushu, 1988).

70 See Liu Zaifu, *Xingge zuhe lun* (On dual composition of literary character) (Shanghai: Shanghai renmin chubanshe, 1986).

71 Liu Zaifu, "Fangzhu zhushen," 306.

72 See Chen Yangu and Jin Dacheng, "Liu Zaifu xianxiang pipan" (A critique of Liu Zaifu phenomenon), *Wenxue pinglun* (Literature review) 2 (1988): 20-23.

73 Xiaomei Chen, "Occidentalism as Counterdiscourse: 'He Shang' in Post-Mao China," *Critical Inquiry* 18 (summer 1992): 692.

74 Ibid., 693.

75 Some British critics have consistently critiqued this aestheticizing tendency in Western postmodernist thinking. See Terry Eagleton, "Capitalism, Modernism, and Postmodernism," in *Against the Grain* (London: Routledge, 1986); and Terry Eagleton, "From *Polis* to Postmodernism," in *Ideology of the Aesthetic*. See also Connor, *Postmodern Culture*.

76 For a more detailed discussion of cultural trends in China in the 1990s, see Liu Kang, "Is There an Alternative to (Capitalist) Globalization? The Debate about Modernity in China," in *Culture and Globalization*, ed. Fredric Jameson and Masao Miyoshi (Durham, N.C.: Duke University Press, 1998).

77 Jacques Derrida, *Specters of Marx* (London: Routledge, 1994), 95.

BIBLIOGRAPHY

Adamson, Walter. *Hegemony and Revolution: A Study of Antonio Gramsci's Political and Cultural Theory.* Berkeley: University of California Press, 1980.

Adorno, Theodor. *Asthetische Theorie: Gesammelte Schriften.* 20 vols. Frankfurt: Suhrkamp, 1970.

————. *Negative Dialectics.* Translated by E. B. Ashton. London: Routledge, 1973.

————. "Subject-Object." In *The Essential Frankfurt School Reader,* edited by Andrew Arato and Eike Gebhardt. New York: Urizen Books, 1978.

Ahmad, Aijaz. "Jameson's Rhetoric of Otherness and the 'National Allegory.'" *Social Text* 19 (fall 1987): 3–25.

Ai Xiaoming. "Hu Feng yu Lukaqi" (Hu Feng and Lukács). *Wenxue pinglun* 5 (October 1988): 40–52.

Althusser, Louis. *Lenin and Philosophy and Other Essays.* London: New Left Books, 1971.

————. *For Marx.* London: New Left Books, 1977.

————. *Philosophy and the Spontaneous Philosophy of the Scientist.* Edited by Gregory Elliot. London: Verso, 1990.

Anderson, Benedict. *Imagined Communities.* London: Verso, 1983.

Anderson, Marston. *The Limits of Realism: Chinese Fiction in the Revolutionary Period.* Berkeley: University of California Press, 1990.

Anderson, Perry. "Modernity and Revolution." *New Left Review* 114 (March–April 1984): 96–113.

Austin, J. L. *How to Do Things with Words.* Cambridge, Mass.: Harvard University Press, 1962.

Bakhtin, Mikhail. *Problems of Dostoevsky's Poetics.* Translated by C. Emerson. Minneapolis: University of Minnesota Press, 1984.

————. *Rabelais and His World.* Bloomington: Indiana University Press, 1984.

Baogang He. *The Democratic Implications of Civil Society in China.* New York: St. Martin's Press, 1997.

Baudelaire, Charles. *The Painter of Modern Life and Other Essays.* London: Phaidon, 1964.

Bays, Daniel. *China Enters the Twentieth Century: Chang Chih-tung and the Issues of a New Age, 1895–1909.* Ann Arbor: University of Michigan Press, 1978.

Benjamin, A., ed. *The Problem of Modernity: Adorno and Benjamin.* London: Verso, 1988.

Benjamin, Walter. *Illuminations.* Translated by Hannah Arendt. New York: Schocken Books, 1969.

———. *Charles Baudelaire: A Lyric Poet in the Era of High Capitalism.* London: New Left Books, 1973.

———. *The Origin of German Tragic Drama.* London: Routledge, 1977.

Berges, Marie-Claire. *The Golden Age of the Chinese Bourgeoisie.* Translated by Janet Lloyd. Cambridge, U. K.: Cambridge University Press.

Berman, Marshall. *All That Is Solid Melts into Air: The Experience of Modernity.* New York: Penguin Books, 1988.

Bernstein, J. M. *The Fate of Art: Aesthetic Alienation from Kant to Derrida and Adorno.* University Park: Pennsylvania State University Press, 1992.

Bonner, Joey. *Wang Kuo-wei: An Intellectual Biography.* Cambridge, Mass.: Harvard University Press, 1986.

boundary 2. Special issues on Antonio Gramsci, vol. 14, no. 4 (spring 1986) and vol. 21, no. 2 (summer 1994).

Bourdieu, Pierre. *Outline of a Philosophy of Practice.* Cambridge, Cambridge University Press, 1977.

———. *Algeria 1960.* Cambridge, Cambridge University Press, 1979.

———. *Distinction: A Social Critique of the Judgment of Taste.* Cambridge, Mass.: Harvard University Press, 1984.

Bové, Paul. *In the Wake of Theory.* Hanover, N.H.: Wesleyan University Press, 1992.

Bradbury, Malcom, and James MacFarlane, eds. *Modernism, 1890–1930.* New York: Penguin, 1976.

Bronner, Stephen. *Of Critical Theory and Its Theorists.* Oxford: Blackwell, 1994.

Brook, Timothy, and B. Michael Frolic, eds. *Civil Society in China.* Armonk, N.Y.: M. E. Sharpe, 1997.

Brugger, Bill, ed. *China: The Impact of Cultural Revolution.* London: Croom Helm, 1978.

Brugger, Bill, and David Kelly. *Chinese Marxism in the Post-Mao Era.* Stanford, Calif.: Stanford University Press, 1990.

Cai Yi. *Meixue lunzhu chubian* (Primary essays on aesthetics). Shanghai: Shanghai wenyi chubanshe, 1982.

Cai Yuanpei. *Cai Yuanpei xuanji* (Selected works of Cai Yuanpei). Beijing: Zhonghua shuju, 1963.

———. *Cai Yuanpei xiansheng quanji* (Complete works of Cai Yuanpei). Taipei: Shangwu yinshuguan, 1968.

Chang, Hao. *Liang Ch'i-ch'ao and Intellectual Transition in China, 1890–1907.* Cambridge, Mass.: Harvard University Press, 1971.

Chen Duxiu. "Ben zhi zui'an zhi dabian shu" (A self-defense of our journal's "criminal case"). *Xin qingnian* (New youth) 6, no. 1 (1915): 1–6.

Chen Wei. *Zhongguo xiandai meixue sixiang shigang* (A brief history of modern Chinese aesthetic thought). Shanghai: Shanghai renmin chubanshe, 1993.

Chen, Xiaomei. "Occidentalism as Counterdiscourse: 'He Shang' in Post-Mao China." *Critical Inquiry* 18 (summer 1992): 686–712.

Chen Yangu and Jin Dacheng. "Liu Zaifu xianxiang pipan" (A critique of Liu Zaifu phenomenon). *Wenxue pinglun* (Literature review) 2 (1988): 18–33.

Chow, Rey. "Response," special issue, "Marxism beyond Marxism?" *Polygraph* 6/7 (1993).

Chytry, Josef. *The Aesthetic State: A Quest in Modern German Thought.* Berkeley: University of California Press, 1989.

Connor, Steve. *Postmodern Culture: An Introduction to Theories of the Contemporary.* Oxford: Basil Blackwell, 1989.

Davidson, Alistair. *Antonio Gramsci: Towards an Intellectual Biography.* London: Merlin Press, 1977.

Deleuze, Gilles. *Kant's Critical Philosophy.* Minneapolis: University of Minnesota Press, 1984.

De Pitte, P. van. *Kant as Philosophical Anthropologist.* The Hague: Hague Press, 1971.

Derrida, Jacques. *Specters of Marx.* London: Routledge, 1994.

Dirlik, Arif. "The Predicament of Marxist Revolutionary Consciousness: Mao Zedong, Antonio Gramsci, and the Reformulation of Marxist Revolutionary Theory." *Modern China* 9, no. 2 (April 1983): 182–211.

———. *The Origins of Chinese Communism.* Oxford: Oxford University Press, 1989.

———. "Post-Socialism/Flexible Production: Marxism in Contemporary Radicalism." *Polygraph* 6/7 (1993).

———. *After the Revolution: Waking to Global Capitalism.* Hanover, N.H.: Wesleyan University Press, 1994.

———. "The Postcolonial Aura: Third World Criticism in the Age of Global Capitalism." *Critical Inquiry* 20 (1994): 328–56.

———. "Mao Zedong and 'Chinese Marxism,'" in *The Encyclopedia of Asian Philosophy.* London: Routledge, 1995.

Dirlik, Arif, and Maurice Meisner, eds. *Marxism and the Chinese Experience.* New York: M. E. Sharpe, 1989.

Duiker, William. "The Aesthetic Philosophy of Ts'ai Yuan-p'ei." *Philosophy East and West* 22, no. 4 (1972): 385–401.

———. *Ts'ai Yüan-p'ei: Educator of Modern China.* University Park: Pennsylvania State University Press, 1977.

Eagleton, Terry. *Walter Benjamin, or Towards a Revolutionary Criticism.* London: Verso, 1981.

———. *Against the Grain.* London: Routledge, 1986.

———. *The Ideology of the Aesthetic.* Oxford: Basil Blackwell, 1990.

———. *Ideology: An Introduction.* London: Verso, 1991.

Easton, Susan. *Humanist Marxism and Wittgensteinian Social Philosophy.* Manchester: Manchester University Press, 1983.

Fan Jun. "Hu Feng: Shang wei jieshu de huati" (Hu Feng: An incomplete issue of inquiry). *Wenxue pinlun* (Literature review) 5 (October 1988): 17–33.

Feng Yu-lan. *A History of Chinese Philosophy.* Princeton, N.J.: Princeton University Press, 1953.

Forgacs, David. "National-Popular: Genealogy of a Concept." In *The Cultural Studies Reader*, edited by Simon During. London: Routledge, 1993.

Foucault, Michel. *Power/Knowledge: Selected Interviews and Other Writings, 1972–1977.* New York: Pantheon Books, 1978.

———. *Foucault Reader.* New York: Pantheon Books, 1984.

Gálik, Marián. *Mao Tun and Modern Chinese Literary Criticism.* Wiesbaden: Franz Steiner Verlag, 1969.

Gan Yang, ed. *Zhongguo dangdai wenhua yishi* (Contemporary Chinese cultural consciousness). Hong Kong: Sanlian shudian, 1989.

Geming wenxue lunzheng ziliao xuanbian (Selected materials from the revolutionary literature debate). 2 vols. Beijing: Renmin wenxue chubanshe, 1981.

Gerratana, Valentino. "Althusser and Stalinism." *New Left Review* 101/102 (spring/summer 1977): 111–21.

Goldman, Merle. *Literary Dissent in Communist China*. Cambridge, Mass.: Harvard University Press, 1967.

———. *Sowing the Seeds of Democracy in China*. Cambridge, Mass.: Harvard University Press, 1994.

———, ed. *Modern Chinese Literature in the May Fourth Era*. Cambridge, Mass.: Harvard University Press, 1977.

Goldman, Merle, et al., eds. *China's Intellectuals and the State: In Search of a New Relationship*. Cambridge, Mass.: Council on East Asian Studies at Harvard University, 1987.

Gramsci, Antonio. *Selections from the Prison Notebooks*. Edited and translated by Quintin Hoare and Geoffrey Nowell-Smith. New York: International Publishers, 1971.

———. *Selections from Cultural Writings*. Edited by David Forgacs and Geoffrey Nowell-Smith. London: Lawrence and Wishart, 1985.

———. *Antonio Gramsci Prison Notebooks*. Edited by Joseph Buttigieg. New York: Columbia University Press, 1992.

Grieder, Jerome. *Hu Shih and the Chinese Renaissance*. Cambridge, Mass.: Harvard University Press, 1971.

Harvey, David. *The Condition of Postmodernity*. Oxford: Basil Blackwell, 1989.

Hirschkop, Ken, and David Shepherd, eds. *Bakhtin and Cultural Theory*. Manchester: Manchester University Press, 1989.

Holquist, Michael. *Dialogism: Bakhtin and His World*. London: Routledge, 1990.

Holub, Robert. *Reception Theory: A Critical Introduction*. London: Routledge, 1984.

Horkheimer, Max, and Theodor Adorno. *Dialectic of Enlightenment*. Translated by John Cumming. New York: Continuum, 1994.

Hsia, C. T. *A History of Modern Chinese Fiction*. 2d ed. New Haven, Conn.: Yale University Press, 1971.

Hsia, T. A. *The Gate of Darkness: Studies on the Leftist Literary Movement in China*. Seattle: University of Washington Press, 1968.

Hu Feng. "Realism Today." In *Literature of the People's Republic of China*, edited by Kaiyu Hsu, translated by Paul Pickowicz. Bloomington: Indiana University Press, 1980.

———. *Hu Feng pinglun ji* (Critical essays of Hu Feng). 3 vols. Beijing: Renmin wenxue chubanshe, 1984.

———. *Guanyu jiefang yilai de wenyi shijian qingkuang de baogao* (A report on literary and artistic practices since the liberation). *Xin wenxue shiliao* (Historical documents of new literary history) 3 (1989).

Hu Qiuyuan. "Langfei de lunzheng: Duiyu pipingzhe de ruogan dabian" (Superfluous argument: Some responses to criticism). *Xiandai* (The modern) 2, no. 2 (December 1932): 2–38.

———. *Wenxue yishu lunji* (Collected essays on literature and art). 2 vols. Taipei: Xueshu chubanshe, 1979.

Hu Shi. "Conflicts of Cultures." In *The China Christian Yearbook, 1929*. Shanghai: Christian Literature Society, 1930.

———. "Du Liang Shuming xiansheng de *Dongxi wenhua ji qi zhexue*" (Comment on Liang Shuming's *East/West cultures and philosophies*) (1923) and "Women duiyu xiyang jindai wenming de taidu" (Our attitude toward modern Western culture) (1926). In *Cong "xihua" dao xiandaihua*, edited by Luo Rongqu. Beijing: Beijing daxue chubanshe, 1990.

Huang, Philip C. *Liang Ch'i-ch'ao and Modern Chinese Liberalism*. Seattle: University of Washington Press, 1972.

Hung, Chang-tai. *Going to the People: Chinese Intellectuals and Folk Literature, 1918– 1937*. Cambridge, Mass.: Council on East Asian Studies at Harvard University, 1985.

Hutcheon, Linda. *Politics of Postmodernism*. London: Routledge, 1989.

Huters, Theodore. "Hu Feng and the Critical Legacy of Lu Xun." In *Lu Xun and His Legacy*, edited by Leo Ou-fan Lee. Berkeley: University of California Press, 1985.

Jameson, Fredric. *Marxism and Form*. Princeton, N.J.: Princeton University Press, 1971.

———. *The Political Unconscious*. Ithaca, N.Y.: Cornell University Press, 1981.

———. "Third World Literature in the Era of Multinational Capital." *Social Text* 15 (fall 1986): 65–88.

———. *The Ideologies of Theory*. 2 vols. Minneapolis: University of Minnesota Press, 1988.

———. *Late Marxism: Adorno, or, The Persistence of the Dialectic*. London: Verso, 1990.

———. *Postmodernism, or, The Cultural Logic of Late Capitalism*. Durham, N.C.: Duke University Press, 1991.

———. "Actually Exisiting Marxism." *Polygraph* 6/7 (1993).

Jauss, Hans Robert. *Toward an Aesthetic of Reception*. Minneapolis: University of Minnesota Press, 1982.

Jay, Martin. *The Dialectical Imagination*. Boston: Little, Brown and Co., 1973.

———. *Adorno*. Cambridge, Mass.: Harvard University Press, 1984.

Kant, Immanuel. *Critique of Judgment*. Oxford: Basil Blackwell, 1973.

Kraus, Richard. *Class Conflict in Chinese Socialism*. New York: Columbia University Press, 1981.

Lacan, Jacques. *Ecrits*. New York: W. W. Norton, 1977.

Laclau, Ernesto, and Chantal Mouffe. *Hegemony and Socialist Strategy: Towards a Radical Democratic Politics*. London: Verso, 1985.

Landy, Marcia. *Film, Politics, and Gramsci*. Minneapolis: University of Minnesota Press, 1994.

Larson, Wendy. *Literary Authority and the Modern Chinese Writer*. Durham, N.C.: Duke University Press, 1991.

League of Left-Wing Writers, *Zuolian huyi lu* (Memoirs of the league of left-wing writers). 2 vols. Beijing: Zhongguo shehui kexue chubanshe, 1982.

Lee, Leo Ou-fan. *The Romantic Generation of Modern Chinese Writers*. Cambridge, Mass.: Harvard University Press, 1973.

———. *Voices from the Iron House: A Study of Lu Xun*. Bloomington: Indiana University Press, 1987.

———, ed. *Lu Xun and His Legacy*. Berkeley: University of California Press, 1985.

Lenin, Vladimir Ilyich. *Selected Works of Lenin*. New York: International Publishers, 1943.

Levenson, Joseph. *Liang Ch'i-ch'ao and the Mind of Modern China*. 3d ed. New York: Harper and Row, 1966.

Li Hui. *Hu Feng yuan'an shimo* (Hu Feng's case of injustice). Beijing: Renmin ribao chubanshe, 1989.

Li Tuo. "Resisting Writing." In *Politics, Ideology, and Literary Discourse in Modern China: Theoretical Interventions and Cultural Critique*, edited by Liu Kang and Xiaobing Tang, 273–77. (Durham, N.C.: Duke University Press, 1993).

Li Zehou. *Pipan zhexue de pipan: Kande shuping* (Critique of the critical philosophy: A study of Kant). Beijing: Renmin chubanshe, 1979.

———. *Meixue lunji* (Essays on aesthetics). Shanghai: Shanghai wenyi chubanshe, 1980.

————. *Mei de licheng* (The journey of the beautiful). Beijing: Renmin chubanshe, 1981. English translation: *The Path of Beauty*. 2d ed. Hong Kong: Oxford University Press, 1994.

————. *Li Zehou zhexue meixue wenxuan* (Collected essays of philosophy and aesthetics by Li Zehou). Changsha: Hunan renmin chubanshe, 1985.

————. *Zhongguo gudai sixiang shi lun* (Essays on classical Chinese thoughts). Beijing: Renmin chubanshe, 1985.

————. "The Philosophy of Kant and a Theory of Subjectivity." In *Analecta Husserlina*, edited by A-T. Tymieniecka, 21: 135–49. Dordrecht: D. Reidel Publishing, 1986.

————. *Zou wo ziji de lu* (Take my own path). Beijing: Sanlian shudian, 1986.

————. *Zhongguo xiandai sixiang shi lun* (Essays on modern Chinese intellectual history). Beijing: Dongfang chubanshe, 1987.

————. *Huaxia meixue* (Chinese aesthetics). Hong Kong: Sanlian shudian, 1988.

————. *Wode zhexue tigang* (An outline of my philosophy). Taipei: Fengyun shidai chuban gongsi, 1990.

————. *On Marxism in China*. Hong Kong: Joint Publishers, 1993.

————. "Guanyu 'shiyong lixing'" (Notes on "pragmatic rationality"). *Ershi yi shiji* (Twenty-first century) 21 (spring 1994): 98–103.

————. "Zhexue tanxun lu" (Notes on philosophical inquiries). *Minbao yuekan*, nos. 7–10 (1994).

Li Zehou and Vera Schwarz. "Six Generations of Modern Chinese Intellectuals." *Chinese Studies in History* (winter 1983–1984), 102–26.

Liang Qichao. *Yinbingshi heji* (Collected essays from the ice-drinker's studio). Shanghai: Zhonghuan shuju, 1936.

————. "Meishu yu kexue" (Art and science). In *Zhongguo meixue ziliao xuanbian* (Selected essays on Chinese aesthetics). Vol. 2, A00–A10. Beijing: Zhonghua shuju, 1981.

————. "Xiaoshuo yu qunzhi zhi guanxi" (On the relationship between fiction and the government of the people). In *Zhongguo jindai wenlun xuan* (Selected modern Chinese literary essays). Vol. 1, 157–61. Beijing: Renmin wenxue chubanshe, 1981.

Lin Fei and Liu Zaifu. *Lu Xun zhuan* (Biography of Lu Xun). Beijing: Zhongguo shehui kexue chubanshe, 1981.

Lin Min. "The Search for Modernity: Chinese Intellectual Discourse and Society, 1978–1988; The Case of Li Zehou." *China Quarterly* 122 (fall 1992): 969–98.

Lin Piao (Lin Biao). *Long Live the Victory of the People's War!* Peking: Foreign Language Press, 1967.

Lin Yu-sheng. *The Crisis of Chinese Consciousness: Radical Antitraditionalism in the May Fourth Era*. Madison: University of Wisconsin Press, 1979. Chinese translation: *Zhongguo yishi de weiji*. Guiyang: Guizhou renmin chubanshe, 1988.

Liu Kang. "Subjectivity, Marxism, and Cultural Theory in China." *Social Text* 31/32 (summer/fall 1992): 114–41.

————. "Politics, Critical Paradigms: Reflections on Modern Chinese Literature Studies." *Modern China* 19, no. 1 (1993): 13–40.

————. "Yi zhong zhuanxing qi de wenhua lilun: Lun Bahejin duihua zhuyi zai dangdai wenlun zhong de mingyun" (A theory of cultural change: Bakhtin's dialogism in contemporary critical theory). *Zhongguo shehui kexue* (Social sciences in China) 86 (spring 1994): 161–77.

————. *Duihua de xuansheng: Bahejin wenhuan lilun* (Dialogism: Bakhtin and cultural theory). Beijing: Zhongguo renmin daxue chubanshe, 1995.

―――. "The Problematics of Mao and Althusser: Alternative Modernity and Cultural Revolution." *Rethinking Marxism* 8, no. 3 (fall 1995): 1―26.

―――. "Is There an Alternative to (Capitalist) Globalization? The Case of China." In *The Cultures of Globalization*, edited by Fredric Jameson and Masao Miyoshi. Durham, N.C.: Duke University Press, 1998.

―――. "The Legacy of Mao and Althusser: Problematics of Dialectics, Alternative Modernity, and Cultural Revolution." In *Critical Perspectives on Mao Zedong Thought*, edited by Arif Dirlik and Nick Knight. Forthcoming.

Liu Kang and Xiaobing Tang, eds. *Politics, Ideology, and Literary Discourse in Modern China: Theoretical Interventions and Cultural Critique*. Durham, N.C.: Duke University Press, 1993.

Liu Mengxi. "'Wenhua tuo ming' yu Zhongguo xiandai xueshu chuantong" ("Cultural will-passing" and the modern Chinese tradition of scholarship). *Zhongguo wenhua* (Chinese culture), no. 6 (spring 1992): 104–13.

Liu Xiaobo. *Xuanzhe the pipan: Yu Li Zehou duihua* (Alternative critique: Dialogues with Li Zehou). Shanghai: Shanghai renmin chubanshe, 1988.

Liu Xiaofeng. *Zhengjiu yu xiaoyao* (Salvation and carefreeness). Shanghai: Shanghai renmin chubanshe, 1988.

Liu Zaifu. *Lu Xun meixue sixiang lungao* (Essays on Lu Xun's aesthetic thought). Beijing: Zhongguo shehui kexue chubanshe, 1981.

―――. "Lun wenxue de zhuti xing" (On the subjectivity of literature). *Wenxue pinglun* (Literary review) 5–6 (May/June 1985): 13–14.

―――. *Xingge zuhe lun* (On dual composition of literary character). Shanghai: Shanghai renmin chubanshe, 1986.

―――. *Liu Zaifu ji* (Selected essays of Liu Zaifu). Harbin: Helongjiang renmin chubanshe, 1988.

―――. *Xunzhao de bei ge* (Tragic songs of quest). Hong Kong: Tiandi tushu, 1988.

―――. "Wusi wenxue qimeng jingshen de shiluo yu huigui" (The loss and recovery of the enlightenment spirit of May Fourth literature). In *Wusi: Duoyuan de fansi* (May Fourth: Pluralist reflections), edited by Ling Yu-sheng et al., 92–122. Taipei: Lianjing chubanshe, 1989.

―――. "The Subjectivity of Literature Revisited." In *Politics, Ideology, and Literary Discourse in Modern China: Theoretical Interventions and Cultural Critique*, edited by Liu Kang and Xiaobing Tang, 56–69. Durham, N.C.: Duke University Press, 1993.

―――. *Fangzhu zhushen* (Exile of gods). Hong Kong: Tiandi tushu, 1994.

Liu Zaifu and Lin Gang. *Chuantong yu Zhongguo ren* (Tradition and the Chinese person). Hong Kong: Sanlian shudian, 1988.

Lu Xun. *Lu Xun sanshi nian ji* (Collected works of Lu Xun over thirty years). Hong Kong: Xinyi chubanshe, 1971.

―――. *Selected Stories of Lu Hsün*. Peking: Foreign Language Press, 1972.

―――. *Lu Xun quanji* (Completed works of Lu Xun). 16 vols. Beijing: Renmin wenxue chubanshe, 1973.

―――. *Lu Xun xuanji* (Selected works of Lu Xun). Beijing: Renmin wenxue chubanshe, 1983.

Lukács, Georg. *Marxism and Human Literature*. Edited by E. San Juan Jr. New York: Delta Book, 1973.

Lunn, Eugene. *Marxism and Modernism: An Historical Study of Lukács, Brecht, Benjamin, and Adorno*. Berkeley: University of California Press, 1982.

Luo Lo. "Sangdai chongxin pingshuo de zhengui yichan: Hu Feng wenyi sixiang pinglun"

(Valuable heritage to be reassessed: Hu Feng's literary thought). In *Hu Feng lunji* (Critical essays on Hu Feng), edited by Wen Zhenting and Fan Jiyan, 15–20. Beijing: Zhongguo shehui kexue chubanshe, 1991.

Luo Rongqu, ed. *Cong "xihua" dao xiandaihua* (From "Westernization" to modernization). Beijing: Beijing daxue chubanshe, 1990.

Lyell, William. *Lu Hsün's Vision of Reality.* Berkeley: University of California Press, 1976.

Malraux, André. *Man's Fate (La Condition humaine).* New York: Vantage Books, 1968.

Mao Zedong. *Selected Works of Mao Tse-tung.* 4 vols. Peking: Foreign Language Press, 1967.

———. *Mao Zedong sixiang wansui* (Long live Mao Zedong thought). Photo reproductions of the Red Guard publications of 1969.

———. *Mao Zedong ji* (Collected works of Mao Zedong). Edited by Takeuchi Minoru. 10 vols. Hong Kong: Po Wen Book Co., 1976.

———. *Maozedong xuanji* (Selected works of Mao Zedong). 5 vols. Beijing: Renmin chubanshe, 1977.

———. *Chairman Mao Talks to the People.* Edited by S. Schram. New York: Pantheon Books, 1984.

———. *The Secret Speeches of Chairman Mao.* Edited by R. MacFarquhar et al. Cambridge, Mass.: Council on East Asian Studies at Harvard University, 1989.

———. *The Writings of Mao Zedong, 1949–1976.* Edited by John Leung and Michael Kau. Armonk, N.Y.: M. E. Sharpe, 1992.

Marcuse, Herbert. *The Aesthetic Dimension: Towards a Critique of Marxist Aesthetics.* Boston: Beacon Press, 1978.

Maruyama Noboru, *Rojin to kakumei bungaku* (Lu Xun and revolutionary literature). Tokyo: Kinokuniya shoten, 1972.

Marx, Karl. *Grundrisse.* Harmondsworth: Penguin, 1973.

———. *Economic and Philosophical Manuscripts.* Edited by Karl Coletti. London: Routledge, 1975.

Marx, Karl, and Friedrich Engels. *The Marx-Engels Reader.* Edited by Robert Tucker. New York: W. W. Norton, 1972.

———. *The German Ideology.* Edited by C. J. Arthur. New York: International Publishers, 1974.

McDougall, Bonnie. *The Introduction of Western Literary Theories into Modern China, 1919–1925.* Tokyo: Center for East Asian Cultural Studies, 1971.

———. *Mao Zedong's "Talks at the Yan'an Conference on Literature and Art": A Translation of the 1943 Text with Commentary.* Ann Arbor: University of Michigan Center for Chinese Studies, 1980.

Meisner, Maurice. *Li Ta-chao and the Origins of Chinese Marxism.* Cambridge, Mass.: Harvard University Press, 1967.

———. *Marxism, Maoism, and Utopianism.* Madison: University of Wisconsin Press, 1982.

Meixue wenti taolun ji (Essays of the debate about aesthetic problems). 5 vols. Beijing: Zuojia chubanshe, 1957.

Miyoshi, Masao. *Off Center: Power and Culture Relations between Japan and the United States.* Cambridge, Mass.: Harvard University Press, 1991.

Miyoshi, Masao, and H. D. Harootunian, eds. *Postmodernism and Japan.* Durham, N.C.: Duke University Press, 1989.

———. *Japan in the World.* Durham, N.C.: Duke University Press, 1993.

Mouffe, Chantal, ed. *Gramsci and Marxist Theory*. London: Routledge, 1979.

Nathan, Andrew. *Chinese Democracy*. Berkeley: University of California Press, 1985.

Nelson, Cary, and Lawrence Grossberg, eds. *Marxism and the Interpretation of Culture*. Urbana: University of Illinois Press, 1988.

Peirce, C. S. *Philosophical Writings of Peirce*. New York: Dover Publications, 1955.

Piaget, Jean. *Genetic Epistemology*. New York: Pantheon Books, 1970.

———. *The Principles of Genetic Epistemology*. New York: Columbia University Press, 1972.

Pickowicz, Paul. *Marxist Literary Thought in China: The Influence of Ch'ü Chiü-pai*. Berkeley: University of California Press, 1981.

Prusek, Jaroslev. *The Lyrical and the Epic: Studies of Modern Chinese Literature*. Edited by Leo Ou-fau Lee. Bloomington: Indiana University Press, 1980.

———, ed. *Studies in Modern Chinese Literature*. Berlin: Akademie-Verlag, 1964.

"'Public Sphere'/'Civil Society' in China?" *Modern China* 19, no. 2 (April 1993).

Qu Qiubai. *Qu Qiubai wenji* (Collected essays of Qu Qiubai). 4 vols. Beijing: Renmin wenxue chubanshe, 1953.

Rubinstein, David. *Marx and Wittgenstein*. Boston: Beacon Press, 1981.

Ryan, Michael. *Politics and Culture: Working Hypotheses for a Post-Revolutionary Society*. Baltimore, Md.: Johns Hopkins University Press, 1989.

Said, Edward. *Orientalism*. London: Routledge, 1978.

———. *The World, the Text, the Critic*. Cambridge, Mass.: Harvard University Press, 1983.

Schram, Stuart S. *The Political Thought of Mao Tse-tung*. New York: Praeger Publishers, 1971.

Schwarz, Vera. *The Chinese Enlightenment*. Berkeley: University of California Press, 1986.

Semanov, V. I. *Lu Hsün and His Predecessors*. White Plains, N.Y.: M. E. Sharpe, 1980.

Shwartz, Benjamin. *Chinese Communism and the Rise of Mao*. Cambridge, Mass.: Harvard University Press, 1951.

Sima Lu. *Qu Qiubai zhuan* (A biography of Qu Qiubai). Hong Kong: Zilian chubanshe, 1962.

Spivak, Gayatri. "Can the Subaltern Speak?" In *Marxism and the Interpretation of Culture*, edited by Cary Nelson and Lawrence Grossberg, 271–316. Urbana: University of Illinois Press, 1988.

Todd, Nigel. "Ideological Superstructure in Gramsci and Mao Tse-tung." *Journal of History of Ideas* 35 (January/March 1974).

Wakeman, Frederic, Jr. *History and Will: Philosophical Perspectives of Mao Tse-tung's Thought*. Berkeley: University of California Press, 1975.

Wang Guowei. *Wang Guowei yishu* (Collected works of Wang Guowei). 2 vols. Shanghai: Shangwu yinshuguan, 1940.

———. *Poetic Remarks in the Human World: Jen Chien Ts'u Hua*. Translated and edited by Tu Ching-i. Taipei: Chung-hua shu-chü, 1970.

———. "*Honglou meng pinglun*" (Comments on *Dream of Red Chamber*). In *Zhongguo meixue ziliao xuanbian* (Collection on Chinese aesthetics). Vol. 2. Beijing: Zhonghua shuju, 1982.

Wang Yao. *Zhongguo xin wenxue shi gao* (A history of Chinese new literature). Shanghai: Xin wenyi chubanshe, 1982.

———. *Lu Xun zuopin lunji* (Essays on Lu Xun's works). Beijing: Renmin wenxue chubanshe, 1984.

Wang Zhanyang. *Mao Zedong de jianguo fanglüe yu dangdai Zhongguo de gaige kaifang* (Mao Zedong's strategies of state building, and contemporary China's reform and openness). Changchun: Jilin renmin chubanshe, 1993.

Wen Zhenting and Fan Jiyan, eds. *Hu Feng lunji* (Critical essays on Hu Feng). Beijing: Zhongguo shehui kexue chubanshe, 1991.

Wenxue zhutixing lunzheng ji (Essays of the debate about literary subjectivity). Beijing: Hongqi chubanshe, 1986.

White, Lynn. *Policies of Chaos: The Organizational Causes of Violence in China's Cultural Revolution.* Princeton, N.J.: Princeton University Press, 1989.

Williams, Raymond. *Marxism and Literature.* Oxford: Oxford University Press, 1977.

———. *Problems in Materialism and Culture.* London: Verso, 1980.

———. *Keywords.* Oxford: Oxford University Press, 1983.

Wolin, Richard. *Walter Benjamin: An Aesthetic of Redemption.* New York: Columbia University Press, 1982.

Wu Jianguo et al., eds. *Dangdai Zhongguo yishixingtai fengyun lu* (Ideological currents in contemporary China). Beijing: Jingguan jiaoyu chubanshe, 1993.

Wylie, Raymond. *The Emergence of Maoism: Mao Tse-tung, Ch'en Po-ta, and the Search for Chinese Theory, 1935–1945.* Stanford, Calif.: Stanford University Press, 1980.

Xu Dachun. "Shu meixue" (Introduction of aesthetics). *Dongfang zhazhi* (The Orient) 1, no. 1 (1915).

Yang Li et al., eds. *Zhongguo xiandai zuojia da cidian* (An encyclopedic dictionary of modern Chinese writers). Beijing: Xin shijie chubanshe, 1992.

Yang Xianzhen. *Wo de zhexue "zui'an"* (My philosophical "criminal records"). Beijing: Renmin chubanshe, 1981.

Yue Daiyun. "Guanyu xianshizhuyi de liang chang lunzhan: Lukaqi dui Bulaixite yu Hu Feng dui Zhou Yang" (Two debates about realism: Lukács versus Brecht, and Hu Feng versus Zhou Yang). *Wenyi bao* (Literature and art gazette), 13 August 1988.

Zhang Longxi. "Western Theory and Chinese Reality." *Critical Reality* 19 (1992): 105–30.

———. "Out of the Cultural Ghetto: Theory, Politics, and the Study of Chinese Literature." *Modern China* 19, no. 1 (January 1993): 71–101.

Zhang Xudong. "On Some Motifs in the Chinese 'Cultural Fever' of the Late 1980s." *Social Text* 39 (summer 1994): 120–56.

Zhao Shilin. *Dangdai Zhongguo meixue yanjiu gaishu* (An introduction to contemporary Chinese aesthetics). Tianjin: Tianjin jiaoyu chubanshe, 1988.

Zhongguo gongchandang di ba ci quanguo daibiao dahui wenjian (Documents of the eighth congress of the CCP). Beijing: Renmin chubanshe, 1956.

Zhongguo meixue ziliao xuanbian (Collection on Chinese aesthetics). 2 vols. Beijing: Zhonghua shuju, 1982.

Zhou Yang. "The Fighting Task Confronting Workers in Philosophy and the Social Sciences." *Peking Review* 1 (1964): 16–27.

Zhu Guangqian. "Wode wenyi sixiang de fandong xing" (The reactionary aspects of my literary thoughts). *Wenyi bao* (Literary gazette), no. 6 (1956).

———. *Xifang meixue shi* (A history of Western aesthetics). Beijing: Renmin wenxue chubanshe, 1979.

———. *Zhu Guangqian meixue wenji* (Collected aesthetic essays of Zhu Guangqian). Shanghai: Shanghai wenyi chubanshe, 1982.

INDEX

Liu Kang is Associate Professor of Comparative Literature and
Chinese at Pennsylvania State University. He is the author of
Dialogism: Bakhtin and Cultural Theory (1995), coauthor with
Li Xiguang of *Demonizing China* (1997), and coeditor with
Xiaobing Tang of *Politics, Ideology, and Literary Discourse
in Modern China: Theoretical Interventions and Cultural
Critique,* published by Duke University Press in 1993.

Library of Congress Cataloging-in-Publication Data
Liu, Kang.
Aesthetics and Marxism : Chinese aesthetic Marxists and their
Western contemporaries / Kang Liu.
p.   cm.—(Post-contemporary interventions)
Includes bibliographical references (p.   ) and index.
ISBN 0-8223-2425-3 (cloth : acid-free paper).
ISBN 0-8223-2448-2 (paper : acid-free paper)
1. Aesthetics.   2. Culture.   3. Philosophy, Marxist—China.
4. Philosophy, German—19th century.   5. Philosophy,
German—20th century.   I. Title.   II. Series.
BH39.L5595 2000   111'.85'09—dc21   99-43220 CIP